UNDAUNTED TRAILBLAZERS

MINORITY WOMEN LEADERS for ORAL HEALTH

SHELIA S. PRICE   JEANNE C. SINKFORD   MARILYN P. WOOLFOLK

Copyright © 2021 Shelia S. Price, Jeanne C. Sinkford, Marilyn P. Woolfolk

All rights reserved. This book or any portion thereof may not be reproduced or used in any manner whatsoever without the express written permission of the publisher except for the use of brief quotations in a book review.

Edited by:
SHELIA S. PRICE
JEANNE C. SINKFORD
MARILYN P. WOOLFOLK

Cover Illustration Copyright © 2021 Liz Weaver

Contributing Editors: Marita Inglehart and Joseph West

978-1-7366735-0-8	Undaunted Trailblazers	Hardback
978-1-7366735-1-5	Undaunted Trailblazers	Paperback
978-1-7366735-2-2	Undaunted Trailblazers	Ebook - EPUB

CONTENTS

The Origin 1
Introduction 5
Canise Y. Bean, DMD, MPH 9
Winifred J. Booker, DDS, FAAPD 17
Sheila R. Brown, MEd, DDS, FACD 25
Marsha E. Butler, DDS, FACD 31
Gail Cherry-Peppers, DDS, MS 37
Agnes H. Donahue, DDS, MSD, MPH 43
Cherae Farmer-Dixon, DDS, MSPH, MBA, FACD, FICD 49
A. Isabel Garcia, DDS, MPH, FACD 55
Leslie E. Grant, DDS, MSPA, FACD 61
Judy Greenlea Taylor, DDS, MPH, FACD, FICD 67
Hazel J. Harper, DDS, MPH, FACD 77
Sandra G. Harris, DDS, FACD 85
Marja M. Hurley, MD, FASBMR 91
Andrea D. Jackson, DDS, MS, FACP, FACD, FICD 97
Ernestine S. Lacy, DDS 105
Ana Lopez-Fuentes, DMD, MPH, FACD, FICD 111
Melanie E. Mayberry, DDS, MS-HCM, FACD 119
Renee McCoy-Collins, DDS, FACD, FICD 127
Vivian W. Pinn, MD, FCAP 133

Shelia S. Price, DDS, EdD, FACD 139
Joyce A. Reese, DDS, MPH, FACD 147
Dionne J. Richardson, DDS, MPH 153
Jessica A. Rickert, DDS 161
Rochelle L. Rollins, PhD, MPH 167
Frances Emelia Sam, DDS 173
Jeanne C. Sinkford, DDS, MS, PhD, DSc, FACD, FICD 181
Janet H. Southerland, DDS, MPH, PhD, FACD, FICD 189
Carol G. Summerhays, DDS, FACD 195
Machelle Fleming Thompson, RDH, HCAP, MPH 201
Jennifer Webster-Cyriaque, DDS, PhD 207
Marilyn P. Woolfolk, MS, DDS, MPH, FACD 213
Poem: This Sisterhood!!! (by Dr. Beverly Y. Murdock) 220
Bio Sketches 223
Minority Women Oral Health Pioneers 281
Epilogue 289
Afterword (Commentary by Dr. Paul Gates) 297
Acknowledgments 301
Visual Resources 303
Recommended Readings 309
Dental History Resources 313

The Origin

♦ ♦ ♦

This book was conceived after a casual conversation between a mentor and two mentees. It was a sunny Wednesday morning in May 2019 when the three of us met in Washington, DC, with the singular purpose to celebrate Jeanne's retirement. Upon meeting in the hotel lobby, we excitedly exchanged hugs and began talking, unconcerned about time and, most importantly, without an agenda. We eventually journeyed across town, chauffeured by Sam, a longtime Sinkford family friend. Sam knew every nook and cranny of the city. He shared a plethora of DC factoids, pointed out historic landmarks, and reminisced about working there.

We had lunch outdoors at the wharf on the Potomac, taking in every detail of our individual updates while basking in the warm sunshine and gentle breeze by the water. From amply available things to enjoy in the nation's capital, the three of us chose to spend the afternoon together at the Smithsonian National Portrait Gallery. There we explored portraits and histories of US presidents and many other luminaries. We took particular note of women represented in the gallery. Michelle Obama's portrait was the first of these notables. We listened attentively to a museum guide explaining the history behind the artist's creative work.

Soon separated from the other tourists, we spotted a large portrait of the women of the US Supreme Court. Seated on a sofa is first woman justice Sandra Day O'Connor (1981–2006), and to her left is Ruth Bader Ginsburg, who followed from 1993 to 2020. Sonia Sotomayor (2009) and Elena Kagan (2010) are also in the portrait. While reading the accompanying placard, Jeanne quietly commented, "RBG and I were born the same year," unknowingly revealing her age to us, something we had not discussed before.

Each exhibit poured out historical tidbits and evoked awe. We also discovered a treasure trove of courageous women who formed a fearless front line in women's suffrage. We lingered in this section, viewing videos, portraits, and print postings about the movement. A 1915 *Women's Journal and Suffrage News* article titled "Equality Is the Sacred Law of Humanity" sums up the impetus for women's legal right to vote protests. The display also honors women of color, including Mary McLeod Bethune (1875–1955), a renowned educator; advocate for civil and women's rights; advisor to President Franklin D. Roosevelt; and founder of the Daytona Normal and Industrial Institute for Negro Girls in Daytona, Florida. Prominently displayed is a quote by African American activist Mary Church Terrell (1863–1954), who proclaimed, nearly 130 years ago, at the National Woman Suffrage Association Convention: "A white woman has only one handicap to overcome—a great one, true, her sex; a colored woman faces two—her sex and her race."

Enthralled by the laudable work of these and other exceptional women, our conversation about women's contributions continued that night and soon turned to our honoree's remarkable achievements. We engaged in unscripted Q and A about Dr. Sinkford's career. Shelia presented her a book titled *Legacy, The Dental Profession*, which she acquired years earlier while researching leadership in dentistry. Aside from a woman dental hygienist, Dr. Sinkford is the featured woman dentist in the 1990 book chronicling essays and bio sketches of a select group of leaders in the dental profession from around the world.

Our visit to the National Portrait Gallery painted a backdrop for impromptu discussion about minority women leaders in oral health. We found ourselves asking an important question: Of all the books and publications on leadership, where could one find a collective historical account of minority women leaders in oral health? The seed had been planted for this book.

Over the next few months, we reconnected by email and telephone. Jeanne took the lead in not letting the light fade on the book prospect. From day one, she was the key source of energy and wise insight. She formulated a content statement. We then began developing a list of minority women pioneers whose contributions to oral health have been somewhat hidden in many arenas, from dental education, public health, and organized dentistry to the military and dental product or insurance industry. The dental profession, as in other areas of science, has not heard the stories of these pioneers, which include their personal challenges, beliefs, and contributions. We felt strongly about uncovering their personal stories and professional contributions and bringing them to the surface for historical preservation and leadership development for the future.

As the list of potential contributors expanded, we realized the book could not encompass a comprehensive accounting of all minority women leaders. The number of contributing authors was limited by what seemed achievable by the anticipated completion date of December 2020, which would coincide with the one hundredth-anniversary year of the ratification of Amendment XIX of the Constitution of the United States. The second-tier consideration was to ensure diverse geographical, educational, and organizational representation. The selection criteria were as follows: contemporary minority women (alive and able to tell their stories), "firsts" in achievement, publication in refereed resources, and awards of recognition. Names were received from peers, women's groups, and other sources. Two women physicians have been included for their outstanding achievements and sustained efforts in research and recruitment that benefit women and the dental profession. Data was secured from contributing authors through online submissions and personal interviews.

As our conversations deepened and teleconference agendas lengthened, it became clear that we needed help on this project. Dr. Joseph West accepted our invitation to be the project manager. Dr. Marita Inglehart encouragingly joined the team as senior editor. Later, Dr. Anne Marie O'Keefe and Mr. Kensley Youte came on board as supporting editor and assistant project manager, respectively. We also wanted someone on the team who could bring the unvarnished historical context and experiential insights needed to unveil this book. Dr. Paul Gates unanimously came to mind as the most fitting voice to capture the relevance of these untold stories. He has been a reliable example to many by mentoring both men and women, channeling courage, opening avenues for professional development, and leveraging financial resources that propel career aspirations of minorities in dentistry. Dr. Gates accepted our invitation to contribute to the book by writing the focused commentary that serves as the afterword.

We have not met face-to-face since our gathering in Washington, DC. Our plan to reconvene in person in March was suspended by the COVID-19 pandemic. Technology has kept us connected and on track to bring this project to fruition. From one conversation, we cultivated a plan to shine the light on minority women leaders in oral health through a collection of personal untold and meritorious stories. Each person's story is framed around a few probing questions to learn preparatory steps taken, mentoring influences, challenges, and competencies needed to lead efforts that are dedicated to advancing oral health. Their stories attest to diligent preparation, unwavering courage, the power of mentoring, and unflinching insistence on succeeding in the historically male-dominated field.

While the collection of stories is not exhaustive, this book illustrates the rise of minority women leaders and how they thrive amid two persistent factors—being women and being women of color. With the blessing of God, we have assembled a gallery of accomplished minority women who have advanced oral health. As undaunted trailblazers, their authentic stories and professional biographies will inspire leadership development and appeal to current leaders and mentors—men and women—who are dedicated to helping women of color push beyond the glass ceiling to the summit of success in the upper echelon of leadership. *Caelum est finis*—the sky is the limit.

Introduction

◆ ◆ ◆

Stories, whether triumphant or troubling, are reflections of our past, pillars for the present, and instruments to help shape the future. Interspersed through this book is a wardrobe of wisdom shared through reflective real-life stories and experiences of a cadre of thirty-one accomplished minority women leaders in oral health. Their poignant responses to probing questions unwrap important lessons learned, challenges surmounted, and advice to women aspiring to leadership roles. Chronicled are achievements of women "firsts" or pioneers, influential champions in their life, and even the role of setbacks in their unrelenting personal and professional climb.

The uncharted pathway into dentistry by women was blazed in 1866 when Dr. Lucy Hobbs Taylor became the first woman graduate from the Ohio College of Dental Surgery. Embarking on the obscure educational highway to the male-dominated dental field was a bold, courageous, and slow-developing movement. Nearly a quarter century after Dr. Hobbs Taylor's pioneering achievement, in 1890, Dr. Ida Gray earned the distinction of being the first female African American dental school graduate from the University of Michigan School of Dentistry.

Historically Black Colleges and Universities (HBCUs), namely, Howard University College of Dentistry and Meharry Medical College School of Dentistry, have been wellsprings of Black women dental graduates. Leading the way in 1896 and 1902 were Dr. Mary Imogene Williams (at Howard) and Dr. Ollie Bryan-Davis (at Meharry), respectively. Also paving the way for women of color was Columbia University dental graduate Dr. Gertrude Curtis, who in 1909 became the first Negro woman to practice dentistry in New York State. Other pioneers in that era were 1918 University of Southern California dental graduate Dr. Vada Watson Somerville and Tufts University graduate Dr. Jessie G. Garnett, who in 1919 became the first Black woman to practice dentistry in Boston.

The 1920s introduced another significant minority woman dentist pioneer. Dr. Elizabeth "Bessie" Delany, a 1923 Columbia University dental graduate, completed dental school as the only African American in a class of 170 students and was the second African American woman to gain dental licensure in the state of New York. At age one hundred this color-barrier breaker gained overdue recognition when she, along with her sister Sarah "Sadie" Delany, an educator, voiced their mountaintop experiences in the best seller *Having Our Say*.

While pursuing a career as a dentist was novel, advancing into the realm of leadership in dentistry was another high hurdle that took years for minority women to overcome. More than a century elapsed between Dr. Hobbs Taylor becoming the first woman dentist to the emergence of the first woman dental dean. Dr. Jeanne Craig Sinkford, a 1958 Howard University dental graduate, broke this long-standing leadership barrier in 1975 when she became the first female dean of a US dental school. The eighty-five-year span between Dr. Gray's and Dr. Sinkford's achievements provides an indelible historical mile marker in minority women's journey into dentistry and eventual ascent to leadership in the profession. What took so long? What were the societal, environmental, cultural, and other barriers encountered by women during this span of time? Answers to these and other questions will be disclosed in the individual and collective stories of the women leaders featured in this book.

Whether leading in the middle, on the margins, or the upper rung of the organizational leadership ladder, the voices captured here inspire and motivate. Threaded throughout this book are patterns of unrelenting courage, grit, perseverance, and achievement of minority women who followed Dr. Ida Gray's wilderness journey into the dental profession and later advanced to leadership positions. These unique, real-life personal stories are stitched together by commonality of purpose, resilience, and resolve to overcome inertia, break "glass ceilings," and achieve prominent roles as scientists, educators, administrators, public health officials, and beyond. Each woman leader shares remarkable "aha" moments and monumental insights that challenge, energize, and provide an indispensable guide for women aspiring to leadership. These women leaders also highlight other individuals—both men and women—who championed their professional rise.

Revealed in this book is a tapestry of talented minority women who, with the aid of allies or an internal drive to prove naysayers wrong, mastered the art of leadership without a blueprint for success. Their substantive stories will provide a timeless compass for generations of women to come. Similar to Dr. Delany, a previous "hidden figure" in the oral health workforce, these pioneering women are having their say and inspiring other change agents. This writing documents and celebrates many other minority women dental pioneers. For example, in 1992, Dr. Juliann Bluitt Foster became the first woman president of the Chicago Dental Society. The following year she was elected as first woman president of the American College of Dentists, the organization that represents gold standard leadership, professionalism, ethics, and excellence in dentistry.

The demographic pendulum in dentistry has slowly shifted from a nontraditional to traditional career path for women. Equally as important, leadership opportunities for women in dentistry are also ticking upward, albeit the cadence of change for women of color has not paralleled the rate of increase for others. In recent years, however, minority women in oral health are rising as opportunities emerge. For example, in 2019, Dr. Lily Garcia was named dean of the UNLV School of Dental Medicine. Four years earlier, she served as chair of the American Dental Education Association (ADEA) Board of Directors. Similarly, in 2020, Dr. Rena D'Souza became the first minority woman appointed director of the National Institute of Dental and Craniofacial Research (NIDCR) at the National Institutes of Health (NIH).

Spanning more than a century, from the early 1900s to the present day, women's emergence in the dental profession rose at a snail's pace from 2 percent to nearly 50 percent, with the greatest increase occurring in the past three decades. Noteworthy is the disparity in percentage between minority women and their majority counterparts in the dental profession. Minority women have never represented more than 5 percent of US dentists, even though their representation in the general population is far greater. These demographic realities are sobering, particularly in light of the nation's rapidly increasing minority population. The data supports a call to examine why minority women are so poorly represented in dentistry, particularly in leadership, and then to identify and implement solutions.

The foregoing demographic snapshot is a compelling reason to capture the voices of phenomenal minority women leaders who have surmounted impediments historically experienced by women, particularly women of color. Their stories uncover the individual and collective characteristics and attitudes necessary to overcome anticipated and unforeseen obstacles.

This book will help crack the shared and unique codes for survival and success of minority women leaders influencing oral health. We hope readers do not underestimate these women's extraordinary achievements based on modesty of the prose but rather use these success stories as motivation to conquer trials and transform travails into triumphs. In the pages ahead, their combined knowledge and wisdom provides a unique compass that will allow their successors to forge new frontiers and advance oral health.

Canise Y. Bean, DMD, MPH

◆ ◆ ◆

My Early Years

Growing up in Lexington, Kentucky, allowed me to have a great childhood experience, although, looking back, I was a bit sheltered. My parents, Calvin and Juanita Wright, were hardworking, law-abiding middle-class citizens. My dad was a brick mason, and my mother was a well-respected teacher. At the time of my birth, my mother was teaching physical education at a local elementary school; she went on to teach physical education at a high school, where she also sponsored and coached the cheerleading team.

I remember traveling by bus to "away" games with the basketball team and the cheerleaders. It was fun to sit in the stands. I knew all the cheers and moves, and I would call the players by name when they made free throws or great plays. After the games, we had pizza before going home. Mother worked for a while in a middle school and then moved to Kentucky State University in Frankfort, where she supervised student teachers. Kentucky State is a historically Black institution and her alma mater.

For my kindergarten year, I lived with my mother's sister, Aunt Connie, and her husband, Uncle Haskins, in Dayton, Ohio, because there was no kindergarten in Lexington at that time. Aunt Connie was the principal of an elementary school and insisted that I attend kindergarten at her school. My mother, and sometimes my father, would come to visit most weekends. This first school experience was a time of great discovery and growth because I had a first best friend, Karen, and the best teacher ever, Mrs. Myers.

Back in Lexington, my family had a small three-bedroom house on a dead-end street in a subdivision of Lexington known as Saint Martin's Village. Saint Martin's was named after Martín de Porres, a Peruvian patron saint of mixed-race heritage. There were thirteen families on the street, and most had children. We always found games to play, and the beauty of living on a dead-end street was that it converted easily to a playground. I recall the time I rode my tricycle on the sidewalk to the end of the street, which had a water drain underneath. The drop to the street was about three feet. I figured I had graduated from the sidewalk and decided to ride over the three-foot drop. Not a good decision! But certainly, a lesson well learned and not repeated.

I always felt like I was the kid who had to go home first. As soon as the streetlights came on and the games and talks with the older kids got really intense, I had to go inside. If I was delayed, my father would come to the front door and call my name. That was very embarrassing in front of my friends, especially because I started my growth spurt early and was as tall or taller than the other kids but not as old.

My elementary school years were spent at three different schools. I attended first and second grades at an all-Black school with phenomenal teachers. For third and fourth grades, I went to an integrated school, which was an eye-opening experience in the early 1960s. My fifth and sixth grades were spent at the neighborhood Black school. It was within walking distance from our home. After school, I walked to my aunt Roe's house. She was my mother's second sister, who owned and operated a beauty salon in her basement. During these walks to Aunt Roe's with my friend Paula, I encountered my first memorable bullying experience.

A classmate named Bobby would walk behind us, throw rocks at us, call us names, rush up behind us, and push and kick us while he laughed. When Paula and I told our parents, they talked to Bobby's parents, and the episodes diminished.

One important formative phase of my early life was that I played flute in the band, beginning in fourth grade. Our next-door neighbor was the band director for a local high school, and he gave me free instruction about proper positioning and embouchure. I enjoyed the band and later played in the orchestra. In high school, I was introduced to the piccolo and marching band, and I was able to play my instrument, march, and be part of various formations at the same time! I was also an avid spectator and cheerleader for my school's football and basketball teams, which reminded me of when my mother was cheerleader sponsor and coach. My intention was to be on the cheerleading squad, but I just did not have the right stuff to make it. As I matured, I came to realize that I was much better suited to being a band member and continued playing in the band in college.

Thinking back to my early years, I am glad I learned that the word *friend* cannot be applied to all acquaintances, neighbors, classmates, and colleagues. A friend accepts and cares for you unconditionally and is able to critique truthfully and with love. A friend does not reveal secrets, hold grudges, envy, or do harm. A friend is a gem, and one must know how to be one in order to have them. Friends can sustain and empower others in their life's journey, including their professional aspirations and goals. Friends are a must for successful female leaders.

Introduction to the Health Professions

The summer before I left for college, I participated in a six-week residential program at the University of Kentucky (UK). It was designed to expose students from minority backgrounds to the health professions. Most program participants wanted to be physicians or nurses, so they were placed in those health-care settings as shadows and student workers. I always wanted to be an obstetrician and deliver babies, but during my senior year in high school, I decided I was meant to be a pharmacist.

After some pre-Google-days research, I determined that Texas Southern University (TSU) College of Pharmacy and Health Sciences in Houston was the school for me. It was a historically Black institution with a well-known marching band that accepted females, while Grambling State and Florida A&M University only allowed them to be majorettes.

When I asked to be placed with a pharmacist during the summer program at UK, I was informed that the program did not have a relationship with a pharmacy program. Instead, they placed me in the UK dental emergency room. Growing up, I had enjoyed good dental care, including orthodontia, and so I resigned myself to that alternative because I felt that I knew what my college plans were. But I fell in love with dentistry. The human interactions were very rewarding, and the services we provided were life changing for many patients. It was truly a team-service delivery model.

Upon arriving at Texas Southern University, I changed my major from pharmacy to premed/predent. I enjoyed playing in the band, especially the away-game trips to Jackson and Lorman, Mississippi; New Orleans and Grambling, Louisiana; Birmingham, Alabama; and many cities in Texas that I would not have chosen to visit in the early 1970s, on the heels of Jim Crow. TSU provided my first taste of the real power and financial influence of athletics when I traveled with the band on a university charter plane to Honolulu for the University of Hawaii season opener. And Texas Southern was not even ranked in football!

I met some incredible people during my college years and was initiated into Delta Sigma Theta (DST) Sorority, Inc. After three years at TSU, I had completed the requisites for dental school and returned to my hometown of Lexington to pursue that career path. After graduating from the University of Kentucky College of Dentistry (class of 1980), I married and moved to Ohio for a general practice residency at Cleveland Metropolitan Hospital. While there, it was my privilege to found the first African American group practice in Cleveland—Shaker Dental Associates. After ten years with Shaker Dental Associates, we moved to Columbus, Ohio, where I completed a master of public health degree. Not being able to find my niche in public health, I returned to private practice part-time, beginning at one day per week and increasing the time to three days.

Becoming a Dental Educator and Administrator

After receiving dental care for my children and myself at the Ohio State University College of Dentistry, I considered that holding an academic position there would be stimulating and provide an opportunity to work part-time. Upon more investigation, visits, interviews, and discussion with faculty and administrators, I accepted a full-time position as an assistant professor.

What I did not know initially was that many dental educators did not expect me to succeed. Being naive, I expected to be accepted as a much-needed addition to the faculty. I recall being "set up" by a colleague in faculty practice who referred a young patient in her twenties who had extensive caries, with reversible periodontal status, and wanted to save every tooth in her mouth. Being new, I was eager to please, demonstrate my skills, and satisfy the patient, and I went to work to achieve a disease-free state for her. About halfway through the treatment, it became apparent that the patient was not sufficiently committed to her desire to "save" every tooth and do her part in assuring success of the treatment plan. Thus, it became necessary to perform multiple extractions and prosthetic procedures. I realized I had received this referral because the "grunt" care, i.e., removal of extensive decay, root canals, and poor patient motivation, were more of a challenge than my colleague had wished to tackle and believed could be accomplished with favorable results. It was more gratifying to watch me struggle and ultimately reach a dead end. I never confronted this faculty member to express my disappointment in the lack of common courtesy, but realized I was not considered a peer.

Additionally, I was not technologically savvy, was not offered assistance, and thus was pretty much self-taught about computer applications and programs. I did get a quick run-through from a female faculty colleague regarding the capabilities and operation of the classroom equipment before my first lecture as a course director. I was thankful for that!

Within a year of teaching at the college, public health came knocking at my door through a five-year grant from the Robert Wood Johnson Foundation (RWJF) known as Pipeline, Profession, and Practice: Community-Based Dental Education to the Ohio State University College of Dentistry. It required placing our dental students in community sites for sixty days, providing direct care to underserved patients, and increasing enrollment of students from underrepresented minority backgrounds. I was honored to lead this effort that became known as the OHIO Project. My priority was to get to work without being concerned with my title, position, or compensation. Other than working as a course director in operative dentistry, this was my first leadership role. Transforming a dental school curriculum from twelve days spent in a campus center for special needs children, a pediatric dental clinic at a local renowned children's hospital, and a few days in nursing homes and geriatric community centers to sixty full days in community dental settings throughout the state that cared for underserved populations was a monumental feat.

Lessons Learned While Advocating for Diversity, Equity, and Inclusion

Implementing community-based dental education during the five-year period RWJF funded our dental school included frequent and daunting challenges. But I discovered that I am a good listener and have the ability to delegate responsibilities that are outside of my expertise. I also learned that it is important to ask for—not demand—assistance, and I began to understand the value of establishing and trusting the capabilities of committees.

While looking to educate faculty members about the importance of diversifying the dental profession and the value of diversity for growth and advancement, I concluded that a more nontraditional and interactive approach might be more effective, meaningful, and enduring. Therefore, I identified and contracted with a theater-based diversity and inclusion consulting firm. They were experts in the field and thorough in their assessment of our faculty. The college leadership declared the training mandatory, so it was well attended and very participatory. However, a colleague forwarded an email trail of a faculty discussion of the training in racial and derogatory terms. References were made to "monkeys" and the "Ku Klux Klan" and the worthlessness of investing in diversity. After all, these faculty members thought Ohio State University was a Big Ten school with a championship football team and a dental school that was capable and proficient at educating "Buckeye dentists."

I expected resistance, but not in such a racist manner. I always worked to accept people for who and what they were, but this was a lesson that face-to-face interactions do not necessarily change hearts.

The Value of Mentors

I did not actively seek a department chair as my mentor. Rather, he came to me. He was a true champion of the OHIO Project and lead author on the RWJF grant proposal. He took me under his wing, saw to it that I was appointed as the program codirector, and assisted in planning and implementing strategies. He also identified other key members of the college leadership who could contribute to the success of the OHIO Project, even though they were not all strong supporters of community-based dental education and diversity. My mentor later included me in his specialty department as a general dentist by expanding its scope to include community oral health and a name change. That was an important and bold move, and the other department members were welcoming, accepting, and helpful.

My mentor and a few other advocates were strong supporters of my promotion to associate professor and, five years later, full clinical professor. As a faculty member involved in the promotion and tenure process in various roles, I understand and appreciate the significance of mentors. They are a necessity in health professions academia.

When my mentor retired, neither the new chair nor the college leadership felt my placement was right for the college structure, and I was moved again. However, at that point, community-based dental education had been immersed into the clinical education curriculum of the college and offered great value on many levels.

Pearls of Wisdom

I wish to share many pearls with future members of the health professions who are from historically underrepresented b ackgrounds. As a graduate of Texas Southern and a proud life member of Delta Sigma Theta, I share the words of a TSU alumnus and sorority sister, also known as a most eloquent US congresswoman from the great state of Texas:

> The women of this world must exercise leadership, quality, dedication, concern and commitment which is not going to be shattered by the inanities and ignorance and idiots who would view our cause as one that is violative of the American dream of equal rights for everyone (Barbara Jordan, 1975).

Be gracious, be grateful, and go high.

Therefore *can't*, *won't*, and *don't think so* will not suffice. You must stand up, stand tall, and be a vessel of change.

Winifred J. Booker, DDS, FAAPD

◆ ◆ ◆

My Family Background

I was born at Georgetown University Hospital in Washington, DC, the fifth child and fourth girl in a family that eventually included eight children. My mother, Martha Cecelia Thomas, was from Bushwood, Maryland. She attended what is now Bowie State University and New York University, where she earned her bachelor and master of education degrees. As an elementary school teacher, and then a corrective reading and writing specialist, she served children and families in the Southern Maryland and Baltimore County public school systems for thirty-three years. Mother loved and accepted each of us for who we were and took great delight in our individual creativities. She was fun, laughed often, and was very patient and gentle.

My father was from Baltimore, Maryland. He was educated at West Virginia State University, New York University, and the University of Maryland, where he earned his bachelor of education, master of education, and doctor of philosophy degrees, respectively. For sixteen years, he served as chairman of the Department of Physical Education at what is now Coppin State University. My dad proudly served our country in World War II and through two tours in the Korean War. We often called him "sir," at his insistence, especially if he was upset with us. He was matter of fact, no nonsense, and unaccepting of rhetoric, so you were best to come with it straight from the outset.

For the first eight years of my life, we lived in Saint Mary's County in southern Maryland, where we owned seven acres of land and did our own gardening. We gathered wild berries and firewood, and we cultivated fruit and flowers for our survival and enjoyment. We often went crabbing and fishing from our uncle's pier in Avenue, Maryland, and frequently shopped for groceries at the Amish markets. We made up games, constructed our own kites, regularly played school, and often hiked through the woods, taking in all that nature had to offer.

One of my fondest childhood memories was when Mother would have us shampoo our hair in the rain. Our property had well water, and our parents were astute about water conservation. As long as there was no thunder and lightning, we would slip into our bathing suits, lather up our hair, and dance to the water music coming from the sky. Attending Mass every Sunday and on holidays was required by Mother. Frequenting church festivals and local tribal powwows were the best of times too. We thoroughly enjoyed our youngest years!

While my parents were my greatest mentors, my education at Tennessee State University and Meharry Medical College was made possible because of the unselfish support of many mentors, including my sisters. These mentorships helped me to become confident and to develop a deep sense of compassion for others, a determination to improve the human experience by helping to advance health care, and a desire to make a difference in the world.

My oldest sister, Jennifer, excelled in academics and was a superior athlete during high school and college. Her intellect and competitive strength assured me that I, too, had such strength and talent. When I was about six years old, Jennifer and I started to listen to music together, which made me feel very calm and loved by her.

While my twin sisters, Cathy and Carol, also excelled at sports, they were different in other ways and totally unafraid to try new things. When we were teenagers, Mother bought us a telephone from Montgomery Ward to share in our bedroom. We were pleased to have our very own telephone in the room where the four of us frequently hung out together. Lo and behold, my sister Carol decided to take our brand-new telephone apart just for the fun of taunting us. There appeared to be a thousand pieces laid out on the white bedspread, but she methodically reassembled it after we had collected ourselves. My sister did not think for one second that she was not going to be able to put Humpty Dumpty back together again! This experience gave me the courage and fearlessness to confront the many challenges that lay ahead.

My sister Cathy, the more settled of the genetic duplicates, once made a blanket out of scraps of material using our mother's sewing machine. I thought it was a most amazing feat, and the patchwork blanket was equally amazing to me. When it was time for her to start student teaching, she drove an old convertible. She never thought twice about the fact that the car was three decades older than she was. In fact, her students excitedly referred to it as their teacher's "summer car." I felt incredibly inspired to see her drive down the street with the top down!

My Irish twin sister, Edwina, was a whole lot of fun to play with when we were children. We held hands all the time. We made mud pies and decorated them with flowers. But the best fun was her talent for making dolls out of literally anything at hand. She used dandelions, honeysuckles, cattails, weeping willow branches, or tall blades of grass. Our tea parties and conversations with these unusual imaginary guests were even more delightful. My relationship with Edwina validated my own out-of-the-box thinking.

My youngest sister, Linda, had an eye for fashion very early. This may have stemmed from the fact that I was the one who most often helped her to dress for school. I would creatively adorn her in mother's broaches and comb her hair into bun styles. Determined not to ever look like an old lady as a teenager, her selection of outfits was always classy. Watching her mature in this way made me proud. At the same time, I felt like quite the accomplished eleven-year-old for having looked after my youngest sister in this way.

Becoming a Pediatric Dentist

Being mentored by Dr. Bettye Jennings during the summer of my third year in dental school exponentially increased my confidence going into my final year. That summer, I had an externship with the Baltimore City Health Department. The externship included rotations through the Cherry Hill, Caroline Street, and Upton dental clinics and working on the mobile dental bus that traveled to community sites and to elementary schools. I took patient histories, cleaned teeth, and assisted with restorative treatments and surgical procedures, all the while maintaining detailed notes about every single patient encounter.

At the conclusion of this externship, I thanked Dr. Jennings for this opportunity and proudly provided a copy of the neatly typed document that I had come to treasure. She looked it over, looked up at me with the brightest smile ever, and said, "When you finish dental school, you have a job with the Baltimore City Health Department." I felt happy, empowered, and validated, and I proceeded to my senior year in dental school on top of the world!

A second important mentor at that time was Dr. Cynthia Hodge. She joined the faculty of Meharry Medical College at the beginning of my third year in dental school, and I was assigned to her preceptor group. She never doubted my capability, even when I doubted it myself. The way in which she communicated never afforded time for self-doubt. I knew I could go to her for help in figuring out what sometimes seemed to be an unsolvable situation. I always left our meetings with a renewed sense of confidence.

Though I had excelled in pediatric dentistry, I was not sure that I wanted to specialize, because dental school had been grueling for me. But Dr. Hodge insisted that I participate in the interview process to understand what was involved in case I would change my mind. In helping to prepare me, she went through her checklist, as she did with all the students she mentored. I am officially the happiest pediatric dentist in the whole wide world, and now we laugh together when we think back to this conversation.

I received my dental license on February 2, 1988, and was immediately employed by two colleagues. In 1990, I opened my first general practice in a community of abject poverty. The unmet needs of children were immense, and the closest pediatric dentist practiced several miles away. Despite being a general dentist in need of further pediatric training, the community embraced me, and I embraced them. I organized programs to further endear families in Upton, providing health education presentations and disseminating promotional products and resourceful literature.

In 1988, following what I was taught while attending dental school, I held my first Healthy Halloween Party, and the children and parents came in droves—they loved it. In the spring, I organized a Project Healthy Easter Basket event. To this day, I remain keenly focused on the continued expansion of family dental care and have developed a revolutionary practice model for infants and toddlers.

After three years in private practice, I applied to a pediatric dentistry residency program. I realized that adults were no longer the population I aspired to treat and that the children in this community needed me more. I had come to appreciate that I connected well with children. At that time, Baltimore had only one pediatric dentist of color.

Being accepted into a pediatric dental residency program in 1994 was the most impactful educational experience of my career. But the pathway to get there required assertive persistence. I matched as the third candidate when the program only offered two positions. Having written down the names of the pediatric dentists who interviewed me, I sent a letter to each of them. I also wrote to the chair of the program and to the president of the Children's National Medical Center. In my letters, I appealed to them to create a third position so that I could be accepted into the upcoming class. I communicated the needs of the underserved community where my practice was established and the limitations I faced in providing care for these children. I stated that I desired this opportunity so much that I was willing to accept the position without the benefit of a stipend. A few days went by, and finally I received a favorable response. I completed this two-year residency program in 1996 while maintaining my private practice in Baltimore.

Going Beyond the Boundaries of My Pediatric Dental Practice

My determination to educate and empower families about good oral health led me to establish Brushtime Enterprises. I formed this company as more and more toddlers and children presented with rampant early childhood caries and when it was not uncommon for me to treat many of them under general anesthesia. My persistent passion to achieve changes in health behavior and to patent oral health-care innovations produced the Brushtime Bunny and Dental Care in a Carrot in 1993. The newly developed Brushtime Baby line of health education products for baby and parents, as well as the patent-pending Mouth Almighty device, uphold this irrepressible desire to advance health outcomes for children and families.

Founding a nonprofit organization—the Children's Oral Health Institute—provided the platform to develop programs to help further empower children and their families. The idea to reach as many families as possible in the largest numbers possible produced the program Lessons in a Lunch Box: Healthy Teeth Essentials & Facts About Snacks. This outreach program expanded to include the support of organized and corporate dentistry and hundreds of volunteers. Now fifty-six of sixty-six dental schools—including their faculty, student dentists, and dental hygiene students—are responsible for helping to implement this program in elementary school classrooms in all fifty states, the District of Columbia, and Puerto Rico, Haiti, and the Bahamas.

In 2012, the Children's Oral Health Institute organized efforts to introduce new health legislation. The state of Maryland now requires all public schools to teach about oral health every year from kindergarten through the twelfth grade. The National Governors Association has referred to this progressive law as a "Best Practice Model."

Winifred J. Booker, DDS, FAAPD

Despite all these sometimes-formidable efforts and successes my career in dentistry has afforded me, and most importantly afforded the beneficiaries of these opportunities, it is still frustrating to face the various and sometimes-senseless barriers. It can be exasperating to not have enough out-of-the-box, progressive visionaries in place to help ensure the expeditious development and advancement of resources for the sake of patient populations in need. It continues to be a challenge to help masses of marginalized children and their families achieve better oral and therefore meaningful overall health. These challenges inspire me to be unapologetically excited about health-care innovation and to create products and resources. While I have gone about the business of doing just this, the needs remain immense. I therefore remain enthusiastically steadfast and willingly committed to continue making every effort to rise to these challenges.

Sheila R. Brown, MEd, DDS, FACD

◆ ◆ ◆

My Life Before Becoming a Dentist

I grew up as an only child of older parents. Both of them had the benefit of a college education; between them they had attended Tougaloo, Fisk, and Howard universities. There was never a question about whether or not I would go to college, only when and where. My paternal grandmother took great pride in announcing to my father that she had purchased encyclopedias for me when I was eight years old.

When I was very young, I learned that my grandmother was ill, and I watched her navigate through the guidelines determined by her physician. I looked at her one day and said, "Granny, I am going to be a doctor so I can cure you." She looked at me and said, "Thank you." And so, my journey began.

In college, I was driven to succeed. Having lost a parent the year before, I understood that I did not have time to waste. I read my catalog of classes to make sure I was on the premed path. I was so immersed in getting all the classes that three years passed before I remembered to sign up for the MCAT (Medical College Admission Test) and the possibility of early graduation was around the corner. However, as fate would have it, I was offered an application for the Teacher Corps / Peace Corps, which provided the opportunity to earn a master's degree in education. So off I went to Houston.

I was assigned, as a Peace Corps volunteer, to teach science in Tamale, Ghana, in West Africa. This experience was transformational. It broadened my vision and my perspective of the world. Being in a country that was run by people of color—a proud people who were well educated and motivated—was inspiring. I taught biology to students at the senior secondary school level. These students were preparing to teach the wonders of science in grade schools. Their thirst for knowledge was amazing and made me rise to being my best self. On my second day in the classroom, I asked a student a question; he looked at me in wonder as he stood to answer. "I am not sure," he said.

The very next day, this student enthusiastically greeted me at the door with all that he had learned the previous night about the subject. All I could do was smile. At that very moment, I could see him teaching others with the same fervor and enthusiasm. I was so proud of him. Learning is a very valuable and powerful force. There is no greater reward than seeing the look on students' faces when they understand. It is priceless.

Giving of one's self, for no other reason than because it is the right thing to do, is the best feeling in the world. What I got from that young man was more valuable than the contribution I made as his teacher. This experience triggered my first life goal—to always try to make a difference.

Becoming a Dentist

I was very fortunate to go into dentistry. I was introduced to the profession by a physician who knew that I was interested in medicine. He asked if I had ever considered dentistry. He added, "It is a wonderful career for a woman. You can practice and meet some of the needs of family life." He also mentioned the growing need for women in the profession. I heard two things in his statement—freedom and flexibility—my second life goal. I started looking at dental schools and requesting applications that day.

After teaching in Ghana, Houston, and Chicago, I was accepted at the University of Michigan School of Dentistry. There were twelve Black students in my class, and we were committed to making sure that everyone succeeded and graduated. My dental school advisor, Dr. Lee Jones, was a powerful influence for me. He inspired me to become the best I could be. I remember telling him that all of my Black classmates were going to graduate on time; that we had agreed to look out for each other and study together when needed. He answered with a supportive smile.

Dr. Jones inspired me to be a leader as a student and as a professional in organized dentistry. My first step toward leadership was founding the King's Feast, a celebration of the life and accomplishments of the Rev. Dr. Martin Luther King Jr. This inaugural event took place in January 1982 and was hosted by the Black students in my class. This event has been celebrated every year and is now part of the calendar of the University of Michigan School of Dentistry. It remains one of the greatest achievements of my life.

At the end of my third year in dental school, I was elected president of the Michigan chapter of the Black Dental Student Association (BDSA), now known as the Student National Dental Association (SNDA). I served the chapter and represented it in the House of Delegates at the national level for one year.

After my dental school graduation, I returned home and worked in established practices for nineteen months. After that, I started my own practice. During this time, I had two mentors who supported me and taught me how to manage a business. They were Dr. James T. Smith, also known as Smithy, and Dr. Marilyn D. Jackson. Dr. Smith watched me work in his practice and recognized my independence. He said to me, "You have your own way of doing things. You need your own practice, and I am going to help you to get it." I will never forget how much he cared about me and wanted me to succeed. He pushed me out of the nest so I could fly.

Dr. Marilyn D. Jackson invited me to join her in my first office as her partner. She also taught and guided me in my education about running a business, which I needed to succeed. In fact, I was able to buy the practice in two years and expand it. Both of these mentors contributed greatly to my growth and development as a person and as a professional.

Becoming a Leader in Organized Dentistry

During this time, I re-entered organized dentistry. I started as a delegate in the National Dental Association (NDA). Next, I served on the board of trustees as treasurer and became the organization's eighty-seventh national president. I resisted the last step for years. Every year, Dr. Jones would ask when I was going to run for president. And every year, I would tell him, "I am not going to run." He would just say okay and grin. But mentors always seem to know. When I called to tell him that I was running for president, he said, "I know."

Being president was exhilarating. It was a great honor to serve as a change agent. In fact, it was the pinnacle of my professional career. During my term and under my leadership, the organization

- developed the research subcommittee of the Minority Faculty Forum;
- established the memorandum of understanding with The Links, Incorporated, as a community partner;
- implemented the inaugural NDA New Dentist Program as part of the annual meeting; and
- launched the first National Dental Association public service announcement on oral health.

And my greatest accomplishment was to obtain an official written apology from the American Dental Association for their participation in the disenfranchisement of African American dentists in the United States. I still have a copy of that letter framed and hanging in my office.

Overcoming Challenges

People will follow those they respect. You must be fearless when working with other organizations so there is no misunderstanding about your commitment to your organization and the individuals you serve. It is equally important to be a consensus builder and remember that it is not always about you. And, last but not least, as a leader you must push those who need pushing and elevate those who need to be elevated due to their hard work and commitment. And always remember—a high tide raises all ships!

I had a rocky path during my education. The road was paved with racism and sexism. At times, I could not figure out whether I was treated in a disparaging way because I was Black or because I was a woman. At first, I could not understand why this time was so overwhelming. I had experienced discrimination before, both in the workplace and in public. But this seemed different. I could have walked away, but I realized that leaving dental school would stop me from accomplishing my life's goals and objectives. So I had a conversation with myself.

"Sheila, your objectives are

1. to be a dentist and graduate on time;
2. to learn all that you can and more;
3. to prepare to associate with a practicing dentist and learn more; and
4. to prepare to open your own practice so you can achieve your life's goal.

So, keep your eyes on the goal."

Words of Wisdom for Future Leaders

My advice to future leaders is:

- Know who you are and who you are not.
- Surround yourself with friends on whom you can depend, who do the work and have your back.

- Associate with qualified people who are up for the task.
- Be a good listener.
- Be a consensus builder.
- Never stop learning.
- Do not be afraid to make decisions. Much of the time you have a fifty-fifty chance of getting it right. There is no shame in making a wrong decision—own it.
- Finally, be flexible. There are many roads that lead to the same place or a better one. Had I not taken the side road to the Teacher Corps / Peace Corps, I would not have met the physician who encouraged me to become a dentist. I thank God for him!

Marsha E. Butler, DDS, FACD

◆ ◆ ◆

My Way to Dental School

As the daughter of two educators from Kansas, I grew up focused on going to college and becoming a doctor. We lived in a segregated section of Wichita. There were four elementary schools in town that African American children could attend. My father was the principal of one of those schools, and my mother was a teacher at another one of them. At that time in Wichita, Blacks were teachers or nurses; a few of them were physicians and lawyers, and the rest of the Black population worked primarily for the airline industry.

My parents were the first in their families to get advanced degrees. From the time my brother and I were very young, it was clear that we were going to college. My father often emphasized that the best thing we could do was to get a good education and give back to those we might leave behind. He and my mother were great influences on my life, ensuring that I understood that God was in the driver's seat and that I could be whatever I wanted to be if I put my mind to it and received the necessary education to facilitate that dream.

I was among the first group of Black children in Wichita to integrate the school system in our district. My dad drove me and a few of my friends daily to a school that was twenty miles from our house. It was my first experience at navigating an integrated school environment—not always a fair or friendly one—to gain an education and continue to excel at the things that I liked to do at the time, including gymnastics, mastering the cello, cheerleading, and dance.

Early in life, I recognized that I liked science and math. Fortunately, I had great teachers who encouraged me to continue on this path. I graduated from high school in the top 1 percent of my class, but I remember being frustrated that I was not considered for valedictorian.

Upon graduation, it was important to me to leave Wichita, spread my wings, and learn more about the world. I did not go far from home, because I accepted a scholarship at Stephens College in Columbia, Missouri. Stephens was an elite all-girls private school that taught me a lot about what I wanted to be. I had a dual major of biology and fashion design. Needless to say, when I got a C in one of my design classes, I dropped the design major. I knew that I wanted to be a doctor. In order to pursue this goal, I decided to transfer to Howard University in Washington, DC.

Coming from a mostly white Midwestern town, it was exciting to attend a college where so many students looked like me. I was inspired by my professors and my friends to seriously consider going to dental school. After three years at Howard, majoring in microbiology with a minor in chemistry, I knew I wanted to stay in Washington, DC. I therefore applied to and was accepted at Howard University's College of Dentistry.

My Life as a Dentist

Being accepted to dental school was like a dream coming true. Drs. Boyd, Sinkford, Duhaney, and Sanders were my mentors while I was there. These seemed to be the best days of my life. I also got married while in dental school. My husband, Larry, worked as a teacher at that time.

Upon graduation, I worked as an associate dentist in Michigan and soon opened my own practice in Detroit. While running my own business, I had the opportunity to promote oral health in the community, including speaking as an advocate on TV and radio. My peers in Michigan and my family in Kansas kept me motivated. But as exciting as it was, running a dental practice and being a young mother and wife was strenuous. My nuclear family and I wanted to move back to the East Coast, so I joined a group practice in New Jersey.

Working in this practice was stimulating and challenging. I learned a lot from a great mentor, Dr. James Lassiter, who believed it was important to have a high-quality dental practice but also to give back by helping dental students and young dentists who needed support to get started. Dr. Lassiter was there for me while I practiced with him, and he was there for me when I decided to leave the dental practice and venture into corporate America. My experience practicing dentistry in New Jersey gave me pride in the quality of my work and the confidence to build relationships with other organizations and institutions that would partner with me in my future endeavors.

Working in a Corporate Setting

I came to the realization that I wanted to have a greater impact on oral health than I could achieve in a group or solo practice. I began researching opportunities to leverage my dental skills and what I had learned in the dental office, and I took courses in marketing to augment my understanding of business. Fortunately, I was hired by Johnson & Johnson Dental Products to educate and market to dental practitioners about infection control and cosmetic dentistry. I entered a working environment that was new and foreign to me. But I was excited about working for a large company where I could reach dental professionals on a larger scale. At that time, we were facing the new challenge of HIV/AIDS, which required educating practitioners about the need to wear gloves and masks.

Working in this industry helped to build my business acuity and my communication, collaboration, and relationship-building skills. I represented the company at many conferences and meetings of dental professionals. I was constantly reminded that I was the only Black female in

Undaunted Trailblazers

the room; most of my colleagues were white males. I joined the company apologizing that I did not have a business degree, but I soon realized that it was my knowledge of dentistry that was my greatest asset in the corporate field of dental products. I also had some valuable peers at Johnson & Johnson who gave me the "inside" information that helped me navigate my way in my first few years.

When Johnson & Johnson sold off their dental products company, I and about 200 other employees were laid off. At the time, I was devastated that this could happen. But when God closes one door, he will open another door for you. About two months later, I was hired by Colgate-Palmolive to create a comprehensive initiative to help improve the oral health of minority communities throughout the United States. This was during a time when the National Dental Association Foundation (NDAF) was negotiating with Colgate to contribute more to help African American dental and dental hygiene students through scholarships and research grants at Howard University's and Meharry Medical College's dental schools. NDAF succeeded in gaining Colgate-Palmolive's financial support, and I was given the responsibility to manage the NDAF scholarship and research programs.

Many people from various organizations were instrumental in supporting me to successfully manage this endeavor. The NDAF leaders—including Drs. Lassiter, Paul Gates, and John Maupin—helped me understand the needs of their organization. I then had to translate those needs to achieve corporate understanding that would propel this relationship to a win-win outcome. Supporters at Colgate—including Mark, Juliber, Cook, and Huston—believed in me and in the oral health initiative. They were important to my career success and to the long-term commitment that Colgate made to the NDAF and to the minority oral health program. Within four years, we had expanded the oral health initiative globally to eighty countries and translated the oral health curriculum into thirty languages. This was possible because many of my colleagues in our local subsidiaries embraced the messages and goals of empowerment and improved oral health.

Of course, along the way, I had to deal with many challenges. I was given the responsibility of leading our professional relations efforts globally. At that time, I was reporting to the supervising manager, who would often travel with the team to various global meetings. We were in Bruges, Belgium, for a team meeting when I first encountered racial bias. My supervisor was informing our colleagues in Europe what it was like to live in the United States, explaining specifically his belief that when Black families move into an area, the value of the homes goes down. As I sat near him at the presentation table, he indicated that he, too, would move out if Blacks moved into his community. Many of my colleagues and I were taken aback by this blatant racism.

This supervisor/manager also had issues with women and with the LGBTQ+ community. With my feedback and feedback from other team members who were also offended by his remarks, Colgate finally let this manager go. The company has a strong focus on diversity and inclusion and would not tolerate this behavior.

Leadership Lessons Learned

It became clear to me how important it was to stand up for myself and, as a leader, to stand up for my team members who were also berated by the aforementioned manager. Leadership sometimes requires that we make tough choices that may have unfortunate consequences for others we know. One of my favorite quotes is from Maya Angelou: "Without courage, we cannot practice any other virtue with consistency. We can't be kind, true, merciful, generous, or honest."

When mentoring others at work, at dental schools, at my church, and in the community, I share how important it is to be *you*, striving to continuously learn and grow to become the best version of yourself. I encourage young people to aspire to do more than what they do at work, to find their passion and their joy in life and to thrive in it. We should look for the new experiences that fulfill our goals and our future ambitions. We need to mentor the next generation of women leaders to be courageous, curious, and innovative and to seek many diverse experiences that can help them inform those at the tables where decisions are made. I have had the opportunity to meet and nurture many of our new, upcoming female leaders who are rising stars. And I am excited about the future.

For me, leadership includes being your most authentic self, encouraging others to trust you and your judgment, collaborating with colleagues to come to critical decisions, and caring about others as you would want them to care about you. I consider myself a collaborative leader. In my position in global oral health, I have the opportunity to work with teams around the world to drive strategies and policies and to implement programs locally.

When I first began in this leadership position at Colgate, it was important to expand the oral health initiative quickly around the world. I realized that I could not do this massive expansion alone. What I quickly learned (my aha moment) is that in order to have a great impact globally, we must empower others to embrace the conceptual ideas and strategies that will support the achievement of our goals. In this case, my team members were included from the beginning in concept development and implementation strategies, with the flexibility to innovate in ways that would make the program relevant to their own communities. Our employees consider the Bright Smiles, Bright Futures program as a valuable opportunity for their subsidiaries to give back to their communities.

I am most proud of this oral health initiative, which I was hired to conceptualize thirty years ago, for its sustainability, its relevance globally, and its ongoing potential for innovation and growth. The Bright Smiles, Bright Futures program is now embedded in the DNA of the Colgate-Palmolive Company. I feel certain that it will continue to evolve and to reach and impact even more children and their families. By building enduring relationships with governments, the dental profession, and local nonprofit organizations, this ambition and ability to change oral health policy will be crucial in eliminating oral disease in children around the world in the next decade. That would be the ultimate dream come true.

Gail Cherry-Peppers, DDS, MS

◆ ◆ ◆

Early Years

I grew up with very meager beginnings, in Washington, DC, two miles from Howard University College of Dentistry. My grandmother cleaned houses as her primary profession and made sure we read and studied for hours after school. She and my mother wanted all children to attend college. My family's motto was "Study hard and get straight As in school." My family struggled to make ends meet but worked hard to provide a happy home. My godmother and my mother were teachers who encouraged me to study hard and obtain high grades in school, college, and professional school.

My role model was my godfather, who graduated from Howard University's College of Medicine and was a family physician. My godmother always told us that we needed more doctors in the family. My godfather found numerous enrichment programs in science for me to attend during the summer. Many of these programs aimed at recruiting future health professionals took place at Howard University, such as Upward Bound and other high school summer programs for students who wanted to become medical or dental professionals. I attended at least three science-related summer programs while I was in middle school and high school. After completing these programs, I knew that I wanted to become a health professional.

During one of these summer programs, I had one of my best teaching moments. It happened when I had the opportunity to watch the extraction of wisdom teeth in the oral surgery department at Howard University Hospital. I remember how excited and fascinated I was to watch these procedures. This experience was my introduction to clinical dentistry, and it influenced me greatly.

Becoming a Dentist

My family wanted me to go to medical school and thought that dentistry would be a limiting profession. While pursuing a bachelor of science degree in biology at Howard University, I had the opportunity to visit the dental school to talk to several faculty members. They provided me with an overview of the field of dentistry. This visit helped me to make up my mind to pursue my dream of becoming a dentist.

When I had the courage to tell my family and my godparents, they were surprised. However, they accepted my decision to go to dental school, and so I attended Howard University College of Dentistry. After graduating with a dental doctorate, I continued my education as a resident in an advanced training in general dentistry program.

The lesson I learned at that time was that it was important to follow my heart and become a dentist. I think this is a valuable lesson for all future leaders. It is crucial to push to achieve our own dreams because it is difficult to be motivated when living someone else's dream. When we work toward our own goals and do what we want to do, we can make great achievements.

Having two very strong mentors was another supporting factor that helped me fulfill my dream of becoming a dentist. One was my high school science teacher, who was influential in my decision to go to dental school. The second mentor was the mother of a friend and high school classmate, who was the only female dentist I knew. It was good to have two high-achieving females as my mentors. They encouraged me to get excellent grades, work hard to get into dental school, and graduate successfully. I've continued these great mentor/mentee relationships to this day. It was extremely helpful to find mentors who could show me the path to success. Over the years, they helped me build my career, advised me on the steps to take to navigate rigorous science programs, and get through dental school. I asked these mentors how to develop résumés, how to interview for jobs, how to sustain a good marriage and raise children, and how to climb the ladder of success.

My experiences have led me to recommend the following to all future leaders: stick with your mentors and share the lessons you learn with others who are trying to become successful leaders. I sought advice because I had so many unanswered questions and wanted some help to become a success. These relationships helped me achieve what I wanted to achieve.

Taking On Leadership Positions

Over the course of my career, I had several leadership positions. I retired from the US Public Health Service as a captain after I had worked at several HHS agencies, such as the National Institutes of Health (NIH), the Health Resources and Services Administration (HRSA), and the Food and Drug Administration (FDA). As a dental clinical consultant in these positions, I focused on the oral manifestations of chronic disease and population sciences. For example, I was the primary oral medicine specialist on the dental section of the AIDS Education and Training Center (AETC). I also led many other initiatives, such as the dental components of the Baltimore Longitudinal Study on Aging (BLSA) and Million Hearts, and I took the lead on the dental component of the FDA and NIH's $40 million PATH (Population Assessment of Tobacco and Health Study) program. I had opportunities to collaborate in the efforts to formulate national guidelines, such as the 2000 and the upcoming US Surgeon General's Report on Oral Health and the Office on Women's Health Tobacco Epidemic Plans.

Since retiring from the US Public Health Service (USPHS) and joining Howard University College of Dentistry (HUCD), I have served as the director of dental public health and associate professor. I enjoy supervising dental students in the clinics, teach several courses, and am engaged in the administration of HUCD's student community outreach and cultural event activities. Our students participate in more than thirty cultural and community service events. These events include health fairs, mission trip externships, remote-area medical events, community chronic disease–screening events, and clinical rotations in underserved areas across the United States.

I still serve as a consultant to the USPHS for disasters and critical emergencies and as a Howard University liaison. I also serve as the dental coordinator of the National HIV Curriculum, an AIDS Education and Training Center (AETC) National Coordinating Resource Center project with the Howard University HIV team.

Thinking back over all these years and the current activities, I realize that I learned several life lessons that are critical in becoming a successful woman leader. First, I think about the fact that it is crucial to work extremely hard and stay focused. As a woman, I encountered men who did not treat me well as their "woman boss" or "female leader." I realized that I had to be prepared to work with them and teach them that if they gave respect to others and demanded the same, they would receive respect. At the same time, it is important to be kind, have compassion, and be reliable. Those are great attributes to have. It is good to be firm, but don't forget to keep the promises you make.

Another critical realization I made was how difficult it is to work hard and raise a family at the same time. I learned that I could not do it without the assistance of others. I sought out wise advocates in addition to my lifelong mentors and learned to seek help whenever I needed advice on how to climb the ladder of success, I continue to use this approach to this day.

Overcoming Challenges

During a reorganization process in the US Public Health Service, I encountered one of my life's most severe challenges when I had to transfer to a job I did not like. As a captain in the Public Health Service, we had to move every few years. At that new job, I worked with staff members who were not friendly or positive. I very quickly realized that I did not like the work or the environment. In this situation, I prayed a lot. Then I began to reach out to colleagues and friends and gave them my résumé. In addition, I also called places at which I would have wanted to work and set up informal meetings with strangers to let them know I was interested in a particular area that matched my skill set. I always asked them to let me know if any positions became available. My persistence paid off, and I started a new job of my choice only four months later.

I also experienced challenges in not being able say no to speaking engagements and participating in professional organizations. It became clear to me that I had to stop trying to accept every engagement because I became burned out and exhausted. Therefore, I became more selective and now enjoy speaking at a few sessions per year.

Looking Back

Over the years, I learned how important it is to take vacations. During most of my earlier years, I did not use my vacation time because I was working so much. However, I learned to take a few vacations per year to add balance to my life. In my job, I did not lose my annual leave if I did not take days off. So, I would take extra vacations days when I was sick. I realized that vacations were important to me to help me relax and rejuvenate. Upon returning to work after a vacation, I always had more energy and was able to give 100 percent of my efforts.

Thinking back over my life, I am most proud of coming from an underserved area and having had a family and mentors who pushed me to achieve a high level of success. This foundation proved to be instrumental in allowing me to give back to my community. I am grateful for my loving husband and children, who strongly support me. In addition, I absolutely love to be a female dentist. I stuck with my dream, worked hard, and stayed focused.

It is important to me to give back through mentoring others who are doing well. Sometimes it is difficult to find the time to give back, but I always try to make the extra efforts needed to help others. My message to the members of the next generation who aspire to become leaders is to work hard and do not hesitate to overcome roadblocks and challenges. I want to encourage them never to be afraid and always trust their own voice and vision.

It is important to aspire to high levels of success, even if you think you are reaching too high. Above all, I want to remind these future leaders to nurture their relationships and friendships. Life will knock us down at times, and sometimes we have trials, make mistakes, or face disappointments. It is important to take those terrible moments in stride and continue to fight for high achievements and success. Having faith, family, friends, and mentors supports our life's journeys. Overall, it is important to learn from the challenges and tough times, to be flexible and redirect one's path, and to celebrate and rejoice in the good times. It is always helpful to seek out individuals in leadership whose work is admirable and ask them for advice. Keep learning, become an expert in your craft, seek to make leadership contributions, and you will make your way to the top!

Agnes H. Donahue, DDS, MSD, MPH

(Sadly, Dr. Donahue suddenly passed away on September 26, 2020.)

◆ ◆ ◆

My Early Years

I grew up in a poor and loving family on the Gulf Coast of Mississippi in the town of Ocean Springs, a quiet, picturesque place where everybody knew everybody and everybody looked out for everybody. My father, Henry Y. Donahue, was a Baptist minister who pastored three small churches along the Mississippi Gulf Coast. My mother, Valletta, played the piano for the services. My brother, Henry, was four years older than me. On Sunday morning, my parents would pack up the Buick and we would head for the one of the three churches we were scheduled to be at that week. There was a lot of singing, Bible reading, preaching, and praying. I particularly loved the singing.

School was a special event. There was a school for Black children (first through twelfth grade) and three schools for white children (elementary, middle school, and high school). I was well prepared by my mother to enter first grade. Upon entry, I could recite the Lord's Prayer, Psalm 23, and could count to a hundred by ones, twos, and fives. I did well in school at every grade level, and by seventh grade I had developed an interest in science. My father had purchased a set of encyclopedias for our home library. I loved perusing them. I already had my mind set on going to college when I finished school. This was a pretty ambitious plan, since no Black person from our town had ever gone to college. Everyone thought my ambitions were cute, and no one tried to discourage me.

By the time I went to college, I had decided I wanted to be in health care. I enrolled in Xavier University of Louisiana. During those years, education was still pretty segregated. Xavier was one of the few Historically Black Colleges and Universities (HBCUs) that offered a premedical degree to Black students. I was a biology major. I had less time for socializing, as I had a work-study job and I was doing extra work to fill in some of my high school gaps. In addition, my mother became ill, and I started to travel ninety miles home to Ocean Springs every weekend to see her. The summer between my freshman and sophomore year, my mother passed. I was devastated.

The next three years of undergraduate school were long and intense. The extra work that I put in to fill in the gaps in my background paid off, and by the end of my second year, I had made the honor roll. I so wish I could have told Mother about that. With graduation approaching, the big question came: What next? My plan to become a physician was tempered by the reality of the cost of education. There could be only one solution—work a few years and save my money.

I went to meet with every recruiter and narrowed down my options, and I met with the recruiter from Brookhaven National Laboratory (BNL) of New York because I'd heard that two Xavier students had had wonderful experiences in a summer program there. Two weeks later, I was offered a position as a biology scientific technician at BNL to start in September. I was so happy. If only I could tell Mama.

My first day at BNL was both exciting and frightening. Madam Curie House, the women's residence, was a very nice dormitory. But there were no Black people around. I had never been in a place where there were no Black people. Beyond that, there were only three people from the United States. The next morning, I made my way to my new job, a biophysics laboratory in the medical building, and met my new boss, Dr. Nicholas Delihas. I would grow to be very comfortable in this work setting. Work done at the lab represented the cutting edge for the study of the structure and function of ribosomal RNA.

Finding the Path to Dentistry

Students and teachers from HBCUs came from all over the country to Brookhaven for a period of study, but it was especially nice to see some people from the Southern states. I became friends with many of them, as well as with the students and fellows from other countries. As a result of connections through one of those friendships, I had the chance opportunity to meet Dr. Otis Maxwell, who was doing a prosthodontics fellowship at NYU while on sabbatical from Meharry Medical College School of Dentistry. When I talked with him about my work at the laboratory and graduate courses in cell biology that I was taking, he asked me if I had ever thought about going to dental school. I said no. He encouraged me to consider it, keep my options open, and send an application to Meharry Medical College School of Dentistry. I warmed up to the idea and applied. I had my heart set on Meharry, and upon acceptance, I packed up and headed to Nashville, Tennessee, for the fall freshman dental class. There were thirty-three people in my class. Six of us were women. In 1971 that made us the largest percentage of women in a dental class in the country: 32 percent.

The years at Meharry passed fast, and soon we would be ready to move on to the next phase. I received a fellowship to the pediatric dentistry program at Boston University School of Graduate Dentistry. I entered the program in 1975, and my mentor there was Dr. Spencer Frankl. Spence, as everyone called him, was a powerhouse in pediatric dentistry.

Mentoring Influence

Toward the end of my training, I focused on returning home to Mississippi. I submitted a curriculum vitae to the University of Mississippi School of Dentistry. The chairman of pediatric dentistry reached out to the chairman of my program in Boston. This connection was solidified on finding that my mentor, Dr. Frankl, knew the chairman at Mississippi, Dr. Rovelstad, very well.

I graduated, left the Northeast, and went back to my home state to live for the first time in ten years. A newly minted faculty member at the University of Mississippi Medical Center School of Dentistry, I learned that there were only eight pediatric dentists in the entire state, and five of them were at the university. I headed the Maternal and Child Health dental program at the university. Dr. Gordon Rovelstad, who had been promoted to academic dean and was now my mentor, supported my professional development. My experience in the area of maternal and child health led to an opportunity to pursue fellowship training at the University of California at Berkeley School of Public Health. He thought it was a great idea and said he could support me to get a sabbatical to do the training.

Career Advancement

I arrived at the University of California at Berkeley School of Public Health and immediately set to work. Upon completing this educational program in maternal and child health, I applied for a three-year fellowship at the National Institutes of Health. I accepted the fellowship and arrived in Washington, DC, at a time when there was a major reorganization happening. At the completion of my fellowship at NIH/NIDR, they offered me a position as a staff fellow. I would report to the Division of Intramural Research, and I informed the University of Mississippi that I would not be returning.

After all my various training, fellowships, and roles of responsibility, I worked with the regional offices in the federal government for the next fifteen years in Washington, DC. I successfully sought support for the Public Health Service's Office on Women's Health (OWH) to be formally added to the organizational structure of the Department of Health and Human Services. I was appointed its first executive director in 1991. I later served as the liaison for Public Health Intergovernmental Affairs and coordinator to the Regional Health Administrators (RHA) and the Office of the Assistant Secretary for Health. I was also coordinator between the RHAs and the surgeons general. I was advisor to seven assistant secretaries for health, eight surgeons general, and seven secretaries of the Department of Health and Human Services.

I remained the liaison between the RHAs, the assistant secretary for Health, and the new assistant secretary for Emergency Preparedness, Response, and Recovery. Until my retirement, I continued to be the HHS department's liaison to the Association of State and Territorial Health Officers, the National Association of County and City Health Officials, and the American Public Health Association. My final activity before my retirement in 2015 was to keep the ASH informed of the pulse in the states regarding the Ebola outbreak and to facilitate the safe return of the RHAs who were deployed to Liberia for the Ebola response back to the United States and eventually to their homes.

Cherae Farmer-Dixon, DDS, MSPH, MBA, FACD, FICD

∴

My Journey to Becoming a Dentist

"Thank you! These teeth make me look twenty years younger."

Hearing these words while participating in a summer science program set me on the path toward my dream. As a high school student, I had the wonderful opportunity of participating in a summer science Health Careers Opportunity Program (HCOP) at Tougaloo College. We shadowed various health professionals. When I shadowed a dentist in a community health center and witnessed the impact that dental care made on the patients' lives, I decided that dentistry was the profession for me.

I grew up in Indianola, in the Mississippi Delta. My parents were both educators and instilled in me the importance of hard work and excellence. Mediocre grades were not an option. They ensured that my life was filled with opportunities that enhanced my academics, supported community engagement, and grounded me in faith, dedication, and integrity. I helped to register people to vote before I was eligible to vote myself. I was active in the church, Girl Scouts, and other school and community groups that taught me foundational leadership, organizational skills, and community awareness.

When I graduated from high school, the question was not if I was going to college but which college I would attend. It was an automatic transition, as education was the foundation of my family. I grew up going to college sports and other activities with my parents and traveling to take my aunts and sister to begin their college careers. I would be part of the third generation of college graduates in our family. The summer science experience was the trajectory for my dental career path.

As I entered college, I was focused on majoring in biology with a plan to become a dentist. I began at Tougaloo College and transferred, in my junior year, to Mississippi Valley State University, the alma mater of my grandmother and my parents. Despite the transfer, my studies were not delayed; I graduated with honors and became the third generation of "Valley" graduates.

After being accepted to several dental schools, I decided on attending Meharry Medical College, the launching pad of many dentists who had impacted underserved areas and minority communities throughout the country. During my freshman year, I had the opportunity to meet the dean at the time, Dr. Rueben Warren. He introduced me to public health by allowing me to serve as a student research assistant. One of his projects was a school-based program that he helped to establish in Port Gibson, Mississippi. As a native Mississippian, this sparked my interest, but research was not on my radar at that time. Still, I had been taught that when you get opportunities to learn and gain new experiences, you should be open and willing. So, I participated and was pleasantly surprised by the breadth and depth of the knowledge I gained. I learned about policies and legislative issues that impacted care, about family and household attitudes that affected the acceptability of care, and about the role of communication and community involvement in the success of the program.

This experience made me interested in looking beyond the oral cavity to see the entire person, including the socioeconomic factors, cultural beliefs, behavioral habits, and perceptions that impacted overall health.

Cherae Farmer-Dixon, DDS, MSPH, MBA, FACD, FICD

I began to see dentistry in the dimensions of availability, accessibility, and acceptability. I knew that I not only wanted to be a general dentist but that I wanted to explore the world of public health dentistry. More importantly, I learned to be open to new possibilities and opportunities and to use these as stepping-stones to grow.

As I matriculated through dental school, Dr. Warren continued to serve as a mentor, and now, thirty years later, he still serves in that capacity. He encouraged me to pursue a master's degree in public health, which I completed at Meharry in 1994. My plan had been to return to the Mississippi Delta after dental school and practice with a dentist who had also graduated from Meharry and was looking to retire. However, God clearly had another plan for me. I decided to complete a general practice residency, and it was during this time that I got the opportunity to join the faculty at Meharry Medical College, my alma mater and the school that gave me my foundation. The chairman of the Department of Operative Dentistry, Dr. Fred Fielder (he later became dean of the School of Dentistry), encouraged me to join the faculty for what I thought would be a year or two to "help out" since there was a shortage of dentists. This was new territory for me. I wanted to be like a sponge and learn as much as I could. I wanted not only to succeed but to make a significant impact on the lives and experiences of dental students, just as I had been positively affected.

Developing an Academic Career

When I joined the faculty, I was given a very valuable resource—the "Appointment, Promotions, and Tenure" document. I was told this was the "academic bible" and to use it as my guide for academic promotion. Following its advice, I began to engage in research and participate in leadership trainings, including the Executive Leadership in Academic Medicine (ELAM) program, sponsored by the American Association of Medical Colleges (AAMC), the American Dental Education Association's (ADEA) Leadership Institute, and the Harvard Leadership Program. Each of these programs taught me valuable knowledge and leadership skills that advanced my professional development. These opportunities took me from being an instructor in operative dentistry to becoming associate dean of Student Affairs, associate dean of Academic and Student Affairs, and finally, dean of the School of Dentistry, while also being a full professor in the department of dental public health.

Over the years, I established a diverse network of colleagues and lifelong friendships that improved my professional decisions and helped me establish a good work-life balance. I met Dr. Jeanne Sinkford early in my career, and we have maintained our friendship and mentoring relationship over the years. I connected with Dr. Sharon Turner when I was an ELAM fellow. She served on my Dean's Advisory Committee and has continued to be a good friend and mentor. Dr. Denise Kassebaum and I met when I was an ADEA Leadership fellow, and we both had two children around the same age. Because she was further along in her career and had already dealt with some of the challenges I faced, I got very valuable advice from her.

My Leadership Experiences

As a leader, I value the opportunity to mentor and inspire others. Whether I am at work, in a meeting, at home, visiting family, at church, attending a sports event, or volunteering at a community service event, if there is an opportunity to serve and mentor, I am excited to do so. Many young people of color from disadvantaged backgrounds have few opportunities to see professional women and leaders who look like them. But if they meet them, they will realize that they can become such professionals as well.

Lifelong learning is also an integral component of my life. I recently obtained an executive master's in business administration (EMBA). People asked why I wanted to get this degree when I already had several degrees. For me, it was not about getting another credential. It was all about having the opportunity to learn about financial management. I firmly believe that we are never too old or know too much to learn more.

As a leader, I also believe it is important to help others by supporting their different leadership styles, giving guidance when needed, and maintaining open lines of communication. There were occasions when I tried to push people beyond their comfort zones. But I realized that this could create problems. I learned that just because I think people can move in a different direction, it will not work unless they believe they can. There are still occasions when my team and I hold different views on a subject, but they always know that I value their opinions and input.

From the start of my academic career, it was challenging to be taken seriously as a young woman in the "good old boys club" of academia. So, I seized the opportunity to become the director of student affairs, to work with several student organizations, and to help with student recruitment by serving on the Admissions Committee. I had to look beyond my peers for help in navigating my professional career. It was also important for me to stay open to self-improvement and accept constructive criticism.

The highlight of my career has been the opportunity to serve students, faculty, and alumni as dean of the dental school at Meharry, my alma mater. This was not something that I planned or even thought about. But when I was given the opportunity, I accepted the challenge. In retrospect, I realize that I have been preparing for this position since my youth. Even at this point in my life, I continue to build on every experience, knowing that it prepares me for the next part of my professional journey.

A. Isabel Garcia, DDS, MPH, FACD

◆ ◆ ◆

The Early Years

My three siblings and I were raised in a close-knit family in a small town in eastern Cuba. Some of my happiest memories as a child were our trips to the beach; I still recall the excitement of seeing the deep-blue and aquamarine colors of the ocean glistening in the hot Caribbean sun as we got closer. My sister Ana and I were born thirteen months apart, and together we navigated the school system and the turmoil brought about by the Cuban Revolution.

I do not remember many discussions at home about pursuing a career. It was an unstated expectation. After we immigrated to the United States in the early 1970s, my parents set an exceptional example of hard work, integrity, and perseverance in the face of many challenges. Undeterred by the typical barriers faced by new immigrants—learning the language and adapting to America—my parents made sure we did not lose sight of the importance of doing well in school.

I recall many lessons from my mother, who, unlike my dad, lived well into her nineties. After my father died, she went to work outside of our home for the first time in her life, supporting us through college, helping my sister through graduate school and me during dental school. I lived at home and worked part-time to help pay for my tuition. I never heard my mother complain, despair, blame someone else, or express doubts about our situation. I vowed to do the same.

I believe it was Susan Jeffers who wrote, "Take responsibility for your life. Never blame someone else for anything you are doing, being, having or feeling." She also encouraged people to "pick up the mirror instead of the magnifying glass." My mother set an enduring example, guiding me throughout my personal and professional life. I would tell future women leaders to seek someone inside, or outside, of their family who can provide that inner compass and guiding light in their life.

Becoming a Public Health Dentist

Of the four children in my family, I was the least likely to pursue a career in dentistry. The town we grew up in had no fluoride in the water, and we kept a traditional diet, along with consuming plenty of sweets. By the time I was a second grader, I recall locking myself in the bedroom to avoid the dreaded visits to our family dentist. Little did I know I would find myself, fifteen years later, calming fearful children as a third-year dental student at the Medical College of Virginia.

Through a college classmate, I became intrigued with the "art and science" of dentistry. Despite my negative childhood experiences, dentistry was a great fit for me. Fortunately, I had very good fine-motor skills and found the clinical curriculum especially enjoyable. I was motivated to help people who were fearful of the dentist like me. After a start as an associate in private practice, my career took a different path, thanks to the influence of several people who widened my outlook. Former Virginia dental health director Dr. Joe Doherty gave me my first job in public health dentistry, allowing me to experience the satisfaction of providing care to underserved children. I loved the job and the community I served, but I became unsettled by the glaring disparities in oral health I saw between some of the children I cared for and those from nearby affluent areas. I realized that a broader public health approach was needed to meet their dental needs in a lasting way. So, I went back to school seven years after finishing dental school. This time, I acquired not just a public health degree but a different way of thinking and solving problems and a greater understanding of the social, economic, and societal factors that contribute to health disparities.

While at the University of Michigan School of Public Health, I learned countless lessons from Drs. Brian Burt, Steve Eklund, and Jane Weintraub. They taught me the basics of scientific inquiry, epidemiology, and public health, giving me a strong foundation for my subsequent twenty-two-year career in the US Public Health Service (USPHS). Through them, I learned to be a more critical thinker, to view the world through a public-health lens, to be data driven, and to write clearly and succinctly. I realized that while dentistry is my profession, public health is my real passion. To young people pondering career choices, I would say: seek something you will love doing for the rest of your life, choose something that is greater than yourself, and never hesitate if you must take a sharp turn along the way; the path toward the future is hardly ever a straight line.

I am fortunate to have met leaders in dental public health and research who paved the way, opened doors for me, and became lifelong mentors. Dr. Bill Maas gave me the chance to work in outcomes research and health-care quality in my first assignment as a USPHS-commissioned officer. Dr. Dushanka Kleinman recruited me to the National Institute of Dental and Craniofacial Research (NIDCR) and patiently and kindly led by example. Rear Admiral Kleinman was polished, smart, and accomplished; everything about her seemed perfect—from the fit of her uniform to her flawless eloquence. Never in my wildest dreams could I have imagined occupying "her office" twelve years later.

Taking On Leadership Positions

My first leadership role came as a big surprise. My first encounter with Dr. Larry Tabak was in 2000. As the new director of NIDCR, he began a critical review of all institute programs. I had to defend the institute's science-transfer program. The day before our first meeting, I "crammed" late into the night. In the morning, I arrived armed with data showing that the program was valuable. I presented the information with sweaty palms and a pounding heart. At the end of the meeting, I stood up to exit the room and he told me, "You did okay, kid." From that experience, I learned that if you are going to meet the head honcho, you better prepare like it is your life's biggest final exam.

Seven years and several assignments later, Dr. Tabak asked me to serve as NIDCR's deputy director. I thought he had lost his mind. I was afraid to say yes but even more scared to say no. My acceptance turned out to be a pivotal decision, allowing me to work closely with him and with NIDCR leadership, as well as many exceptional people at the National Institutes of Health (NIH). My world grew exponentially, and I studied everything closely, including the management style, professional demeanor, problem-solving approaches, and even the presentation style of some of the best people working at NIH. Dr. Lois Cohen and Dr. Norm Braveman were among those who had extensive federal government experience, and I could count on them for guidance and candid advice. Three years later, Dr. Tabak moved up to become NIH's principal deputy director, and I served as acting NIDCR director from 2010 to 2011, another incredible opportunity and growth experience. I guess I had finally learned to be open to new opportunities, even if my first instinct was to run and hide!

Of special note among my mentors and supporters is my late husband, partner, and public health colleague, Dr. Ric Bothwell, whose unwavering support helped me gain confidence to take on positions of greater responsibility. The support and flexibility of Ric and my son, Adam Bothwell, have been essential through my career, often providing the perspective and balance that only spouses and children can give.

There is no magic formula for attaining success as a leader. From an early age, I had a stubborn streak. If challenged with something "impossible," I would set out to prove it could be done. But many times, I had to push through the doubts and insecurities, knowing that to complete some tasks, I had to work harder than anyone else. I have found it essential to build my leadership based on trust and credibility, and to never compromise my integrity, even if it means making painfully difficult decisions. I am not really sure when it finally clicked, but I realized along the way that I did not have to act like a man to be successful. I could be myself, be empathetic and firm but kind. I learned to make decisions as a person and as a leader and not "as a woman."

Finally, a great deal of success comes with the realization that you have to be open to taking that fork in the road that you did not anticipate and to embrace the tough times that, without fail, will come along. American writer and former pediatric surgeon Bernie Siegel said, "One cannot get through life without pain. What we can do is choose how to use the pain life presents to us."

Being a Minority Woman Leader

As I look back, it never occurred to me that I could not be successful because I am a woman and a Cuban American, yet the challenges were there. By nature, I am introverted, which, combined with speaking English as a second language, meant that I lacked the confidence to seek student government or other leadership roles while in school and during the early phases of my career. I nearly changed my chemistry major in college when I found out that seniors had to present their seminar project in front of the entire class! Over time, I learned that being the loudest voice in the room is not the hallmark of leadership. Understanding the right balance and knowing when it is crucial to speak up is something deeply personal that requires confidence, emotional intelligence, and patience. Pushing against that natural tendency to not speak up has been a lifelong journey and hard work, but I believe it made me a better listener. My family may or may not agree. As for mastering English, I am very proud of my skills, but I still butcher certain words from time to time, if I lack focus or if I am tired.

Like many people who are attracted to dentistry, I am a perfectionist. This was a clear strength during my years of clinical work, when it is critical to get things "just right," as we learned in dental school. Once I transitioned to administrative and leadership roles, I struggled with how to balance my perfectionist mindset with knowing when to let go. As life got busier and multiple competing priorities became unavoidable, I learned to manage my time a lot better and to not become paralyzed by chasing perfection. It is a good thing to seek growth and improvement in our everyday lives and our work, but does perfection exist in anyone's daily life? I admit that this issue is still sometimes difficult for me, and I have to remind myself that the data will never be unimpeachable and that it is better to take a chance to start a project and improve it over time than to let an opportunity pass me by. Asking others for help, recognizing the need for broad input when needed, and inviting honest feedback have all been helpful strategies that I continue to use every day.

I am proud of the career I have built and the people whom I have helped along the way. I am in touch with former residents, trainees, and colleagues, and I try to follow their careers and support them as they mature in new roles. I believe that a true measure of success is not a thicker CV or a bigger title. You are only as good as the teams you build and the people you nurture.

In my leadership position as a dental school dean, I have come to accept the need to welcome—and at times deflect—criticism, to develop a sense of humor, and to resist the temptation to take the easy way out when the going gets tough. Especially during difficult times, I appreciate having lifelong mentors and trusted advisors I can rely on. My advice to women aspiring to be future leaders is to seek mentors early on and to listen to them. Establish partnerships and see them as a two-way street—not simply for your own gain but as a means to offer something in return. Choose guiding principles to live by and set up guardrails to keep from getting pulled off course by things that are too good to be true. Listen to that inner compass and do not let negative self-talk take over when things get tough. And remember that being a mentor is part of leadership. Embrace that role early on, and your accomplishments will be richer as a result.

Leslie E. Grant, DDS, MSPA, FACD

◆ ◆ ◆

My Early Years

I spent my early childhood in Charlotte, North Carolina, in a great community-centered neighborhood. This was, in retrospect, a wonderful, affirming, and supportive experience that helped to conceal the reality of the segregation in the city, state, and region. My favorite childhood memories are of summer and the freedom we had to play with friends all day until the streetlights came on in the evening. Our communities were stable. Families did not move around as much as they do now, and restrictive covenants often prevented African American families from venturing away from our long-established neighborhoods.

Education has always been revered in my family. Every generation since the Emancipation has attended college. My great-grandmother was a teacher, and my great-grandfather was an African Methodist Episcopal Zion minister. Many people are not aware that, a century ago, not every town had public high schools for people of color. My grandmother and her siblings had to leave home to attend a church-run boarding school in a different town just to earn their high school diplomas. Their perseverance and drive taught our family that with educational achievement comes an obligation to the community and to our African American institutions.

During several of my childhood summers, both my mother and grandmother left home to pursue their graduate degrees. For those months, I stayed with my great-aunt in Connecticut and was able to experience life in a whole new world. We went to a local beach, ventured to Manhattan for shopping and entertainment, and dined at any restaurant we wanted to try out. At my young age, I understood that places like Connecticut and New York were not only fun, they were places without the boundaries of segregation. In my time in Charlotte, there were only a few places where we could dine out. For special occasions, we often went to the airport restaurant because we were not refused service there.

Becoming a Dentist and Taking On Leadership Roles

All these childhood experiences and family guidance helped to shape my mind and aspirations. But my path to dentistry was not a direct one. My undergraduate and graduate training was in speech and language pathology. My interest in dentistry grew out of my fascination with the functions of the oral mechanism, particularly related to mastication and swallowing. The dental profession provides many intrinsic rewards—the ability to restore a smile, alleviate pain, recognize pathology, and care for multiple generations of a family. This very special profession also provides opportunities for leadership and advocacy.

For most of us, leadership roles come gradually and sometimes even by surprise. A pivotal moment for me occurred in my early years as a member of the Reference Committee for the National Dental Association's House of Delegates. Our committee chair was an excellent leader who encouraged debate, deliberation, and dissection of materials, and who reminded committee members to always be prepared. She provided regular updates and recommendations to members of the House and responded deftly to probing questions. She made certain that each committee member had the opportunity to provide reports, field difficult questions, and offer sound reasoning to counter differing points of view.

It is essential to seek mentors who know how to instruct, guide, and lift you up while also demonstrating the importance of fully incorporating the team, sharing responsibility, and listening intently. For those who are ascending to leadership, the mutual respect that comes from collaborative effort is part of what builds reputations and respect.

Perseverance is a quality that all strong leaders must possess. Pathways to and through leadership are often not straightforward, and challenges are a given. But if the cause is right and the knowledge base is sound, those who work with you will be confident in your dependability. However, perseverance does not negate flexibility. Issues evolve, players change, and priorities shift. Without jeopardizing integrity and core values, leaders recognize when modifications are required. Leaders make decisions that are grounded in sound knowledge by doing their homework and by seeking input from a team that has appropriate expertise. Honesty, attention to detail, and the ability to acknowledge mistakes are essential qualities for a leader. The capacity to understand and the ability to listen to other points of view are core attributes of leaders who are responsive and willing to continue growing. It is also important for those in leadership roles to follow up with key individuals or sponsors after meetings and events. This helps to build and sustain relationships and inspires others to trust your sincerity.

Sometimes unanticipated circumstances arise. Several years ago, I walked into a small meeting representing an organization with the previously determined agenda in my hand. But the meeting never got there! A completely unexpected topic took precedence; it had emerged from a prior meeting in which I had not been involved. I set aside the predetermined agenda, listened intently, engaged with the participants, answered questions straightforwardly, and readily acknowledged what I did not know. Most importantly, I took notes and advised when my organization's response could be expected. I tell this story because even with the best preparation, sometimes it is awareness and good communication that will guide you through uncertain arenas.

For several years, I had the privilege of serving in the House of Delegates of the National Dental Association as a representative of the

Maryland Dental Society. Many of my peers and the NDA leadership already knew me from my Student National Dental Association activities and service as SNDA vice president. Once in the NDA House of Delegates, I served on the By-Laws, Reference, and Legislative committees. My colleagues and many NDA members eventually encouraged me to run for the position of Speaker of the House. I was successful in my campaign and became the first woman elected to that position.

At the time, my son was two years old, I was still quite encumbered with student loans, and I owned and operated a solo dental practice. These were very real but not insurmountable challenges in facing the tremendous time commitment, travel, and intraorganizational communication requirements. I admit that there were many late nights and very early-morning hours spent at my computer, but I managed. A few years later, I became the forty-second president of the NDA. Children who grow up in families with busy schedules seem to accommodate change. Quality time and being present for hallmark events are essential. That is what my now twenty-year-old son remembers—that I was always there for important events and celebrations, that he sometimes got to travel with me, and that I brought dental goody bags when I spoke to his elementary school class about how to take care of their teeth. Great family support and dependable childcare are important in the equation. Early in my career, many sacrifices were required, but the rewards and positive outcomes made it worthwhile.

Lessons Learned

It has been my great honor to serve the noble profession of dentistry by providing direct patient treatment, mentoring new and future colleagues, participating in organizational leadership, and advocating for policies that improve oral health care. It would never have crossed my mind when I was growing up, or even during my college years, that my professional activities would lead me to spend time advocating to members of the House and Senate on Capitol Hill. Dentistry has served me well, and I have humbly tried my best to give back to the profession and to our community.

We are at a reckoning point where the growth and advancement of dentistry require heightened visibility, improved oral health care, parity, and greater interprofessional collaboration. My best advice for our future leaders is to continue seeking educational advancement throughout life. Growing and evolving with the times are essential to leadership, and knowledge is the key. It is important to connect with and seek out a diverse composite of individuals. Their varying perspectives will challenge preconceptions and enhance understanding of how people draw different conclusions. Know your strengths and confront your limitations. Do not let setbacks deter you. The unexpected happens to all of us. We learn to adjust, remain focused, and know when to seek assistance so that we can stay the course. Be well acquainted with the mission, legacy, and inner workings of the organizations with which you are directly involved and with those who sponsor and support you. Be receptive to mentorship, and be ready to become a mentor. Be determined to leave an imprint for the future.

Judy Greenlea Taylor, DDS, MPH, FACD, FICD

◆ ◆ ◆

My Early Years

"What do you want to be when you grow up?" I remember my kindergarten teacher asking one day as I sat in class at the tender age of four.

Without any forethought, I responded with, "A pediatrician, veterinarian, and a ballerina." Perhaps this was due to having numerous dolls and family pets that required patchwork and Band-Aids. The ballerina "side gig" was likely due to starting ballet lessons. At this young age, I saw no boundaries to doing all three, due to my imagination of possibilities and having a village that supported me. As the question tagged along through high school and college, the answer became more of what the Chinese philosopher Confucius, once said: "Choose a job you love, and you will never have to work a day in your life." To this day, I encourage my students with this philosophy.

I was born and raised in Atlanta, Georgia, surrounded by women and men of color who were well-educated, accomplished trailblazers, respected in their communities. My mother had a bachelor's and master's degree and worked as a primary school educator for over thirty-five years; she was also an entrepreneur, working full-time, and caring for the family full-time. At that time, Atlanta was the center of the civil rights movement, and my father was one of the most charismatic activists of his time. He was highly respected as a journalist for one of the most notable Black news publications in Atlanta and as the executive director of the NAACP. He was campaign manager, advisor, speechwriter, and mentor to some of the most notable mayors, politicians, and civil rights activists of the 1960s, 1970s, and 1980s, while additionally helping to build and grow Black communities economically. A third major source of support was my stepfather, who helped raise me from the age of three. He was one of the first aviation electronics technician chief petty officers in the US Navy. After retirement, he worked in the school system as a vocational guidance counselor. He was the voice of reason whom everyone went to for advice. My great-grandfather had been the first African American school principal in Atlanta, and many of his children and grandchildren also became educators.

Having this family support system taught my brothers and me important life lessons such as the value of self-identity, perseverance, strength, courage, confidence, education, compassion, generosity, care, humility, work ethic, faith, and hope. As we went on to become doctors, pilots, and entrepreneurs, we learned that this background did not protect us against racial biases and the injustices of the world.

My Path to Dentistry: Guidance Counselors, Mentors, and Pipelines

My path to dentistry was not influenced by a family member in medicine or dentistry. The closest health-care role model I had was my father's best friend from his Morehouse College days, Dr. Asa G. Yancey Sr., who was a medical pioneer. There were no dentists in my "immediate" circle of influence other than my childhood dentist and some classmates' parents who were dentists. I often spoke about becoming a physician, and Dr. Yancey and my family physician encouraged me. In primary and secondary school, some great teachers supported my quest for knowledge, and I participated in many science fairs and competitions. During high school, I shadowed physicians and attended summer and weekend enrichment programs that supported my interest in science and medicine.

My first leadership experience was in high school. With the encouragement of some good friends, I became class president and was voted by my peers as one of the students "most likely to succeed." It was my first understanding that effective leadership is not about esteem but about earning the respect of peers, creating positive energy, taking responsibility, and sharing the glory. This lesson would prove valuable later in life when I became an entrepreneur and accepted other leadership positions.

When asked why I chose dentistry as my profession, I usually mention pipeline programs and mentors. Guidance counselors, advisors, mentors, and pipeline programs guided my career path, leadership roles, and discovery of what was possible based on my talents and drive. In high school, a great guidance counselor knew my interest in natural sciences and becoming a doctor. She introduced me to a pipeline program with a historically Black college and university (HBCU) in Texas, Prairie View A&M University (PVAMU), which was part of the Texas A&M university system. This university started its first honors college, the Benjamin Banneker Honors College. It was dedicated to science, technology, engineering, and mathematics (STEM), and I was happy to join it.

At PVAMU, Dr. George E. Brown, my academic advisor and biology professor, became a great mentor. I enjoyed my academics and graduated a year early, despite being fully engaged in social activities, sorority life, and the college experience. With medical school application deadlines having passed for that year, I used my last two semesters to explore the health-care field of dentistry by working with the on-campus dentist. As I learned more about the field, its career flexibility for women, and the opportunity to use my artistic abilities and manual dexterity, dentistry seemed like a great fit. My final semester became rather fast paced, with exploring dental schools, dental admission testing, and dental school application deadlines. I received several offers, some with full scholarships. But then a pipeline program changed my trajectory.

The University of Iowa College of Dentistry was looking to increase its diversity and actively recruited promising students. When I visited there, I met Dr. Nelson, who served as the associate dean at the time and was the developer and recruiter of this new diversity initiative. The University of Iowa had a phenomenal dental school and also a great research institute, and I felt this program was a good fit. I had started grade school early and skipped over a couple of years, and therefore was very young when I accepted this offer. This fact was of concern to the administration, my college mentor, my parents, and even myself, not because of lack of confidence in my abilities but because of the psychological maturity required for professional school. Only a few weeks after receiving my bachelor of science degree, with a dual major and minor, and being the first graduate of the Benjamin Banneker Honors College, my dental school journey began.

Lessons Learned in Dental School

I had grown up in a predominantly African American community and public school system in southwest Atlanta, and I had attended an HBCU with a primary circle of friends who were all shades of black and brown. I thought I knew how to thrive in diverse settings, but Iowa was far from my previously experienced background. There were only two African American students in the entire dental school at that time, which created unfamiliar territory for everybody. There had been some minority students before, but there was never a significant number of students of color at any given time. I did not notice any blatant racism. But some professors and students had biases against minority students, including the belief that people of color were inherently inferior or possessed unfavorable qualities. These biases were well hidden but were manifest in subtle ways, via comments or actions.

As I adjusted to the rigors of academics and this new cultural climate, I often felt I had to work harder to prove myself than my Black male classmate or white female counterparts, and my stress level increased. I had never been a "quitter" and had always been a source of strength for others. But my mentor Dr. Logan sensed how uncomfortable I was and recommended that I consider a position as a minority recruiter. He also connected me with the Student National Dental Association (SNDA), the student organization of the National Dental Association (NDA), which helped me to take on leadership roles. I reactivated the Iowa chapter of the SNDA and was its local president. Then I became active on a national level as a student executive officer, which helped me navigate dental school and learn from individuals with similar experiences.

During my dental school years, I learned my first life lesson that helped me professionally and as a leader: what does not break you makes you stronger. I received an excellent professional education and developed perseverance, a sense of confidence, and the passion to make a difference. While I took these opportunities to recruit students of color and pave the way for others, I became interested in clinical dentistry, research, and community outreach. At my graduation, I received the Dean's Leadership Award and the Dean's Achievement Award. Years later, a colleague told me that when he attended dental school there, one of my professors who initially displayed biases against minority students had changed his attitudes so much that he was my colleague's biggest support for pursuing his specialty. I knew at that moment that my participation in this dental pipeline program had happened for a reason.

My Professional Journey

After dental school, I did an advanced general practice residency (GPR) program, which allowed me to bridge the gap between dental school and the professional world. Looking back, I realize that this was an excellent choice, and I now recommend that my mentees consider a GPR if they do not choose a specialty. Emory University's combination GPR/oral surgery fellowship program provided a phenomenal experience in various care settings and an opportunity for hospital certification.

Working with attending physicians and chief residents, I learned many lessons. One especially important life lesson was that as an African American woman, I had become so sensitized to experiencing biased behavior that it was difficult for me to differentiate between someone talking down to me versus someone genuinely trying to teach me. I realized this fact one day when my attending specialist at the VA hospital proceeded to guide me through a surgery case, and my confidence, faith in my abilities, and the fact that I was a licensed dentist made me resist his feedback. As his demeanor changed, I realized his intent was to teach me new techniques. This was a valuable lesson for me. No matter how much you think you know, you do not know it all and never will. There are always new skills to learn, no matter how they come to us. Some came to me through mentors who offered gentle guidance, support, and encouragement and helped me to develop in a positive way.

Leadership Challenges and Triumphs

My leadership roles have come in many forms, from being an entrepreneur and small business owner to being a leader in my community in organized dentistry and a member of senior management in nonprofit and corporate arenas. I encountered challenges and triumphs in each of these realms but with a common thread of resilience.

Despite the advantages of my background, I often felt uncomfortable. As early as high school, I knew I wanted my own dental office someday. After my residency program, I decided to open my private practice. I approached seven banks for a business loan and was turned down by all seven. Even coming from a Southern family of faith, discouragement set in. When I was at the brink of giving up, the female vice president of a local bank offered me a loan at a very good rate.

While patients and staff tend to respect doctors, it seems as if minority women must earn this respect. Having a solid work ethic is essential, especially as a business owner. Taking an associateship or salaried position might have been better for achieving a good work-life balance because being a Black small business owner came with double-duty time and challenges. An important lesson learned at this phase of my life was that you can have it all, but maybe not all at the same time. I am convinced that work-life balance is an essential ingredient of health, happiness, and well-being.

Being an Advocate for Underserved Communities

Over the years, I became increasingly more active in community outreach and giving back time, service, and donations. Recognizing the social determinants of health and the injustices in access to health care increased my interest in public health and resulted in my serving on committees and advisory boards for the Department of Health and Human Services (HHS). I also attended a health disparities research program at Columbia University and continued my outreach initiatives. Additionally, I started mentoring high school and college students. I also reconnected with the local and state chapters of the NDA, and I ultimately served as the ninety-second NDA president. While still practicing dentistry, I studied for my master's degree in public health. As my public health career expanded, I was appointed as the first African American—and only dentist—to the Georgia Department of Public Health. Most recently, I took on the role of dental director for a Medicaid managed care organization to help improve access to care. While my plan was never to join corporate America, I learned to navigate my role in senior management as a minority. Women of color have a long way to go in terms of achieving diversity and inclusion in corporate America and among top political and health officials in this country. But with great talent emerging in the national spotlight, we will get there soon.

Lessons Learned as a Woman Leader

During my professional life, I've had good and bad experiences. But there are things I wish I knew then. So here are lessons I've learned and want to offer to future women leaders:

- You cannot let fear or doubt keep you from being a leader. As a leader, you face decisions almost constantly. Do not fear making wrong decisions, because even the best leaders make bad decisions sometimes.

- As a leader, you are going to have your own style. Not everyone will like you or what you do. No matter what, you will be criticized by some and accepted by others. Pick the style that suits you best, and don't let anyone interfere with your vision.

- Sometimes minority women face a double-edged sword: if you voice your opinion, you might be seen as the stereotypical "angry Black woman," but if you remain silent, you go unnoticed. Insert grace into any situation, pray, and let the adrenaline settle before reacting.

- Speaking publicly and with authority may be one of your biggest fears, making you vulnerable whether speaking to your staff, a boardroom, or an audience of thousands. Relax before you speak, prepare as much as possible in advance—even if you are a natural-born speaker—and remember that you may not always say the right things. Remind yourself that you are human, and the people in your audience will see you as a human as well. Even if you make a mistake, it will be alright if your heart is in the right place.

- We are all looking for answers, but sometimes the answer is just time. Giving yourself enough time to outlive the struggles in your twenties and thirties will give you the experiences to balance the challenges that come in your fifties and beyond. Do not rush. Life is a marathon and not a sprint, and the finish line God has in place may not look the same for all of us.

- Surround yourself with positive people, support other women, and do not compete—we are all in this together.

- Stop and enjoy life. Give yourself permission to say no, relax, and breathe. You have and will make a difference in the lives of others, but do not feel you have to save the world in one day.

Historically, not enough minority women have had a seat at the table, so they often had to build their own. As young sisters find their voices and trailblazers shatter glass ceilings for them, we will see more women in leadership roles in health care, administration, academics, corporate settings, politics, and other areas. My experiences, from childhood to adulthood, have shaped who I am and allowed me to achieve the positions I had. I am proud that I followed my dreams on a path that was not always easy or in the direction planned. I am grateful for my family, close friends, and mentors who encouraged, supported, prayed for, and nurtured me. I tried to and will continue to stay true to my values and use every platform, no matter how big or small, to improve life for underrepresented and underserved communities and add another crack to the glass ceilings for the young women who come after us.

Hazel J. Harper, DDS, MPH, FACD

◆ ◆ ◆

Growing Up

I was born in the United States, but my roots are in Guyana, South America. My mother and father were immigrants from Guyana—then called British Guiana. My father had received the Guyana scholarship that would allow him to study in the United States when the sudden death of his father thrust him into the role of family patriarch at the age of seventeen. He immediately forfeited his scholarship and did not come to the United States until ten years later. When he arrived, he had twenty-five cents in his pocket and the dream to attend medical school at Howard University. He sent for my mother, who was a trained midwife and nurse, to join him. I was born before my father started his first year in medical school. He and my mother both worked full-time while he was in school. He was a third-year medical student when my beautiful mother died in childbirth along with my baby sister. My heartbroken father made a promise to my dying mother that he would raise me in her religion, Catholicism, and that he would find another mother for me.

Despite this tragedy, my father kept his promise and raised a happy, healthy, well-adjusted daughter. He was gentle, generous, and a strict disciplinarian who insisted on academic excellence and inculcated a strong work ethic. I did not like to disappoint my father, a remarkably busy family practitioner and surgeon. In addition to building a thriving medical practice and raising four children, he was the Olympic physician for Guyana and attended seven Olympic Games, as well as Wimbledon and the Pan Am Games. My father was my guiding light and hero. He made me determined, tenacious, and resilient, and he taught me the principles that I live by: stand up for what you believe in and don't let anyone tell you what you can't do, because you can do anything you set your mind to.

When I had to decide which college I would attend, I did not really want to go to Howard University. But going to HU was one of the best decisions of my life. I was fortunate to be a first-year student during the revolutions of the 1960s, i.e., the Black Power movement, the women's liberation movement, and the student movement. I left home for college as a polite, polished, scholastically inclined graduate of a private Catholic high school and returned home for Thanksgiving sporting an Afro hairstyle (like Angela Davis, who had become my "sheroe"), a dashiki, and beads. My family asked me what I had done with their daughter and who I was. I had become a fierce revolutionary activist.

When I was a couple of weeks away from following in my father's footsteps and taking the Medical College Admissions Test (MCAT), my stepmother encouraged me to talk to her sorority sister, Dr. Jeanne Sinkford, who was an assistant dean at Howard University College of Dentistry (HUCD). I took her advice and contacted Dr. Sinkford, who invited me to her home to talk. Within ten minutes, she had convinced me that dentistry would be a better career for me. I took the Dental Admission Test, and the rest was history.

Becoming a Dentist

In addition to being accepted into HUCD, I had also been accepted by nine other dental schools that offered me scholarships. Howard was the only school that did not. Although I did not get a scholarship from HUCD, I made up my mind that working part-time and going to HUCD would be better for me than going to a school that would try to break rather than strengthen my spirit. And I was right. At HUCD, I was blessed with two lifelong mentors who shaped my personal and professional life in many ways: my dean, Dr. Joseph L. Henry, and the assistant dean at HUCD, Dr. Jeanne C. Sinkford. She became my mentor, confidante, and cherished friend. She has the standard of excellence to which we all aspire but that we rarely, if ever, achieve. Drs. Henry and Sinkford pushed me to excel, and neither of them tolerated mediocrity. Admittedly, I was a diamond in the rough, with a lot of edges to smooth. Drs. Henry and Sinkford let me know that their expectation of me was to use my God-given talents to become the leader they were training me to be. Dean Henry said to me, "When it is your turn to lead, you cannot turn your back." When I started working part-time as a dental assistant with no experience in Dr. Floyd C. Keene's office, he became my third mentor.

During the time at HUCD, my classmate George Jackson introduced me to the National Dental Association (NDA). He knew that I was a class organizer and thought it was important that I meet with some of the NDA leaders. He took me to visit his uncle Ellard "Punjab" Jackson and his father George Jackson Sr. in Charlottesville, Virginia. They sat me down and told me stories about the Black dental organization that had its beginnings in 1900 at HUCD. They spoke about their father Andrew Jackson, who had been one of the founders of the NDA and its first secretary-treasurer. As they took turns talking, I became more and more fascinated. In 1900, dentists had not been allowed to join the all-white American Dental Association because of racial discrimination. So, a small group of dentists identified Black dental professionals across the United States and invited them and their families to convene every summer for educational sessions and family gatherings. Because of racial discrimination, they were not allowed to stay in or meet in hotels. So, they stayed in each other's homes and held their meetings in churches and schools. I was mesmerized by their compelling stories. As an undergraduate student at HU, I had listened to many revolutionaries who visited Howard's campus. But these stories were different. After several hours, Uncle Punjab said to me, "We are tired, and we are ready to pass the torch."

In 1972, I was part of a group of African American dental students from across the United States who came together at a meeting of the Student National Medical Association in Detroit and formed the Student National Dental Association (SNDA). I became its first secretary. The first SNDA president, Lewis Proffit, and I were tasked with meeting with the NDA leaders and trustees to appeal to the parent organization to not only endorse the SNDA but to embrace it. Dr. Eddie G. Smith, the NDA president, and Dr. Punjab Jackson, the volunteer NDA executive director, became staunch advocates for the SNDA, and they argued that the students were "the lifeblood of the organization." We needed their support to achieve four goals: (a) the full inclusion of the SNDA into the NDA, (b) for the NDA to become the parent organization of the SNDA, (c) for the NDA to host the SNDA conventions during the NDA conventions, and (d) having student representation in the NDA House of Delegates and on the Board of Trustees. The House of Delegates narrowly adopted all four demands.

During the next few months, I heard my name mentioned as a possible candidate for the SNDA presidency. I felt I could not afford to accept this position because of an intensely rigorous academic schedule. Dean Henry heard that I was reluctant, called me to his office, and asked me if it was true. I told him I felt that accepting the nomination would jeopardize my academic standing and was stunned by his response. He said, "You will accept the nomination. You will win the election, and you will locate and identify every Black dental student in the United States, and I will help you. I will assign one of my administrative staff members to help you and the organization." I tried to argue my position, but it was fruitless. I knew it would be my biggest challenge yet. I traveled to many dental schools to meet the students, and everywhere I went, the schools rolled out the red carpet. The deans were supportive and encouraged their students' involvement in the SNDA. By the end of my SNDA presidency, every dental school in the United States that had Black dental students had an SNDA chapter.

Becoming an Advocate

In 2007, the death of twelve-year-old Deamonte Driver from untreated tooth decay changed my life. I found out about the tragedy from a newspaper article in the *Washington Post* and realized that his school was five minutes from my house. One of the leaders of the local chapter of the Robert T. Freeman Dental Society (RTFDS) went with me to meet with the school administrators at Deamonte's school. I became obsessed with finding ways to solve the problem of the lack of proper dental care for children. All the latent leadership skills my mentors had seen in me surged to the surface. I sat down at my computer and quickly galvanized a network of volunteers to screen and treat the other children at Deamonte's school. I could not bear the thought of another preventable tragedy. Although I was the owner of a busy group practice with five dentist associates and fifteen staff members, this project became all consuming. I realized that the issue was a lack of access to dental care for underserved children because the Maryland health system was broken. Our children were being neglected, and their poor parents could not find any dentists to help. Before I knew it, I was writing proposals and delivering testimonies for the Maryland state legislature and sending letters to the health department, school board, school nurses, and the governor. I met with legislators many times in Annapolis, the state capitol, to enlist their support of my plan to bring increased access to dental care to the children of Prince George's County, Maryland. I did not stop until Dr. Belinda Carver-Taylor and I had founded the school-based, mobile Deamonte Driver Dental Project; had support from the NDA; and had obtained funding from the state of Maryland to purchase, operate, and staff a brand-new, state-of-the-art mobile dental unit.

Next to being installed as the first woman president of the NDA, the ribbon-cutting ceremony for the Deamonte Driver Mobile Dental Unit was the proudest moment of my life. I was overjoyed that the ceremony was held on Capitol Hill and that there was an appreciation reception hosted by the late Honorable Elijah Cummings in the Rayburn House office building. The Deamonte Driver Dental Project (DDDP) laid the groundwork for my next undertaking, the NDA-HEALTH NOW project.

Overcoming Challenges

By 1993, I had risen through the ranks of the NDA, had been elected vice president, and was in line to become the first woman president of the NDA. Then, in 1994, in a stunning upset, I was defeated in my path to become president-elect by a male-driven political machine that was not ready for a woman to be in charge. I lost by two votes. It was a very bitter defeat for me and the individuals who had supported me, especially my mentor, Dr. Eddie G. Smith. Viewing the defeat as a vote of no confidence, my first instinct was to resign from the organization. But others who had supported me were already orchestrating my campaign to run again the next year. At first, I resisted their suggestions to run again. But Dr. Smith told me, "This is not only your decision. You just start learning how to act 'presidential.' We'll handle the rest."

So, I sought out an African American female leadership coach, who prepared me for what to expect during my presidency. I read countless books on leadership and studied the differences in leadership styles between men and women. I devoured minutes and notes from the past ten years of the organization's meetings. I intently studied the constitution and by-laws. And most importantly, I contemplated how I could make the organization better, not only during my one-year presidency but for the next generations. I began drafting proposals for a strategic planning retreat, a corporate roundtable, the long-range impact of women dentists to the NDA, a leadership institute, spokesperson training, increased support of the SNDA, and increased involvement in legislative advocacy. In 1995, I was elected as the organization's first woman president, and I started the NDA-Women's Health Symposium, the NDA Corporate

Roundtable, and the Eddie G. Smith Leadership Institute during my term, among other accomplishments.

I encountered a second major challenge in 2011. At this time, the Deamonte Driver Dental Project was going into its third year of operation and had been progressing according to plan. The mobile dental unit was visiting twenty-one Title 1 elementary schools in Prince George's County, Maryland, and had received many awards and accolades from the state. Suddenly, there was dissension within the RTFDS Foundation Board and accusations of impropriety. Although I had been solely responsible for garnering financial and volunteer support, the board ousted me from my position because I was the project director.

This was a difficult time for me. But within a few months, I had conceptualized another program for the NDA. It was one that would replicate and go beyond the Deamonte Driver Project. I suggested calling this new program NDA-HEALTH NOW (Health Equity, Access, Literacy, Technology, and Hope, National Outreach on Wheels) and launching it in five major cities with a strong NDA presence. It would provide service, education, and access to underserved families and would include not only dental care but also medical services, for children, adults, and senior citizens. In 2012, the NDA received a planning grant from The Links Foundation to start pilot programs in Chicago and Dallas. I later secured funding from the Kellogg Foundation and the Coca-Cola Foundation, and by 2019, the project had supported programs in fifteen US cities and seven countries.

Lessons Learned

My life's work has been devoted to improving health in underserved populations, to continuing the NDA legacy, and to mentoring students, the next generation of leaders. My father never allowed me to use the word *can't*. So, I grew up believing that success and achievement were not optional. I echo the same sentiment to future leaders and want to share some additional lessons I learned. Very early on in my professional education, I learned that it is important to surround ourselves with mentors and role models who support us and build our confidence. Having mentors who will not tell us what we want to hear but rather tell us what we need to hear is crucial, and listening is an art form. I believe that mediocrity is not an option and one should always exceed expectations. Channel your passion with preparation and perseverance. Never forget that the only constant in life is change and that change is inevitable for progress. My final advice is to never forget that God gave women instincts, intuition, and intellect. Use your faith and gifts to lead through turbulent times with honesty, integrity, and fairness.

Sandra G. Harris, DDS, FACD

◆ ◆ ◆

Growing Up in Nashville, Tennessee

My life began in Nashville, Tennessee, where I lived across the street from Fisk University and Meharry Medical College. I grew up in the segregated South but in a neighborhood filled with love, surrounded by aunts, uncles, cousins, and good neighbors. Everyone watched out for everyone. It was truly a "village raising a child." The pursuit of education has always been very important in my family. My great-grandfather, Richard Harris, a former slave, was the first Negro to sit on the Board of Trustees at Fisk University. His son, Eugene Harris, was among the first Negro faculty members at Fisk in the 1800s. In addition, most of my aunts and uncles chose careers in education.

When I had to decide where I would attend college, I decided to become an undergraduate at Fisk University, a historically Black college. While I was a student at Fisk during the early 1960s, I participated in peaceful civil rights demonstrations in downtown Nashville. On more than one occasion, I was arrested for nonviolent protesting and spent time in jail with other college students. A few years ago, someone asked if I was afraid of being hurt during the demonstrations. I answered, "No, because the purpose of the sit-in demonstrations—equal rights for all people—was much more important than being jailed or injured." I had learned not be afraid to speak up for what is right and unbiased.

Becoming a Dentist

During my childhood, I lived across the street from Meharry's School of Dentistry (SOD), and so I received all my dental care from Meharry dental students. One of Meharry's graduates, Dr. Henry Lucas, married my cousin, and he and I developed a close friendship. Because of him, I began considering a career in dentistry and applied to Meharry's SOD.

While I was a student, I took great inspiration from Dr. Robert Donald Wood, the chair of the radiology and oral diagnostic sciences departments. I admired him not only for his expertise in the classrooms and clinics but also for his integrity and the manner in which he treated all students, equally and with respect. He was the first person to suggest to me that I should pursue a career in dental education. Later, he helped me to become an assistant professor in orthodontics at Meharry.

After graduating from dental school, I applied for orthodontics residency programs and was accepted into the graduate program at Howard University's College of Dentistry. Dr. Jeanne Sinkford was the dean at that time. I learned later that she was responsible for five women being accepted into the orthodontic class of 1986. During the previous nineteen years of its existence, the orthodontics department had only accepted two or three women. But in 1984, six residents were accepted—five female and one male. When the male student withdrew after a few days, the class of 1986 became the first all-female orthodontic class to graduate from Howard University and probably the first in any dental school in the United States.

Influence of Mentors

In addition to Dr. Wood, Dr. Kenneth Chance, the current dean of Case Western's School of Dentistry, supported my goals and professional advancement. Earlier in his career, Dr. Chance had been the dean of Meharry's School of Dentistry and my supervisor. At that time, in the late 1990s, there were very few female faculty members at Meharry, but Dr. Chance encouraged all of us to become leaders in the dental profession, and he assisted us in reaching that goal. In my case, he nominated me for the inaugural class of the American Dental Education Association's Leadership Institute, in which I had the privilege of participating. Dr. Jeanne Sinkford has been a mentor for many dentists, especially women and minorities. After she retired as dean of the Howard University College of Dentistry to become director of the Center of Equity and Diversity at the American Dental Education Association, I reached out to her for advice during my year as a Leadership Institute fellow and also while serving as the first African American president of the American Association of Women Dentists. It was commonly known that she was always readily available to share her wisdom and knowledge. I chose her for counsel and advice in part because she was the first African American and the first female in many roles in her career, and I was beginning to enter positions where I would be the first.

Although in recent years more females have been admitted as dental students, there are still few female administrators in dental schools or officers in dental organizations. Things are improving slowly, but we must continue to persevere. Men face fewer obstacles along this path, but the end results are what really matter. We must remain focused on our goal of equality.

Becoming a Leader

For me, the characteristics, attributes, and philosophies most important to my success as a woman leader are basically the same as for being a good person. I never strove to be a leader, just a good person. However, when leadership opportunities were presented and I was asked to assume them, I usually agreed, in large part to assist women and minorities in achieving greater equality. The characteristics most important to me are honesty, integrity, doing things to the best of my ability, maintaining a positive attitude, and observing the "Golden Rule" of treating others in the manner that I wanted to be treated. Behaving in this way may be the reason I have been asked to assume leadership positions. I think that one can succeed by adhering to these attributes and can persevere while remaining focused on one's goals.

My first leadership position was in the School of Dentistry at Meharry Medical College as chair of the Admissions Committee. I believe I was the first female to serve in that role. This occurred after the dean of the SOD at that time learned that I was one of twenty-three orthodontists from the Southern region of the United States selected to attend the American Association of Orthodontists' National Leadership Conference.

Surmounting Leadership Challenges

In another leadership position—as the first African American and third female to serve as president of the Nashville Dental Society, the local component of the American Dental Association (ADA)—I was challenged. The organization was founded in 1865 and had a membership of approximately five hundred mostly male dentists when I served as president from 2012 to 2013. During my term as president, I met an unprecedented challenge from several members of the organization who disliked a particular decision the organization's board of trustees made. One of the two members told me that I could and should change the decision since I was president of NDS. Instead, I convened a special session of the board and invited the disappointed members to speak and express their reasons as to why the decision should be changed. As the president, I conducted the meeting where everyone listened to both people, and the matter was handled in a democratic manner. For weeks after the meeting, I received compliments from board members on how fairly and professionally I had presided over a difficult situation that had never occurred before. I felt that I overcame the challenge by abiding by my values of integrity and equity.

When I became the chair of the Department of Orthodontics at Meharry Dental College, I was the first female to serve in that position. I was also the only female faculty member in the department, and the other two faculty members had taught me as a student and had chaired the department in the past. Initially, they were not happy to have me as the chair and created problems whenever possible. However, I was determined to do the job I had been assigned by the dean. Therefore, I stood by my principles until the challenges were resolved.

I was fortunate to be offered many opportunities for leadership in dentistry. Since starting my career in dental education in 1987, I have chaired most committees in the SOD at Meharry. I have also served as chair of the Department of Orthodontics, the Department of Growth & Development, the Department of Orthodontics / Pediatric Dentistry, as executive associate dean of Academic and Student Affairs, and as vice dean. The role in which I currently serve—chair of orthodontics—has been my favorite. It has given me the opportunity to mentor and teach students, especially those interested in a career as an orthodontist, and to watch them enter the profession and excel.

Looking back on my life, I am most proud of the years I spent opposing discrimination due to ethnicity and gender. I am also proud of the fact that I attended three historically Black colleges/universities—Fisk University, Meharry Medical College, and Howard University. These institutions nurtured me and also prepared me for adversities that I would encounter throughout life and especially during my career.

Wisdom for Future Leaders

For women who aspire to be future leaders, my advice is to always be honest, maintain integrity, display professionalism, be genuine, and be true to yourself. Remain strong and resilient because you will meet adversity. But you will also experience great joy.

Marja M. Hurley, MD, FASBMR

◆ ◆ ◆

Growing Up in Jamaica

I grew up in a small seaside community in Jamaica, West Indies, and left the island after completing high school to continue my education. I still remember being a small child the day a Caucasian officer came to our home to inform my mother that my father, who was a sailor and a ship's engineer, was missing after swimming in shark-infested waters. Although I was very young at the time, I knew that my mother had received very bad news, because she began to cry. I did not realize how profoundly that news would affect us. Although I am fascinated by the ocean and find listening to the waves very soothing, especially in times of stress, my fear of the ocean meant that I never learned to swim.

The most profound effect of that devastating news was that my mother became a single parent. Although we had enjoyed a very comfortable life while my father was alive, my siblings and I realized that we would all need to study very hard to get scholarships to private high schools to obtain the fundamental high school education that would best prepare us for college.

A fond childhood memory was spending summers in the country with my grandmother, siblings, and cousins, and most importantly, being able to visit the office of my grandmother's family doctor, who noted my interest in how he took care of his patients. He took the time to answer all of my questions and served as my first mentor. For me, becoming a physician was a decision I made at a very young age.

My Journey to Becoming a Physician

The most impactful educational moment in my life was when I found out that I had been accepted to the University of Connecticut School of Medicine, which led to a series of "firsts" in my medical career as a physician, scientist, and educator. Specifically, I was the first Black woman to graduate from the UConn School of Medicine—a very proud day for my mother. I was also the first, and so far, the only, Black woman to become a tenured full professor on the basic science track there.

My first mentor, the family doctor of my childhood, was a Black male. My college and medical education occurred during a time when there were very few women serving as professional role models or mentors. In college at UConn, my mentors included an African American male, Dr. Frederick Adams, who was the first African American assistant vice president for student affairs. He was a dentist and also the first African American commissioner of public health for the state of Connecticut. He advised me how to balance being engaged in community activities and being a premedical student during a time of racial unrest on college campuses, including UConn. He continued to mentor me in medical school when, as a first-year student, I established the first chapter of the Student National Medical Association at the UConn School of Medicine. He also encouraged my efforts to increase the number of underrepresented students in medicine and dentistry. Before his untimely death, he established a scholarship in the UConn Foundation that I still use to support African American students enrolled at the School of Dental Medicine there.

My second important mentor in college was Professor Heinz Herrmann, who had immigrated to the United States to escape Nazi Germany. Professor Heinz was my cell and molecular biology professor. He is also

Marja M. Hurley, MD, FASBMR

known as the "father of cell biology" in the United States. Professor Herrmann guided me through the process of applying to medical schools, wrote very strong letters of support for me throughout my career, and was present when I received such prestigious awards as the first Martin Luther King Award for Achievement in Science from the University of Connecticut. We remained friends until his death at the age of ninety-five.

Becoming a Physician Scientist and Faculty Member

In medical school, I had two primary mentors—both were Caucasian males. As a third-year medical student, I met Professor Lawrence Raisz, who had recently joined the faculty as chief of endocrinology. Dr. Raisz fostered my interest in endocrine disorders and a potential career in academic medicine. He continued to guide my career, especially at critical decision points in climbing the academic ladder. I was married while in college and medical school, and my husband and I also had a social relationship with both Larry, as he was affectionately known by his friends, and his wife, Helen. I was at times discouraged about being able to develop a research program. But receiving a minority supplement to Larry's program project grant provided me with the financial support I needed to be engaged in research and to submit my first R01 grant proposal to the National Institutes of Health (NIH).

Receiving this R01 funding boosted my confidence in the possibility of achieving a successful academic career as a physician scientist. Larry, who passed away in 2010, would have been extremely proud that I was inducted as a fellow into the American Society for Bone and Mineral Research, and received the Lawrence G. Raisz Esteemed Award from the American Society of Bone and Mineral Research for outstanding achievement in preclinical translational research. This award is one of the highest awards given annually by the society.

My second faculty mentor in medical school was Dr. Eugene Sigman. He subsequently became the dean of the UConn School of Medicine and offered me my first academic position. Upon completing my endocrine fellowship, he also asked me to serve as associate dean for minority student affairs, a position that he created. His decision to make this position one that reported directly to him, and the negotiating advice that Larry gave me, allowed me to navigate the hazardous position of being a Black woman physician serving as an associate dean while providing clinical care to patients in my specialty of endocrinology, serving as an attending physician on the general internal medicine wards, and teaching medical and dental students, while trying to establish a basic research laboratory and securing extramural funding from the NIH for the laboratory.

My major challenges were balancing the components of being an administrator, educator, clinician, and basic science researcher. Although I did not have "impostor syndrome," because I felt that I was as qualified, if not more so, than my peers at my career stage, I realized very early that I would need to identify colleagues within and outside of my institution to achieve the goals I had for myself in so many different domains. There were many supportive colleagues, but there were also individuals in positions of authority in the organization who were not supportive of the creation of an administrative position that reported directly to the dean / executive vice president for health affairs in order to promote diversity in the medical and dental student bodies.

As many Black women in leadership positions know all too well, although you are often the only person of color in the executive suite, your contribution to the conversation is sometimes ignored, and you may even be perceived by some as aggressive, arrogant, or intimidating. It was at times very difficult to know whether I was doing the right thing in trying to balance these competing interests. I began to look outside of my institution for successful African American women role models in the health professions, such as Dr. Jeanne Sinkford and Dr. Vivian Pinn. These two women influenced my career in ways they may not even realize. They were my role models because they were able to achieve great professional success while being incredible champions and implementers of national programs to support all women and to promote diversity for underrepresented men and women in the health professions.

Marja M. Hurley, MD, FASBMR

From Being Mentored to Becoming a Mentor

I am very proud of achieving success as a physician-scientist who has been able to maintain an NIH-funded research laboratory for more than twenty-five years. I am also proud to have been recognized nationally and internationally for my contributions to understanding the role of fibroblast growth factors in bone and phosphate homeostasis. For more information, please visit my research website: https://health.uconn.edu/hurley-lab/. But I am most proud of the science, technology, engineering, and mathematics (STEM) initiatives that I developed for underrepresented students at every level of the educational pipeline. These initiatives have resulted in hundreds of first-generation and underrepresented students graduating from high school; college; and dental, medical, and biomedical research programs. More information can be found on the department website: http://health.uconn.edu/hcop/.

I am very proud that these programs are endowed as the Aetna Health Professions Partnership Initiative at UConn Health. Finally, given the continued lack of African American researchers in the biomedical research area, I am extremely proud that I was able to train more than sixty students in my research laboratory, the majority of whom are students from historically underrepresented minority backgrounds. Some of these mentees have built outstanding careers in academic medicine and biomedical research. They are continuing to "lift as they climb" by providing opportunities and serving as role models for minority students interested in careers in STEM.

Andrea D. Jackson, DDS, MS, FACP, FACD, FICD

◆ ◆ ◆

My Early Years

I grew up in Southeast Washington, DC, with one sister, who was three years younger, my mother, and my father. My mother completed one year of college but moved to a mid- to upper-grade level in the federal government before retiring. My father attended college until enrolling in military service in WWII. Following his military commitment, he returned to college part-time before marrying. He worked in the motion picture business part-time while working a full-time job in the federal government, from which he retired at a mid- to upper-grade level. While working, he eventually returned to complete his bachelor's degree in 1976, when I was in my first year at Howard University. My parents always stressed the importance of a good education and hard work for succeeding in life, and the value of being able to support oneself and take care of one's responsibilities. My sister and I went to DC public schools for most of our education.

My Way to Dentistry

I always had good grades, and that was expected by my parents. I was good at art and attracted to science. While I attended junior high school, my uncle was in dental school at Howard. He once brought his articulator to our house and was setting teeth in our basement. I found that interesting. My uncle also took my sister and me to the dental school so that my sister could get an orthodontics consult. My paternal grandfather often spoke about going to have his teeth made at Howard's dental school. I always was intrigued by the dental office, how clean it smelled and how professional the office environment was, but had no idea how much it actually had impressed me.

Before entering high school, our junior high school counselor asked us to indicate on a form if we were going the college preparatory route or the business route. I brought the form home and told my mother I wanted to go the business route. She quickly changed my mind and said, "Oh no! You will go to college." That was probably the most significant moment during my education.

When I started HD Woodson High School, I was assigned to tenth-grade biology. This class made me appreciate science and dissections and anatomy, and I began to think about health care as a career. My teacher was inspiring, and my classmates and I often thought about our futures. I first considered medicine but did not want to make life-or-death decisions. I then reflected on my experiences with dentistry and thought that becoming a dentist would be a good fit. It would give me flexibility and the ability to use my artistic talent, and it would satisfy my interest in health care and science. When I found out that Howard University had BS/MD and BS/DDS programs, my mind was made up. In addition, both my biology and my chemistry teachers were Howard graduates. I continued to take science courses in high school, performed well, and got accepted into Howard University.

Once I arrived at Howard, I connected with the preprofessional office and was set on my path to dental school. In dental school, I was committed to doing well and graduated as number twelve of 110 students.

Andrea D. Jackson, DDS, MS, FACP, FACD, FICD

Becoming a Dental Educator

Originally, I thought I would go into private practice, but I changed my mind during my training as the years went on. After graduation, I attended a General Practice Residency (GPR) program at Howard University Hospital. During that year, I began thinking about becoming a dental educator. I always admired the faculty at our dental school, and so I approached the chair of restorative dentistry and asked about a teaching position. He quickly gave me an application, and the rest was history. I completed my GPR on June 30 and started my teaching appointment on July 1.

As soon as I joined the faculty, my former instructors and our dean, Dr. Jeanne Sinkford, began to mentor me on the benefits of academia as a career choice and how rewarding it is. They also encouraged me to pursue postdoctoral training to advance my career. With an affinity toward the artistic part of dentistry, I chose prosthodontics as the specialty I wanted to pursue. After my second year in the Department of Restorative Dentistry, I was accepted to the thirty-month master's program in prosthodontics at Georgetown University School of Dentistry and enrolled there after my third year of teaching. Dean Sinkford assisted me with choosing this program, and I received the Louise C. Ball Fellowship for faculty development to support my graduate education. For repayment, I had to return to the faculty to teach two years for every fellowship year I would receive, which added up to five years of faculty commitment after completing my program.

My choice to go to Georgetown was significant, and Dr. Sinkford played a major role in that decision. When I became interested in prosthodontics, I started to accompany a prosthodontics faculty member to the monthly study club meetings of the local chapter of the American College of Prosthodontists, where all the local program directors and residents met for dinner and to hear residents present their research. I had first applied to a prosthodontics program after my first year of teaching but was not accepted. At the monthly meeting, I saw the director of the program where I'd been denied admission. I asked him if there was something I could do to strengthen my application but quickly realized that he had not reviewed my application at all, because he said that I should do a GPR first, and I had completed one already.

I did not let this rejection deter me, and I applied to the same program and to Georgetown during the next cycle the following year. I interviewed at both programs. At Georgetown, I was welcomed, treated like family, and spent the entire morning with the residents and talking with faculty and the program director. At the other program, I had to stand outside the office of the director and department chair. When he finally shook my hand, he turned me around to look at my back and then asked if I had lost weight. The interview took forty-five minutes, and they asked me questions such as, "What makes you think you can be a prosthodontist?" It was not a comfortable environment. When I was accepted to both programs, I went to Dr. Sinkford for advice concerning which program I should choose. After my explanation, she encouraged me to go to Georgetown because she thought it would be a better environment for learning. That was the best decision I could have made.

Being a resident at Georgetown was a great time in my life, as I learned new things and became excited about what the future had in store. The environment was quite different from Howard because I was the only US citizen—and the only African American—in the program. We took our literature review class with the navy residents at Bethesda Naval and regularly attended continuing education programs and guest speaker events with the navy and army residents. The discipline of prosthodontics and the military programs were dominated by white males. The speakers were usually well-known prosthodontists and prosthodontic board examiners for the American Board of Prosthodontics. They would provide excellent presentations on current practices unique to the specialty and speak to the residents about the board examination, encouraging us to take it. Listening to them made me determined to become a board-certified prosthodontist.

I knew achieving this milestone would help me to be competitive for opportunities in the future. My program director, Dr. Richard Grisius, was very supportive and put me in position to conduct my research for my master's thesis at the University of Michigan with the department chair of prosthodontics there, Dr. Brian Lang, who was also very supportive and influential in my prosthodontics education. They understood that I was to return to Howard University upon completion of my training and supported me along the way.

Lessons Learned

My time at Georgetown taught me some very important lessons: Always seek out information that will allow you to achieve your goals. Do not let circumstances or not knowing be reasons for not finding out and working hard toward what you want to do. Don't accept the word *can't*.

I sought mentoring to get the opinion of others who had done things that I wanted to do, to see how they did it, to gain advice and recommendations. Dr. Sinkford was an important role model for me, and this became even more evident as time went by. When I came to dental school, I had never seen a dental school dean before, so having a female dean did not seem unusual. The longer I remained in dentistry, especially in organized dentistry, the more I realized that this was not the norm. I also became aware of how well respected she was. Not only did my program director speak highly of her, but as I began to go to meetings and became involved in dental organizations, I noticed more and more how well known and respected she was throughout the profession.

Taking On Leadership Roles

Upon returning to Howard University College of Dentistry, I began to work in the Department of Prosthodontics, Fixed Division, and became the course director of the preclinical fixed prosthodontics lecture and laboratory courses. The previous course director had been in the position for more than twenty years and had been my teacher. He mentored me as the new course director for one year and then retired. All faculty teaching in this course had been my teachers. Being the youngest, a woman, and their former student was challenging. But they were very cooperative, helpful, and a pleasure to work with, and they played a great part in my success, both in dental school and after I became the course director.

After about two years being back on staff at Howard, I decided to engage the examinations needed to become certified by the American Board of Prosthodontics. The written part was in February 1991, and I was successful. After that, I requested permission from the dean of our dental school to complete the clinical portion, which involved the treatment of my board patients at the College of Dentistry. With the support of my dean, Dr. Robert Knight, and the encouragement and advice of my prosthodontics program mentor and board-certified prosthodontists on faculty at Howard, I was able to successfully pass the board to become a diplomate of the American Board of Prosthodontics. In 1993, I and another woman were the ninth and tenth African American diplomates of the American Board of Prosthodontics, respectively, and the first women of color. While preparing for my boards, four of the African American board-certified prosthodontists were faculty members at Howard University. All four had been in the military, where board certification was tied to rank. These retired colonels helped me by reviewing my cases with me and giving advice.

While being on the faculty a few years following my return to Howard University College of Dentistry and becoming board certified, I was selected as the representative to the Council of Faculties of the American Association of Dental Schools (AADS) and also to attend the AADS Summer Leadership Conference. These experiences were the beginning of me being selected for leadership opportunities in the college. Soon after, the dean appointed me as the director of Fixed Prosthodontics and Restorative Dentistry, when the Restorative Department and the Division of Fixed Prosthodontics were merged due to faculty shortages and retirements. Again, I was in a new leadership position where several faculty members had been my teachers. But for the most part, everyone was helpful, understanding, cooperative, and hardworking. A few years later, as a result of reorganization, I became the chair of Restorative Services, the largest department in the College of Dentistry, combining restorative dentistry, prosthodontics, and community dentistry. My department had twenty-three faculty and three staff members. This leadership position was the most challenging role up to that point. I was in charge of mentoring a large number of faculty, the curriculum, numerous courses, as well as the students, and was still directing courses myself. It took a lot of organizational skills and delegation of responsibility. Several department members had been my former teachers, but there were also younger faculty in the mix whom I had hired. Additionally, we were going through a transition as a college and rebuilding.

I remained in this chair position for sixteen years and then was appointed to the position of associate dean for clinical affairs. Being responsible for clinical operations was something I was very familiar with because I had chaired the largest clinical department in the college for sixteen years. This position was also new because I did not have faculty reporting to me. They reported to their chairs. I would regularly meet with the department chairs to discuss clinical competencies and protocols, getting their input and implementing changes to improve related operations. After six years as associate dean, I was appointed the interim dean, and one year later the dean of the College of Dentistry.

Throughout my tenure in dental education, I became more involved with professional organizations, such as the American Dental Education Association (ADEA) and the American College of Prosthodontists, and I attended the ADEA Leadership Institute. I was selected to become a national board test writer, a consultant examiner for the clinical board examinations, and a site visitor for the Commission of Dental Accreditation (CODA). My involvement in these positions helped me to better assist my students and my school in being successful.

Lessons Learned

I adjusted to new leadership roles by being a good listener and team player, treating everyone with respect and how I would want to be treated. When decisions had to be made, I informed myself about everyone's opinion in meetings; then I would move forward based on collaborations and inclusiveness. I got along well with others and was able to gain consensus and reason with people to gain their support and buy-in.

I always attended professional meetings, maintained membership in various professional organizations, and applied for opportunities that interested me. I never let my race or gender affect my ability to seek information and go after what was important to me.

My leadership style is collaborative, but when I need to make decisions, I put the best interests of the organization first. Professionally, I am most proud of achieving the dean's position, having worked at every level from being an instructor through the ranks to full professor, and now being dean. I am most proud to follow Dr. Sinkford as the second woman dean of Howard University College of Dentistry, my alma mater and the university I gave my adult life to. I am proud of my students and of their achievements in the profession and how they elevate the reputation of the College of Dentistry. I love Howard and will continue to support its mission to become recognized among the best universities in the world. If I had to choose, I would do it all over again.

Personally, I am most proud of my son and my family. I am very thankful for them. We are a small, close-knit group of people who support each other in good and not-so-good times. We have each other's back.

I always wanted to be recognized and respected for my knowledge and abilities, for presenting myself in a professional manner and working hard for my achievements. I want people to think of me as respectful, that I treat them the way I would want to be treated. I want my patients to know that I care about their well-being and provide them with the best care. I want my students to know that I am fair, that I want to provide them with the best educational experience possible, and that I have their best interests at heart. I want my faculty and staff to feel appreciated and respected and realize that I always have the best interests of our organization in mind, especially when hard decisions have to be made. I am grateful for my mentors along the way; I hope that they feel I was worthy of their support and assistance and that I have never let them, my parents, or my family down.

Ernestine S. Lacy, DDS

◆ ◆ ◆

My Path to Dentistry

I grew up in a large family from a lower socioeconomic background and was the first person in my family to attend college. My family was typical of the majority of families living in our neighborhood. Although neither of my parents had completed high school, I always expected to go to college. This expectation was instilled in me by my elementary and high school teachers. My parents raised me with a great work ethic and the expectation to strive for excellence.

While in high school, my educational goal was to go to medical school and become a doctor. I am not sure where that desire came from because I did not know anyone who was in the medical field, and my family only saw health-care providers in emergency situations. But the thought of being a doctor felt right!

In college, I ended up majoring in mathematics and minoring in physics and French because I liked those subjects when I was in high school. I also majored in mathematics because I changed my mind and decided to go into the business world, thinking that math was a good major for that kind of career. While earning a bachelor of science degree, I also earned a teaching certificate in secondary education as a backup plan. I was offered a teaching position while looking for a job in business and took it. I taught math and science for fifteen years before an old interest in medicine resurfaced. It was at a time when I had gotten braces and had oral surgery to correct an underbite. When these procedures took place, my interest in dentistry was born. I shadowed my oral surgeon and other dentists, and I was hooked.

My Professional Development

When I finished dental school, I was admitted to an advanced education in general dentistry (AEGD) postdoctoral program at my dental school. At the same time, I applied for a teaching position there. It was unheard of that residents could both work and be a resident in the AEGD program. But I was fortunate. My department chair allowed me to pursue the AEGD program in the mornings and teach in the fixed prosthodontics lab in the afternoons, and my AEGD director allowed me to earn my certificate in AEGD over two years instead of one.

After I graduated from the AEGD program, I decided to approach my department chair about a raise, which was granted. However, the pay for teaching was still dismal. Fortunately, an opportunity became available to start working in the Office of Academic Affairs. The position was one that worked on increasing the diversity of the student body and the retention of the college's students. My formal mentor at that time was my immediate supervisor, the associate dean for academic affairs. However, my primary informal mentor was Dr. Jeanne Sinkford, who offered ADEA's annual workshops on diversity.

Fairly early in my academic career, the position of associate dean for student affairs became vacant at my dental school. At the recommendation of a colleague, I applied for that position, which, fortunately, I did not get. Subsequent to the position being filled, I became aware of the requirements of the job and the experiences and knowledge needed to successfully perform it—experiences and knowledge I did not have at that time. I am so grateful that I was not appointed as the associate dean for student affairs at that point in my career because I was not ready for it. But this experience taught me an important lesson. I know now that I should not act on the recommendation of others alone. Instead, it is important that I assess the requirements of the position of interest, determine my skill set, and see if there is a good fit between my skills and the position. It became clear to me that I need to always do what is right for me and not what others think is right for me. I think this is an important lesson for future leaders: listen to others but be led by your own heart and head. Assess your situation and determine the best route.

My Mentors

When I think about the mentoring relationships that supported me on my journey, I realize that I had very few formal mentors. But what stands out about them all is that they had my best interests at heart. Looking back, I see that my mentors gained very little, if anything, from the guidance they provided me. Most of my mentors more than likely did not even know they were mentoring me at that time, because the relationships were informal and indirect. My mentors were individuals who I admired, watched, and learned from as they engaged in the responsibilities of their leadership positions. I sought them out because I could see that they would guide me and help me to grow as a leader and person. In addition, they also had knowledge and skills that I clearly needed.

Becoming a Woman Leader

When I think about the characteristics or attributes that are most critical for attaining and sustaining success as a woman leader, I have a straightforward philosophy. I firmly believe that success and quality outcomes are not determined by gender or luck, but by hard work, knowledge, experience, motivation, tenacity, and integrity. It is crucial not to wait for others to advocate for us or plan our advancement. Instead, we need to determine what our professional goals are, prepare ourselves to achieve those goals, develop a strategic plan, and work that plan. Above all, we cannot allow ourselves to get discouraged by setbacks and disappointments. On the contrary, every setback and disappointment carries a lesson for us, and we can use them as motivators.

One other lesson I learned on my professional journey to become a woman leader was that age is just a number. I was thirty-eight years old when I started dental school, and I was forty-two years old when I earned my DDS degree. My age never deterred me, nor did it ever negatively affect my education or my career. Instead, I believe that it was an asset for and enhanced both.

Thinking back on my career, I realize that all professional journeys are not without challenges. Understanding how we overcome these challenges is important. My first leadership position was director of academic programs from 1996 to 1998. This position was created for me when I requested a raise in salary. One major challenge in this position was that I had to raise funds to sustain the dental school's pipeline programs designed to increase student diversity. This was a new challenge for me, and I overcame it by asking my supervisor to mentor me so I could learn how to successfully apply for funds and secure external grants.

At the same time, I faced another challenge: I had to take responsibility for growing and expanding pipeline programs that another faculty member had started. Unfortunately, this colleague took it personally and thought I was taking credit from him and taking over his programs. I tried to overcome this challenge by reaching out to him and tried to ease the tension by letting him know that it was time to expand the programs. I always gave him credit for his role in getting the programs started and tried to keep the lines of communication with him open.

When I think about what I am most proud of on a professional level, I think of helping to offer the opportunity for educational advancement to students from backgrounds similar to my own. It is important to me to assure that we "count in" those students who have been "counted out." I am proud that by doing so, I help to diversify the dental school student body and ultimately create more access to care for patients from underserved communities, such as those from socioeconomically disadvantaged backgrounds and/or from historically underrepresented minority backgrounds.

Ernestine S. Lacy, DDS

Words of Wisdom for Future Leaders

My words of wisdom for future leader fall into three groups. First, I think about our personal attributes and how being who we are can help us as leaders. My advice is as follows:

- Be patient and empathetic.
- Have the ability to let things roll off your back and to take nothing personally.
- Be logical.
- Be open and transparent whenever possible.
- Be able to suspend your own prejudices.
- Be curious about people and ideas.
- Be humble.
- Be tenacious.
- Be confident without being arrogant.
- Be passionate about positions and responsibilities.

The second group of words of wisdom is concerned with knowledge, specifically how we think about the world:

- Know when to be decisive, but know your limits.
- Welcome/respect ideas different from your own.
- Try to see all sides to every question.
- Look at challenges as opportunities to learn and grow.

The third and final group focuses on what our actions should look like (a) in relation to working with others and (b) for ourselves.

When working with others:

- Have and generate excitement.
- Ask for help and delegate when necessary.
- Recognize strengths and use them.

- Always and truly give credit to others and appreciate them.
- Do not micromanage; instead, accept things as good if they are worthwhile alternatives that had not occurred to you.
- Be a team player and value every member of the team.
- Use hierarchies to achieve success (someone has to make a decision)—not to discount people or their ideas.
- Learn from and freely discuss your mistakes.
- Share useful emotions.

Concerning yourself:
- Recognize areas of weakness and work on making them stronger.
- Be able to sleep at night and work hard during the day.
- Prepare for and advocate for your advancement.

Ana Lopez-Fuentes, DMD, MPH, FACD, FICD

◆ ◆ ◆

Growing Up in Puerto Rico

I was born in Puerto Rico, the first of three daughters in a middle-class family. Both my parents are devout Catholics, and my mother, as in many Hispanic families, comes from a family of courageous, strong women. I have fond childhood memories of playing with my sisters, spending weekends with my parents and cousins, enjoying summer road trips around the island, and being active at church. With lots of personal sacrifices from both of my parents, we all attended a fully bilingual Catholic school from kindergarten to twelfth grade. My leadership experience started in sixth grade when I became the class representative to the junior student council. In eighth grade, I became the Junior National Honor Society vice president and president of the Junior Catholic Daughters of America, both at the island level. During my senior year of high school, I was elected to be president of the student council. These leadership opportunities shaped me into an independent, organized, and service-oriented individual who cares for the needs of others. When I gave my first speech in elementary school, I was so short that I had to stand on wooden steps behind the podium to be seen. But I remember my teachers' and parents' expressions of pride when I addressed the audience and made my speech.

Our home became the gathering place for most of my friends and for many of my school's committee meetings. We made posters, flyers, and signs for student council elections and met with students from other schools for debates and sports events. My mother always asked what my plans were for the weekend because there were always activities such as gatherings, dances, prayer groups, retreats, community services, or cookouts. I will never forget the many ways in which my parents supported all of them. Our parents shielded us from harm and are, even now, a source of advice and comfort for all of us. Their support, sacrifices, and love were instrumental in my leadership development.

As a child, I learned how to deal with obstacles. I had a lingual frenum that affected my pronunciation of some words in Spanish. But I did not let that stop me from teaching my younger cousins how to read and write. As a result, they started speaking with the same speech problem I had. We still laugh about that today. I also taught English and math to elementary school children from low-income families at a nearby church. Although not planned, those were my first steps in teaching and leadership. As a child, I wanted to become a dancer, an actress, or a singer. My first dance lessons were when my mother and father danced in our living room. Reading and singing out loud to the Carpenters, Bread, and many other bands in English helped me a lot with my pronunciation and grammar; this was my speech therapy.

Getting a College Education

Sacrifice, hard work, persistence, and *commitment* are words that describe what many families go through to help their offspring have a better future. My parents are no exception. They sacrificed a lot to make it possible for us to have an education. My mother knew that an educated woman would have freedom of choice and could make dreams come true. While I was in college in the United States, my middle sister started her college years at the University of Puerto Rico. When political unrest became widespread in the early 1980s and the university closed because of a major strike, my parents became concerned for my sister's safety and decided to help her transition to another college on the mainland.

To support two daughters in college and make ends meet, my mother started selling clothes and purses and making home deliveries at night while my father stayed home, helping my youngest sister with homework and fixing dinner for them. My sister remembers vividly how she would go with my mother and help her with deliveries and women's requests when she did not have homework. My parents rarely went out for dinner or to the movies while we were in school and college. Money earned was used for essentials and our education. My parents were our role models. They taught us how important family support was, to work hard to reach our goals, and to be grateful each day for all our blessings. They taught me the importance of pursuing my goals and at the same time accepting responsibility for the well-being of others. I learned how important resilience was, and these experiences shaped me.

With my parents' support, I became the first college graduate in my family and the first woman in my extended family to go to college in the United States. This was a milestone for the whole family. Needless to say, the pressure to perform well was constantly present, but so was the support from the strong women in my family. My mother always reminded me that an educated woman can be independent and can take care of her family. I graduated with a bachelor of Science in biology from Tulane University in New Orleans, Louisiana. My college experience exposed me to racism and bias and instilled in me the need to excel in whatever I did. I worked during my college years and had leadership positions in college associations. I decided to apply to dental school after one of my summer jobs. It felt like the right thing to do because of my love for science, education, and the arts. It represented an opportunity to express myself and to help underserved and less fortunate individuals. After much hard work and commitment, I was accepted by a dental school in Puerto Rico.

Becoming a Dentist and Dental Educator

I encountered many challenges in dental school. The curriculum was difficult, the environment was competitive, and gender bias was a problem. Thanks to hard work and my organizational skills, I finished the graduation requirements early. This allowed me to volunteer at the dental assistant clinics where I perfected my clinical skills and practiced for the local boards. My graduation from dental school was a major milestone for everyone in my family.

A year after graduation, the University of Puerto Rico (UPR) offered me a position as an instructor for their dental assisting and hygiene programs. Although I enjoyed private practice, I accepted because I knew that this position would give me the opportunity to teach, learn, and contribute to dental education. One of my first leadership opportunities came when I was asked to implement and direct an expanded-function dental assistant program as part of a collaboration between UPR and the University of Granada, Spain. This project ignited my passion for dental education. I was a young professional with limited experience but a strong desire to learn and challenge myself with new opportunities. With full support from my husband, we embarked on a new journey.

Teaching in Granada came with many challenges. I had to relearn the language and deal with biases as the administrator of the program because of my age and gender; I also had to cope with cultural differences and a new and sometimes harsh environment. Changing the program from stomatology to dentistry was a paradigm shift that many did not want to accept. In addition, there were no regulatory laws for the profession at that time. I was unaware of all these circumstances, but there was no turning back. The decision to work in this program in Spain was made, and I needed to make the best of this experience. With persistence, diplomacy, hard work, and respect I rose to the occasion. I found lifelong friends and made lasting memories. It made me realize that no matter how complicated things are, we can make the best of the situation through tolerance, respect, communication, empathy, and resilience. One of my mentors said, "It is a matter of how you decide to navigate and embrace challenge. Your attitude and constant learning and relearning while never forgetting to have fun in the process are the critical elements for success."

After the first year in Spain, I was offered a faculty position in Granada, which I gracefully declined. I returned to Puerto Rico but continued my commitment as codirector of the program by returning to Granada every three months. In Puerto Rico, I became a full-time instructor in the dental school, finished a master's in public health, and was asked to assist in the accreditation of the dental school. I have stayed at UPR ever since. Throughout my academic career, I have served on almost all the committees and advisory boards at the dental school, Medical Sciences Campus, and at the university level. At the university level, I was able to participate in major decisions and had the honor of being the executive secretary of the President's Board.

Becoming a Leader in Dental Education

Giving back to the community is very important to me. Fifteen years ago, I became involved with the Give Kids a Smile program. It started on a small scale and grew into an island-wide event, sponsored by the University of Puerto Rico School of Dental Medicine (UPRSDM) and private practitioners. On our tenth anniversary, the Puerto Rican government acknowledged our event. In 2007, I started the "Sonrisas para el Éxito" as a collaboration with the American Association of Women Dentists (AAWD) student chapter, which I mentor. This annual event provides oral health care, beauty makeovers, and psychological support free of charge to female victims of violence. All of these experiences helped me understand the importance of having women represented in leadership roles.

The day I became dean of the dental school at UPR was one of the biggest milestones in my career. It was a long, polarized battle to get there, and I endured many forms of harassment. I accepted the position with one goal in mind: to change the political paradigm and open the door for other women, especially Hispanic women, at the local and national level. For a woman to be a dean of a dental school is still a challenge and a great opportunity. One has to work twice as hard and be present and available three times more. My first American Dental Education Association (ADEA) meeting as a dean was a celebration of my appointment. It meant a lot to me to have my mentors, friends, colleagues, and especially Hispanic women from other dental schools there to celebrate. I knew I had to leave a sound legacy and its execution needed to be exemplary, not only for my academic community but for all women, underrepresented minorities, and especially Hispanics, who not only have a glass ceiling but sometimes a multilayered concrete ceiling to break through. Success in this case is not an individual achievement, it is a team achievement.

As dean of the dental school, I created a political paradigm shift. I kept the same appointed administrators with the goal of not creating too much change. We adopted new technologies, such as the electronic health record, a new webpage, social media, and innovations through the technology center. I led our work on creating a new faculty practice and new academic programs such as the periodontics graduate program. We fostered research, alumni relations, and amendments to the local dental law to help our students and graduates address our challenges. I became the first dean from the UPR School of Dental Medicine to be elected to the ADEA Council of Deans Administrative Board. I will never forget my first speech at graduation. The honor and joy of celebrating our student and faculty accomplishments is something that can never be understated. I enjoy mentoring students and faculty, being an advisor to students' associations, and representing Puerto Rico at the national level.

The only constant in life is change, and my leadership was tested in many ways when Hurricane María hit our island in 2017. Our economy was already challenged, the university's budget was shrinking, and then came the devastation. The experience was a test in strength, discipline, organizational skills, family needs, resiliency, communication, and, above all, faith. Thanks to donations, our school became a safety net for many. We managed a quick response, established a sense of normalcy, fed our students in need for three months, and helped our communities.

Ana Lopez-Fuentes, DMD, MPH, FACD, FICD

For that work, I was honored with the 2018 Chair of the ADEA Board of Directors Citation for significant contributions to dental education. The citation recognized my leadership during my tenure as dean of the dental school after Hurricane María, maintaining the school's accreditation, keeping the school open, and helping our communities. It was recognition for the teamwork and sacrifice of many devoted human beings.

Lessons Learned

The leadership path can be filled with risks, challenges, disappointments, and harsh learning experiences. We have to prepare our minds, bodies, and souls to come out of these experiences stronger, resilient, and ready for what comes next. A balance of family life, rest, leisure, and spiritual activities are needed for health and wellness. I learned that one has to enjoy the ride and have fun in the process. When confronted with bias and challenges, I chose the path of hard work, entrepreneurship, and resilience. I accepted challenges and opportunities while balancing my personal life. For every administrative milestone, I had the opportunity to participate in a leadership institute or program. I also empowered other women and men to become leaders and to progress through their academic careers. While we cannot control our challenges, we can control how we react to them.

My career pathway has taught me to be an active learner and to listen to advice and to what people from different walks of life teach us. When listening to staff and having conversations with neighbors and those who cross our paths, I am amazed about all the things people in my immediate circle can teach me. I learned how to prioritize, think outside the box, follow my instincts, ask for advice, take time for crucial decisions, and say yes to opportunities. We learn how strong and resilient we can be while facing major challenges and turning them into opportunities. It is important to look for the positive in everything we encounter and be grateful for all.

My grandmother and mother taught me the importance of courage and to be a humble servant to others. You can be a leader, leave a positive legacy, and have an impact on society no matter what pathway you choose, as long as you do it for the greater good. It is all about passion, hard work, commitment, consistency, and perseverance. Love what you do, be passionate about what you believe in, and never forget to enjoy the simple things in life. A balance in life is crucial for happiness and well-being. Never stop dreaming, and never ever lose faith!

Melanie E. Mayberry, DDS, MS-HCM, FACD

◆ ◆ ◆

Growing Up in Detroit

Detroit in the late 1960s and early 1970s was a city emerging from the burning ashes of the 1967 race riot to the election of Mayor Coleman A. Young, the city's first Black mayor in 1974. It was famous for the Motown sound and as the Motor City. It had a solid Black middle class, safe neighborhoods, and sizeable homes filled with children of doctors, lawyers, judges, white middle-management auto workers, school principals, and dentists.

I was born there and grew up in a strong, loving, and solid middle-class family as the youngest of five children of Dr. Robert J. and Mrs. Catherine L. Mayberry. My father was a dentist, and my mother, as she proudly says to this very day, was a domestic engineer, or in the jargon of her five children: a stay-at-home mom. Both were very modest. No extravagant spending, no cable TV, no big family trips every summer—a one-car household. My mother would often say, "Every day with your dad is a vacation." And my father equally loved and respected my mother. His joy in caring for her and us was evident every day. My parents had three generations of children, four daughters and one son. My oldest sister is twenty-one years older than me, and the sibling closest to me in age is five years my senior. My older sisters grew up in the Jim Crow era in the segregated South and experienced all its pain long before I arrived.

During those times, my father was evolving into the revered dentist he would later be. But his life was not without challenges. Early in his dental career, he drove a bus instead of practicing dentistry, due to discrimination. No white dentist would practice with him, and no banks would loan him money to build his own practice. So he drove a bus to earn a living and take care of us, and saved money to build his own dental practice. As a dental student from 1942 to 1945 at the University of Michigan, my father faced many moments tainted with loathsome racial hate. One story he often shared to illustrate the goodness of humanity and his reason for unceasing hope was about the day a faculty member intervened on his behalf when a patient refused to be treated by an "N-word student." The professor told the patient he could either accept treatment from the Negro student or leave. That story held much more meaning to me fifty years later as I began to navigate the dental profession.

My mother is warm and loving. She was also the disciplinarian. My father was a quiet, strong, humble, intelligent, and revered dentist in the city of Detroit. Both were people of faith and believed firmly that education was crucial to the advancement of one's life. Their goal was that all five of us would be college educated. They often would say, to each of us, "You are my Cadillac." When most of my parents' contemporaries were contemplating big trips and retirement, our parents were thinking about how they would pay for my education. My father decided to get a second job, working as a dentist for the city of Detroit in addition to his private practice.

My Journey to Dentistry

My parents did not pressure me to pursue dentistry, and I wanted to be a veterinarian while growing up, with my parents nurturing my love for animals. I knew that in order to get into veterinarian school, I had to get into college and do well. While not an A student, I was disciplined and focused because I knew what I wanted. I was fortunate that I had supportive parents and family and an innate drive, because my high school guidance counselor was not supportive. She tried to make me settle for a lesser dream as opposed to stretching my arms to higher stars. But in the end, it worked out. Taking science and math courses beyond the required allotment to prepare myself for veterinarian school was an uphill battle, but it was a victory in the end when I was college bound.

The next decision was which college to attend. My two oldest siblings attended in-state, majority-serving institutions. My brother attended a historically Black college and university (HBCU) in New Orleans, followed by my youngest sister, who attended the same HBCU. Their experiences helped me to appreciate the beauty, scholarship, social, and nurturing characteristics of an HBCU. Tuskegee University was the only HBCU with a veterinarian school, so I attended this wonderful place for learning, exploring, testing my ethos, and refining it further. The faculty was warm and nurturing, with a vision of all the possibilities that I could consider. It was also a fun place, with sororities and fraternities helping to shape our social-justice awareness and hosting parties with a purpose. My official and unofficial guidance counselors and mentors offered me a much different experience than the one I'd had in high school. Dr. Benford and Dr. Carter—one a woman and one a man, one white and one Black—were both dedicated to guiding my career path and saw something in me that I did not see in myself. After my first few semesters at Tuskegee, they suggested changing my major from veterinary medicine to biology in the event that I decided to go to medical or dental school. They argued that this background would broaden my career choices.

Their advice was great! Whenever I returned home during school breaks, I would work in my father's practice. These experiences gave me an intriguing glimpse into the world of dentistry, and my father and his appreciative patients made a significant impact on my career choice. I wanted the opportunity to be able to serve and provide the healing touch to patients that I saw my father demonstrate day in and day out. In my sophomore year, I changed my career choice to dentistry. It is one of the best decisions I made in my life. Because of the vision of my two mentors, I was still on track to be adequately prepared for the DAT entrance exam and admission to dental school.

Being a dental student at Meharry Medical College (MMC) was inspiring. No other place has as many Black scientists, physicians, or dentists. I was surrounded by greatness in scholarship, resilience, education, patient care, perseverance, and a rich tradition of service to mankind. Meharry prepared me well for all that I would encounter. Many patients looked surprised when I walked into the dental operatory and said, "Hi, I'm Dr. Mayberry. How are you?" Some would be speechless. Some would say, "You are Dr. Mayberry? I expected you would look different."

On one particular day maybe six to seven years into my career, while working in a small town in northern Michigan, I introduced myself in this way to a new patient. He was an older white man, perhaps in his late seventies or early eighties. As I presented myself, he displayed that look I had come to know. In his case, it was reasonable to be shocked, as this was a small, white town, where everyone knew everyone. You could go for months without seeing anyone of color. He was quiet during our initial interactions. But over time, our exchanges increased because I provided a lot of care to him, from exams and extractions to denture fabrications. As our patient relationship grew, he shared with me, "You know, there was a time when I would not have let someone like you treat me." I asked him what he meant, as if I didn't already know. In the most loquacious manner, he began to share how he used to be a racist, but that he had evolved. Our conversation was so meaningful. Just when I thought our interaction could not get any better, he presented me with a meticulously folded US flag in a perfectly sized box and said, "I had this flag flown at the state capitol in your honor." I was stunned, and tears came to my eyes. This was the type of man my father had encountered during his dental school days over fifty years ago. But this man in my chair was my father's hope realized. It was a meaningful moment that showed me the goodness of humanity will always prevail.

Melanie E. Mayberry, DDS, MS-HCM, FACD

My Mentors

I could not have done it by myself. I had many mentors along the way. Some were my peers, and some my seniors. What they all had in common was the ability to see me and my future possibilities. This is a powerful gift that helps the mentee take risks and meet challenges head-on.

After graduating from dental school, I completed a residency in hospital dentistry general practice at the University of Michigan Medical Center. I then went on to practice dentistry full-time in a Federally Qualified Health Center (FQHC) and started a hospital dentistry program. After several years, I decided to experience practicing in a corporate dental practice in a dental service organization (DSO). Shortly thereafter, the time had come to open my part-time private practice and pursue my interest in dental education. One of my most impactful mentors in academia was my department chairperson. She created an environment that facilitated my growth and created a space for me to thrive. I did not intentionally seek her out as my mentor and was not looking for one, but I needed one. During our frequent interactions, our mentorship relationship grew. I am not even sure she saw herself as my mentor, but she was and still is.

Lessons Learned

"I am qualified to do the job and I know it." Sometimes this sentence is just what we have to tell ourselves, especially when validation may be lacking. Nothing replaces a skill set and, even more important, knowing you have that skill set. This is important for women, especially women of color. Constant self-affirmations and reaffirmations are important because women leaders in the workplace are still not common. We do not always have the luxury, as our male counterparts do, to model same-gender leaders. Sometimes we forge the path as we lead. Confidence with humility is essential. Respect and trustworthiness are key. The respect we give speaks volumes, whether merited or not. We have to be tough and yet tender, compelling and yet compassionate, and think of people first and then of our job. Encouraging others and speaking to the heart is just as important as speaking to the mind. As a result, people do not do the work because they should but because they are motivated to do it for you.

One of my biggest educational moments was when I became chair of one of the largest departments in our school, with very strong male personalities. I decided to have departmental goals and initiatives that would support individual professional development, faculty calibration, and the mission of the University of Detroit Mercy School of Dentistry. When I proposed these initiatives at our first departmental meeting, there was not much conversation. I did not consider that a problem and planned to make another attempt to broach the topic at the next meeting. When there was no progress in the second meeting, I could not understand why this discussion was so difficult and taking so long. So I turned to a trusted confidant and asked how I could get the faculty to identify with these goals. He patiently listened and then said, "You have to give people time to catch up to where you are. Do you want to lose quickly or win slow?" This made me realize that I had spent more time on identifying the goals than I gave to my faculty and that I had not made a collaborative effort. I learned that everybody has to start with what they know and that this might be quite different from the leader's—in this case, my—perspective. So, I gave my team time, and our departmental conversations became richer and more productive. In the end, the department selected the goals, identified goal leaders, and began working toward them.

My first leadership post in academia was being the director of predoctoral education at the University Health Center on the Detroit Medical Center Campus. I was not the first woman in this role, but I was the first woman of color and certainly the youngest. When the dental school leadership asked me to assume this role, I was reluctant. But I had strong support and saw an opportunity to grow and make contributions in a broader way. Even with support, this role was not without challenges. Learning the different personalities of the mostly older male faculty, building new relationships, learning my new role, and communicating a team message were challenging. It required time because trust would not happen overnight. It happened through one-on-one and group interactions both on and off the clinic floor. As I reflect back, the most meaningful time I spent with my team was lunchtime. We ate together and shared what we did on the weekends and what happened in our families. This was the pathway to building the relationships that led to teamwork and made it easy to communicate the clinic's mission and the importance of each member's intricate role for our success.

The Power of Lifelong Learning

As I observed how health care and the world around me were changing, I knew I had to update the tools in my toolbox and contemporize my thinking, especially related to what future health care would look like. So, I decided to go back to school and committed to studying again for entrance exams and completing essays and admission applications. Two years later, I graduated with a master's degree in health-care management from Harvard. It was tough and at times brutal, but it was worth it. You can never go wrong with investing in your education.

My career is still unfolding. I had great experiences and opportunities to make meaningful contributions and create innovative curricula in dental education and patient care. It is difficult to decide which accomplishment I am most proud of. However, all truly meaningful accomplishments are those that directly or indirectly positively impact the lives of those we love, those we care for and treat, and those we serve. In the end, the thing I will be most proud of is the woman I continue to evolve into.

It is important that as people of color, especially women, we protect the dreams in our hearts. One should also know that the dream seed was given to us to plant, grow, and realize its full potential. Sometimes the dream seed is not the problem. The soil is the problem. Be mindful to plant your seeds in fertile ground, and if the ground around you is not fertile, save your seeds until you find a ground that is. Dreams may change. But the important thing is to have a dream.

Renee McCoy-Collins, DDS, FACD, FICD

◆ ◆ ◆

One Defining Moment

The beepers went off and the trauma code team assembled as the formerly quiet corridors of the hospital sprang to life. A teenage male was bleeding profusely from a gunshot wound to his face. His mother was hysterical as the police tried to make sense of another needless tragedy. The patient fought us as he yelled, "But I shot him dead; he is dead!" Those words squeezed my heart as the news was shared in hushed whispers. His victim was only fifteen years old, and our patient, struggling for his life, was only sixteen. Our patient was transferred to the intensive care unit after a sixteen-hour multispecialty team operation. I was weary and swept with emotion.

How Did I Ever Get Here, and Why Have I Chosen a Career That Will Bear Witness to Such Carnage?

I was born in New York City and raised on Long Island. I have six siblings and was the middle child of a family that valued education and community service. My parents always encouraged us to excel in our studies and volunteer for charitable organizations. We chose to volunteer at the neighborhood cerebral palsy center where my mother also volunteered. Leadership in all capacities was expected so that we could learn to be a voice for others in need. Evening dinner table conversations with family always consisted of current events, sharing scholastic achievements, and discussing how education and commitment could lead to societal progress.

My father, Dr. Rhody A. McCoy, was the first African American to pass the NYC school system's principal examination. He then tutored other minority teachers, who also successfully passed. My father was a renowned educator and a leader in the NYC school system's Ocean Hill–Brownsville District Project. My mother, Edith Bowman McCoy, was a homemaker until my siblings and I were in college. She served as an officer and president of the local parent-teacher association. She obtained her master's degree and was ready to defend her dissertation for her Doctor of Education degree at the time of her early death.

My parents made sure our family home was always a site of weekend social gatherings of family and friends. As a young teenager, I began to understand why my family opened their home to so many others. One reason was so that we could gather while being protected from racial segregation and discrimination at local recreational facilities. As a child, I remember two of my classmates telling me they were "white" and inquiring, "What color are you?" Proudly, I answered, "Peach!" At dinnertime, I shared this declaration and was told I was a Negro and that Black was listed as my race on my birth certificate. The next day, I proudly announced to those classmates that I was in fact a Black Negro. Alarmed, they responded, "Well, you must have had too much chocolate milk to drink." We all laughed, satisfied that I was a chocolate-milk consumer and thus looked different.

My maternal grandfather, Dr. James Bowman, was a dentist in Washington, DC. He served as president of the Robert T. Freeman Dental Society and president of the National Dental Association. My uncle, Dr. James Bowman II, was a pathologist specializing in genetic red blood cell research and was mentored by Dr. Charles Drew. My uncle

Renee McCoy-Collins, DDS, FACD, FICD

coauthored numerous publications and books with members of Howard University and Chicago University Medical School faculty.

Becoming an Oral Maxillofacial Surgeon and a Community Educator

While I was on a full academic scholarship at Howard University studying early childhood education, I took a part-time job as a receptionist in my uncle Dr. Elmer Bowman's dental office. I took this opportunity to learn about dentistry with his support and encouragement. During this time, I was fortunately introduced to many leaders in organized dentistry who would also one day become mentors as I pursued a career in oral and maxillofacial surgery.

When I applied to oral maxillofacial residency programs, all of my mentors in the specialty and interviewers asked me a question they never asked my male counterparts. The question was whether I was strong enough to function at the highest level during the greatest moments of duress. My response was always an emphatic yes. Even with my determination to become an exceptional oral and maxillofacial surgeon, I had to reflect on whether this would be sufficient to make a meaningful difference in the community, because contributing to the community was a principle instilled in me since childhood.

Being confronted with the consequences of gun violence among young people led me to write a grant proposal in 1983 to get funding for providing educational forums for young people to understand the recovery process after survival from violent facial trauma. After receiving funding from the Reverend Sullivan Write to Read Foundation and the Coors Foundation, I visited elementary and high schools and correctional facilities for over a year, giving presentations on head and neck trauma and the recovery process. Whenever I asked during these presentations, "How many of you have had a family member or a loved one shot?" almost all hands would be raised.

During this time, my father called one day and asked if I had forgotten to tell him something. He had attended a Black History Month event in California, and in the program, I was featured as one of the recipients of the Black History Month awards in acknowledgment of my contribution to the fight against gun violence among youth.

Making a Difference

Meeting so many young people increased my determination to make a difference in their lives through organized dentistry and larger group efforts. When problems arose, I tried to solve them through leadership and mentoring. I developed a program with a group of physicians to coordinate primary medical care for patients who came to the District of Columbia General Hospital (DCGH) dental clinic for a dental emergency and had no primary care doctor. We agreed to set aside appointment times for these often young and uninsured patients so that they could receive primary care.

As I migrated to serve on the DC Board of Dentistry and worked in private practice, I coordinated with one of my patients with expertise in scholarship counseling to provide pro bono financial aid counseling services to my young patients in high school so they could apply to college scholarship programs. Throughout this time, I fortunately had a young doctor, dental, or medical student whom I mentored to not only provide clinical services but also to provide community services for oral or medical health. I supported the American College of Dentists and the International College of Dentists, recognizing African American applicants and/or those from other historically underrepresented minority backgrounds, who were typically not considered for fellowship unless they had minority mentors.

The Importance of Mentorship

James T. Jackson, my mentor in the fellowship in the American College of Dentists, told me that it was my duty to nominate a deserving colleague each year. The impact of having had mentors in my career cannot be understated, as I needed their support on every level of my career. As one of the first female oral and maxillofacial surgeons in the eastern

Renee McCoy-Collins, DDS, FACD, FICD

United States, and as the first female graduate from Howard University's OMFS program, it was a great challenge to gain acceptance. I know now that it was made easier through the support of my dental school faculty mentors and Dr. Jeanne Sinkford, dean of Howard University College of Dentistry. I decided I had to earn better grades than my dental school classmates and worked harder on and off the oral surgery rotations. Dr. Thomas Jeter, Dr. James Stanback, and Dr. Thomas Pinson advised me to read the OMS journal and shadow the OMS residents in the hospital. These efforts helped me gain the respect of my colleagues and faculty members and get admitted as the first female oral and maxillofacial surgery resident at Howard University.

I appreciate the opportunity I received at Howard University College of Dentistry to demonstrate my abilities. It allowed me to be successful and to give back to the community in all phases of my career and in my personal life. Two mentors in particular, Dr. Pinson and Dr. Calhoun, encouraged me to become active in organized dentistry and hospital staff activities. I was the first female to be the president of a local society of oral maxillofacial surgeons, I became president-elect of Howard University Hospital medical-dental staff, and was president of DC General Hospital medical-dental staff.

Becoming a Leader and Advocate

As one of a few female members of the American Association of Oral and Maxillofacial Surgeons (AAOMS), I was often ignored. But I never stopped being assertive at meetings and in educational forums. There were only a few African American oral and maxillofacial surgeons in the country, and most had graduated from Howard University's specialty program. At one of the annual AAOMS meetings, a group of colleagues and I met and discussed the apparent lack of acceptance of qualified African American applicants by OMS training programs. African American oral maxillofacial surgeons were also not represented in the American Association of Oral and Maxillofacial Surgeons advertising campaign, and African Americans were not being accepted into leadership positions within the organization. The importance of equal representation led me to become a founding member of the National Society of Oral and Maxillofacial Surgeons and its second president. Today, membership in the organization has grown, and its foundation offers educational assistance, research projects, and scholarships to minority residents.

When I became the first female chairperson of the District of Columbia Board of Dentistry, I learned about another component of regulatory guidelines in health care. This led me to become involved with the American Association of Dental Boards and to being elected the East Caucus chairperson. We worked as a team to mentor newer members to take on roles and represent our district caucus on the national level while appointing other DC board members to national positions.

My leadership and mentoring were recognized by the American Association of Dental Boards when they featured me in their November 2019 newsletter and gave me the President's Leadership Award in January 2020 at the annual meeting of the Commission of Dental Competency Admissions, formerly the North East Regional Board.

As I reflect on the commitment and enduring spirit of those who came before me, the mentorship relationships I was fortunate to forge, and the work I have done throughout my career, I remain optimistic about the future of dentistry. The leadership and dedication the next generation of dentists have shown is a positive indicator that quality of and access to health care will continue to expand in the future.

Vivian W. Pinn, MD, FCAP

✦ ✦ ✦

Growing Up

I was born in rural Halifax County, Virginia, but grew up largely in Lynchburg, Virginia. Both of my parents were public school teachers who had to teach in different school systems because married couples at that time could not be employed in the same one. So I spent much of my early years with my maternal and paternal grandparents. It was in those situations that I first desired to become a physician. My paternal grandfather needed shots for pain because of his colon cancer, and it was my father who usually administered them to him. As the oldest grandchild, my grandfather encouraged me to help with the injections. My paternal grandmother had diabetes and also required injections—of insulin—which my father also administered to her.

Because our other relatives were squeamish about "giving needles," my dad eventually taught me how to administer the injections. Physicians made house calls in those days, and it was very apparent that after the doctor visited, everyone seemed much better. My grandparents benefited from the medical attention, and other family members were relieved by seeing how much they benefited from the visits. Those are my earliest recollections of how a physician made a difference. I am told

I was four when I first announced that I wanted to be a doctor, and that never changed.

As a pre-fluoride child with many dental issues, I think my early experiences in the dentist's chair did not warm me to the idea of becoming a dentist. I did not know any Black women physicians, but I greatly admired Dr. Clarissa Winbush, the first Black female dentist in Virginia, who had a dental practice in Lynchburg. She was utterly unique and highly respected by our community as a woman in what was still regarded as a man's profession.

I give my parents a great deal of credit for my continued interest in medicine and for my choice to eventually become a physician. There were no health professionals in our family, only four male African American physicians in my hometown, and except for Dr. Winbush, no African American women dentists. But my parents never told me that I could not become a physician. Instead, they told me that I would need to study hard if that was what I wanted to be.

Becoming a Physician

The next memorable moment on my pathway to becoming a physician was the summer after my sophomore year in college. My mother was experiencing severe hip pain, and I went with her to see the doctor. I remember clearly how cold and authoritarian the doctor was to her, telling her that if she had worn the Oxford shoes he had told her to wear and done her exercises, she would not have pain. This was while he treated her with "gold shots" for arthritis. About a month later, my father discovered a lump while massaging her hip to relieve the pain. She actually had a chondrosarcoma on her ilium bone that the physician had totally missed. I took a leave of absence from college to care for her until she died the following February.

I never forgot that experience. It taught me how important it is to listen to patients and not feel omnipotent just because there is an *MD* behind my name. I also learned firsthand how fulfilling it can be to postpone my own goals to care for a beloved family member. The experience also made me decide to go into medical research.

I had always been rather shy, but my personality changed when I stayed with my mother while she was hospitalized for several months at Sloan Kettering in New York. We had hoped that surgery could save her life, but her cancer had progressed too far. It was then that I learned to "speak up" and be persistent, even demanding, at times. My mother needed care and attention, but the environment seemed huge and inhospitable. I even felt that she was disregarded by some of the staff because she was a minority.

After Wellesley College, I entered the University of Virginia School of Medicine, where I discovered on the very first day that I was the only woman and the only person of color in my class. If there ever was a time that I had to learn to be independent, it was during those years. There was only one female professor on the faculty, and she was definitely not interested in mentoring me. And there were no faculty members of color. So, except for occasional professional advice from a few professors, I depended on my father, even though he had never gone to medical school.

Becoming a Faculty Member

To this day, I believe that the time I spent mentoring others was rooted in the experience I had without a faculty mentor who could relate to my needs as a lone woman of color in that environment. I came to believe that I have a responsibility to be available in whatever way needed to help students, colleagues, and others, even if it just means being someone to talk with or ask for advice. In my first years as a faculty member, I worked to be available for the students. This eventually led to my appointment as assistant dean for student affairs at Tufts University School of Medicine.

My experiences as a research assistant, then a research fellow, and my postgraduate training in pathology were very different. I had many supportive and helpful mentors who helped to guide me in my career. The most meaningful mentor was Dr. Martin Flax, who encouraged me to enter the field of pathology. I did my fellowship in immunopathology with him and followed him from Massachusetts General Hospital to Tufts Medical School. Dr. Flax remained a mentor to me for more than twenty years, and he was especially supportive when I became a department chair. Dr. Flax taught me to have self-confidence, be prepared, accept and not resent constructive criticism, and to continue getting better, even when I thought I had done my best. He encouraged me to make presentations to groups of experts as long as I was well prepared. And he supported the time I devoted to mentoring other students and becoming involved in organized medicine, which advanced my own career priorities.

Taking On Leadership Responsibilities

My first major leadership position was as professor and chair of the Department of Pathology at Howard University. This felt like an important accomplishment to me because, as a senior in medical school, on the day I learned I had been granted a fellowship for postgraduate training in pathology, a faculty member told me to be aware that "women don't become chairmen of pathology." Yet, some fifteen years later, I became the third woman in the United States, and the first African American woman, to chair an academic pathology department. I faced many challenges when I assumed that position. A few faculty members, and some administrative staff, were not used to women in leadership positions and rebuffed what I thought were reasonable expectations for the department. But fortunately, Dr. Jeanne Sinkford was serving as dean of the dental school at that time and acted as an inspiring role model for me. I learned from her how important it is for a leader to be "nice" and approachable but also firm. Dr. Sinkford epitomized all these qualities. I also made many calls to Dr. Flax in Boston, who continued to guide me as a well-established and highly respected pathology chair himself.

The most challenging and most fulfilling leadership position for me was my appointment as the first director of the Office of Research on Women's Health (ORWH) at the National Institutes of Health. This "dream" opportunity came about because the then director of NIH, Dr.

Bernadine Healy, the first and only woman to serve in that position, knew me when she was a Harvard medical student and I was a resident physician who reviewed some of her patients' biopsies with her. The Office of Research on Women's Health was a brand-new concept. I learned a great deal about the challenges for women in unique leadership roles by observing how Dr. Healy overcame some of the subtle, and sometimes not so subtle, defiance to her authority. My major responsibilities were to develop and implement policies and programs to increase research on women's health, implement inclusion policies for research studies, and increase opportunities for women in biomedical careers while assuring the doubters that these were all science-based initiatives worthy of NIH sponsorship.

I had never served in a government position before, but with Dr. Healy's support and guidance, I learned a lot quickly. Only a few women of color were in leadership positions at DHHS, so we formed a support group that allowed us to call on each other for advice and support, or just to vent our frustrations. Dr. Marilyn Gaston, who had years of government experience, was one of those women, and I owe a great deal of my survival in the world of federal politics to her advice and support. Being new to NIH, I decided to retain the previous deputy director of the Office of Research on Women's Health, which turned out to be one of the smartest decisions I made. She knew how to make things happen at NIH, so if I had a good idea, she had the contacts and knowledge to make it happen. Now, almost thirty years later, we remain close colleagues and friends. Knowing that I needed support from the NIH community of scientists, as well as the extramural communities of advocates, scientists, and women's health groups, I set up a series of committees including representatives of all the NIH institutes and centers. This expanded participation in, and ownership of, the office's programs and goals. I did the same with external groups and consulted with them on program developments. This also extended investment in, and ownership of, the programs and policies that we implemented.

Because mentoring had been such an important force in my own career advancement and leadership development, I incorporated it as a formal and required component of many of our office's new programs and efforts. This continued even after my retirement.

When I look back on my career, I think the accomplishments that make me most proud are not my personal honors or awards but witnessing and sharing the many achievements of my former students and mentees in medicine, dentistry, and other fields, some of whom I have followed now for more than thirty years. I brim with pride as I learn of their personal and professional achievements.

I have learned many important things about leadership. Women are often lonely in leadership positions, so there is a need to support them, especially through networking and communication. A good leader must have self-confidence, but without the arrogance that sometimes develops from being "in charge." A good leader must know how she wants to lead others by defining and pursuing specific goals. A good leader must understand that her personal advancement is not nearly as important as the professional advancement and sense of ownership of those whom she leads. And, finally, a good leader must practice and exhibit what I call the "Four *E*s"—empathy, ethics, excellence, and equity.

Shelia S. Price, DDS, EdD, FACD

◆ ◆ ◆

The Beginning

My childhood days were carefree. Playing hopscotch in the sandy lane between our home and my paternal grandparents' yard and chasing fireflies on the adjacent grassy hillside are among my favorite memories. I loved tossing rocks in the river near our home and watching the resulting rings slowly expand. Swinging on the front porch while listening to nature's music, talking with family, and greeting friends are other fond memories.

I grew up in rural Madison, West Virginia, as the youngest of seven children. My father was a brick mason and farmer. My mother, a homemaker, took on domestic jobs to help make ends meet, particularly when my father's workload slowed in the winter. She sewed most of my clothes, sometimes using fabric from hand-me-down garments. She taught me how to sew and instilled the value of making something out of nothing. I learned the importance of hard work from my parents. Attending Sunday school and church service each week were formative parts of my life.

We were poor by the world's standard. But I never defined myself as poor because I had everything I needed to be happy.

Despite their lack of a high school education, my parents encouraged me to achieve academically. My older sisters brought me books on their visits from college. Mama read to me every night. But I was a shy child, and when it was time to start school, I cried profusely every morning. My first-grade teacher, Mrs. Baldwin, played vinyl records at rest time that were intended to soothe students. But I cried. She attempted to console me with her pillow-soft arms. During spring break of my senior year of dental school, Mrs. Baldwin invited me and my mother to have tea at her home. While there, I learned how she remedied my sadness: she identified the music that triggered my tears and placed a "do not play" note on the album cover to remind herself. She explained that, gradually, I began enjoying school. I mention this early history because Mrs. Baldwin beautifully illustrates the power of a compassionate, caring teacher who is sensitive to a student's individual needs. Reflecting on my reluctance to attend first grade, no one would have guessed that I would finish college, dental school, and eventually graduate school.

My fifth-grade teacher introduced me to the word *perseverance*, which became part of my life's motto. After a visit to the dentist during this year, I declared that I would become a dentist and never changed my plan. In middle school, I began playing the clarinet. I joined the high school band and later became a majorette. Throughout high school, I worked at the local jewelry store as a clerk and engraver on most weekends and holiday breaks. My extracurricular and early employment experiences taught me teamwork, time management, and interpersonal skills. I was the first African American valedictorian at my high school, sharing the honor with two white girls who also earned 4.0 GPAs.

Becoming a Dentist

I knew that dental school would be expensive. Summer jobs in college included working at an auto assembly plant in Lorain, Ohio, and a manufacturing company in Macon, Georgia, where I stayed with my sisters

Shelia S. Price, DDS, EdD, FACD

and their families. I was offered an academic scholarship to attend Morris Harvey College (later named University of Charleston) in Charleston, West Virginia, where I majored in biology, worked as a work-study student for my microbiology professor, and graduated cum laude.

In 1982, I started dental school as one of forty-six students at West Virginia University (WVU). I was the only African American dental student during the entire four years of my dental education. I got married after the first year. In 1986, I became the first African American woman to earn a dental degree at WVU and the first person in my family to embark on a health profession career.

My time as a dental student was not always uncomplicated. I was raised with the Golden Rule ingrained: do unto others as you would have them do unto you. A lesson learned in dental school tested my commitment to this moral value. For a preclinical exercise, we were paired and then practiced taking each other's medical and dental histories. I, a first-generation college student, was partnered with a classmate on track to becoming a multigeneration dentist. My classmate role-played the "dentist" and asked me, the "patient," about the last time I had my teeth cleaned. I replied that I never had my teeth cleaned. My classmate smirked, jumped from the chair, and loudly exclaimed to the class, "Shelia never had her teeth cleaned!" I was humiliated by this breach in the fundamental principle of patient confidentiality. Thinking about this situation, I remembered a poster that hung in my college dormitory room. It read, "Experience is a hard teacher; she gives the test first and lesson later." My test here was either to harbor bitterness about the incident or to forgive my classmate. I chose the latter. The lesson here was twofold. Remember, people are imperfect and may knowingly or unknowingly humiliate another person from a background unlike their own. The Golden Rule applies in both directions. One should always be willing to forgive as easily as one receives forgiveness.

Mentoring

I pursued higher education with full support and encouragement from my family and my teachers. But as a first-generation college graduate, I had limited knowledge about dental career options. That changed when Dr. W. Robert Biddington, the dean of the WVU School of Dentistry, began discussing a career in dental education with me. I was awed by his enthusiasm and encouragement for me to become a dental educator. He opened the door to my career, coached me along the way, and connected me to prominent leaders in dental education who later joined him in guiding my professional development.

I enjoyed my faculty assignments and soon, in consultation with Dr. Biddington, began thinking about leadership roles. He recommended that I should earn a doctor in education degree with a concentration in higher education leadership. I was able to continue my full-time faculty position by primarily enrolling in evening and summer courses at WVU. He also nominated and supported me to participate in the Pew National Dental Education Leadership Program. The group of approximately twenty fellows included my coauthor, Dr. Marilyn Woolfolk.

Dr. Biddington inculcated the importance of a strong professional network and advocated for my involvement in the American Association of Dental Schools (AADS), now known as the American Dental Education Association (ADEA). While attending an AADS annual session, he introduced me to Dr. Jeanne Sinkford, the dental dean of Howard University, and WVU alumnus Dr. Paul Gates, who was the dental dean at Fairleigh Dickinson University. These two leaders in dental education became important mentors in my professional journey. Dr. Sinkford facilitated my involvement in several ADEA initiatives, including the Women's Liaison Officers and Women's Health in Interprofessional Education Workgroup. Dr. Gates nominated me to be one of the first recipients of a National Dental Association Foundation / Colgate-Palmolive Postdoctoral Scholarship, which supported my doctoral work in higher education leadership. Dr. Biddington served on my doctoral committee. The advice and support of this remarkable mentor triad guided the development of my career.

In addition, I was fortunate to have had other mentors at various stages in my career. Dr. William Graham prepared me to succeed him in the office of admissions. Dr. Pete Fotos mentored me in the early years on research protocol and preparing my first national presentation, which was on practice characteristics of female dentists. Dr. Richard Crout collaborated with me on research addressing student body diversity and women's health promotion. WVU School of Medicine leaders and clinicians Dr. Rashida Khakoo and Dr. Melanie Fisher provided invaluable interprofessional mentoring and collaboration.

Becoming a Successful Leader and Sustaining Success— Ten Lessons Learned

On my way to becoming a successful leader and sustaining my success, I learned ten important lessons. The first lesson is that effective communication, including active listening skills, forms the bedrock of great leadership. The most practical advice about communicating came from my father, who pointed out that God gave me two ears and one mouth, and I should utilize these gifts proportionately—listen twice as much as I talk. Communicating truthfully and respectfully is important because words are assets when in sync with actions.

A second lesson focuses on going after what we love. Hard-earned credentials, such as DDS and PhD, are alphabet soup unless generously seasoned with compassion and genuine concern for others. If we go after what we love, the third lesson comes naturally, namely, to love learning more. Continually acquiring new information, sharpening skill sets, seeking diverse perspectives, and sharing our knowledge with others will be satisfying if it is concerned with the things we love. Lesson four is to develop strong interpersonal skills. Considering how others feel when stepping onto your leadership "front porch" and making sure that they experience a sense of welcome, belonging, and individual importance is crucial.

No matter how well prepared we are, challenges are inevitable. The fifth lesson therefore is to persevere and push through difficulties. In those situations, it is sometimes difficult to stay positive. But lesson six is to keep a positive mindset. One of my favorite Bible verses, Philippians 4:8, summarizes what this lesson implies: "Whatsoever things are true, honest, just, pure, lovely, of good report, think on these things." One aspect of a positive mindset is lesson seven, to be grateful and thank more than to be thanked.

The eighth lesson focuses on collaboration and the fact that some of the best professional achievements are products of collaboration. Sharing ideas with others, planning, and identifying solutions to challenges can be very rewarding. Collaboration is closely related with lesson nine, to pay attention to our sphere of influence. We never know who aspires to be like us, but I believe in tossing pebbles of hope in the stream of people behind me, producing swells of encouragement and guidance for not only one person but for many, via the ripple effect. My final lesson is to let smiles and laughter have a special place in your life. Smiles are commonly contagious, reciprocal, and cost nothing—pass one on. Laugh often. A merry heart is good medicine (Prov. 17:22).

Challenges

In 1992 I earned tenure, and in 1998 I was promoted to professor. From 1995 to 2001, I served as director of admissions and student affairs and the last year concurrently as interim associate dean for academic and postdoctoral affairs. From 2001 to 2002, I became the first WVU dental faculty to complete the one-year Executive Leadership in Academic Medicine (ELAM) program for women aspiring to leadership in health professions. In 2003, I started in my current leadership position as associate dean for admissions, recruitment, and access to care.

Over these years, I encountered many challenges. As admissions dean, delivering disappointing news to prospective students has been a recurring challenge because each year the number of competitive applications far exceed the available positions in the class. Denial of admission is often met with hateful responses and hostility toward me despite my efforts to communicate these unfavorable decisions with keen objectivity, sensitivity, and sincerity. For many years, I was the only African American dental faculty member at WVU. This reality was intensified by the lack of women dental faculty role models and mentors in the school.

A white female colleague once asked me, "Why do you stay here? It is lily white."

"If not me," I replied, "then who will be here as role model, advocate, and sounding board for students and junior faculty who share my background and experiences?" My response was reinforced not long afterward during a hallway encounter with a young African American woman in a white doctor's coat. She smiled, addressed me as Dr. Price, and told me she admired me. She added she had heard me speak at events and wanted to be like me someday. The encounter touched me deeply because she, a medical student, had formed this opinion by observing me across disciplines.

Despite racial and gender gaffs, I stayed the course with the support of a small group of colleagues, realizing that my journey is bigger than me. With thimble-like spiritual fortitude, I persevered in piercing situations. This quality, along with my first mentor's advice to develop strong professional networks, helped me to overcome challenges and flourish as an African American woman in a nondiverse work environment.

Looking Back and Ahead

My family is a source of pride and joy. Their values of hard work, faith, courage, generosity, and respect shaped my life and influenced my career. It is impossible to describe sources of pride without intertwining gratitude. I am grateful to my first dean and mentor for setting me on the course to become a leader in academic dentistry. I am proud of my collaborative record to promote inclusive and humanistic learning/work environments, address health inequities, and foster workforce diversity. Leading the WVU School of Dentistry's multiyear Robert Wood Johnson Foundation grant entitled "Dental Pipeline, Profession & Practice:

Community-Based Dental Education," dedicated to reducing oral health disparities, is a cornerstone of professional pride. I am also very proud of having ushered former students into dentistry. They overcame hardships and are now professionals, creating new ripples of excellence.

My advice to women aspiring to leadership roles is to dream beyond burdensome societal boundaries and to set and achieve bold goals. Developing personal and professional networks of good-hearted, well-intentioned people and not yielding to naysayers will help you on your journey. It is important to persevere in challenging circumstances with grace and grit and to be unafraid to go out on a limb for what is just.

Maya Angelou once said, "People will forget what you said, people will forget what you did, but people will never forget how you made them feel." This quote should remind us to help others feel good about themselves. Additionally, reach out. In the leadership context, I use my dominant hand to serve, mentor, and encourage others, and I use the other hand to receive advice, mentoring, and different perspectives.

Exercising humility and remaining grateful will serve you well. It is important to rejuvenate regularly and not be too hard on oneself. Enjoy the journey!

Joyce A. Reese, DDS, MPH, FACD

◆ ◆ ◆

Early Experiences

I was born in Richmond, Virginia, into a working-class family that consisted of my parents and sister. My parents valued the pursuit of attaining a postsecondary education and provided my sister and me with rich cultural experiences. My mother was a very active stay-at-home mom. She enrolled my sister and me in ballet and piano lessons at an early age, although finances were scarce. My family enjoyed watching dance and musical performances.

My parents encouraged both of us to excel in whatever we pursued, so I became a dentist and my sister an elementary school teacher. We attended segregated public schools throughout our early education. For high school, we were bused to one of the only two Richmond, Virginia, high schools for colored students. High school was a good experience for me. I discovered that I was especially interested in my science classes and excelled at this course of study. In addition to my classes, I became the feature editor for the school newspaper, a member of the debate team, and queen for one of the cadet corps. In short, I enjoyed high school and was a high achiever.

Becoming a Dentist

My cousin, Dr. Xenobia Gilpin, was a physician. She was the first person who influenced me to consider a profession in the health sciences. Her personality and accomplishments were intriguing and led me to enroll in the premedical program when I attended Virginia Union University. While there, I met a young female dentist who worked for the public health department. I had never heard of a female dentist at that time, and she sparked my interest in a career in dentistry. My family dentist, Dr. Frances Foster, encouraged my interest. He opened his office so that I could observe the practice of dentistry. He also encouraged me to bring classmates to experience the same. He later helped my classmates and me with dental board examinations. I will always remember how encouraging Dr. Foster was during my preparation for the dental licensing board examination.

Throughout my years of attaining a higher education, I struggled financially. While I attended dental school, I worked as a dental assistant to help pay my tuition and other expenses. Often, I had to borrow books from students ahead of me in dental school because I could not afford to buy my own. It was not an easy journey. However, studying was my primary focus during my time as a dental student at Howard University School of Dentistry. It was at Howard that I first took an interest in research and found a research mentor in Dr. Harold Fleming. He contributed greatly to the development of my research skills, which would benefit me later in my investigative scientific pursuits. He also introduced me to Sammy Davis Jr., who was his good friend.

I graduated from dental school as the only female in a class of eighty students. Fortunately, my male colleagues treated me with dignity and respect because I achieved at the same level as they did—sometimes even better—and because I comported myself with dignity and respect. In dental school, I learned the value and art of perseverance and hard work, which would serve me throughout my career. After graduating in 1963, I accepted a job at the City Dental Clinic in Portsmouth, Virginia, for one year. At the end of that year, I returned to Washington, DC, to work as a pediatric dentist at the Group Health Clinic before joining a colleague in private practice and the District of Columbia Division of Dental Health. I began working in public practice during the day and in private practice in the evening.

Working for the Federal Government

My career in the federal government began in 1972, when I joined a new Interpersonal Agreement (IPA) program to observe dental programs, both intramural and extramural, for direct dental care to minority group patients. Dr. Frank Shuford, a public health officer in the District of Columbia, was my sponsor. He supported me, and that allowed me to be accepted for the IPA priority assignment. The Bureau of Health Manpower Education (BHME) sponsored the IPA program, and I became one of the first dentists to participate. It was my first appointment in the Division of Dental Health (DDH) in the federal government. Dr. John Green was the director of the DDH, and his associate chief was Dr. Meryl Packer. Both of them were pioneers in public health and intergovernmental training. Drs. Green and Packer served as my mentors and influenced my decision to remain in the federal government. They also encouraged me to pursue my postdoctoral dental degree in dental public health at the University of Minnesota on a full scholarship and per diem. Dr. Lawrence Meskin, a professor at the University of Minnesota, greatly influenced my decision to attend the program there. During my time as a graduate student, Dr. Ralph Katz and Dr. Meskin mentored me. I graduated in 1974 with a master's in public health.

While pursuing my career, I married Dr. Frederick Douglas Peagler. He was a dental professor at Howard University and became a visiting professor at the University of Minnesota while I studied there. My husband was supportive of my career, and we complemented each other very well. For example, we collaborated in our lectures to various dental groups and societies. In 2006, my husband passed away. His death was related to the diagnosis of glioblastoma, which allowed him only thirty-eight more weeks of life after his diagnosis. After his death, for the first time in my life, I experienced the loneliness and depression that can come from losing a loved one—especially a loved one whose career had been so intertwined with my own. During those times, I realized that I needed professional help to move on with my life. I was fortunate to find a female psychiatrist who helped me to refocus my life and rely on my own inner strength for a sense of well-being.

Taking On Leadership Positions

During my professional career, I was fortunate to have colleagues who were involved with emerging science and opportunities. I did not hesitate to take their advice and to contribute ideas and expertise for the sake of career development. It was amazing to me that so many new opportunities were opening up at that time for individuals from different backgrounds and with different interests. While working for the biomedical grant program at the National Institute for Dental Research (NIDR), I was fortunate to receive an opportunity to spend two years at the National Institute of Standards and Technology (NIST). In this capacity, I was part of the technology development program, serving under Dr. Bruce Mattson. The program implemented joint research and development (R&D) arrangements, patents, patent licenses and other institutional R&D working arrangements. I served as the NIST/NIDR technology transfer liaison in the technology development program. The National Institute of Science and Technology and the National Institute for Dental Research worked together with industry to identify factors that influenced commercialization of dental technology.

Upon returning to NIDR, I became director of the Small Business Innovation Research (SBIR) program. Before retiring, I was elected to serve on one of the four commissions of the Federation Dentaire Internationale (FDI). As a member of the FDI, I served on the commission on dental products and later became its chairperson. FDI continues to be the one dental commission that is recognized by the World Health Organization (WHO). Dr. John Stanford, from the American Dental Association (ADA), was an important colleague and mentor for me at that time. He supported me in my leadership role for the advancement of the science and art of dentistry as an objective of the FDI.

My career-long challenges were accepting and mastering new roles and titles as they emerged from R&D. I was on the cutting edge of policies and programs that required a longstanding strong rapport with manufacturers and consumers in the dental industry. At that time, there were very few women in dental biomaterials, and I am proud to have helped pave the way for other women in my field.

These are my words of wisdom to future leaders: be ready for hard work, recognize your own value, and have faith in yourself and in God.

I have a sense of joy as I reflect back on my career of service and caring for others. I will be forever grateful to the male colleagues who respected women when there were still only a few of us in leadership roles in the sciences and who supported my own advancements throughout my career.

Dionne J. Richardson, DDS, MPH

◆ ◆ ◆

My Early Years

Growing up in New Orleans gave me a great appreciation of family, culture, and community and influenced me, my journey, and my career path greatly. I had excellent role models in my family and community and consider Desire in the Lower Ninth Ward the root of my beginning. I saw much of society's ills as well as its crowning achievements. In the midst of the disparities in this community, leaders in politics, education, professional sports, medicine, and dentistry emerged. The ability to rise above unyielding circumstances was manifested in a community that was undeniably blemished by disparities. Yet individuals did great things at every turn. I always admired those who rose above the odds and became worn and weathered.

The post-civil-rights era in the 1970s was a pivotal time in the lives of African Americans. My parents and other relatives were young people entrenched in supporting the civil rights movement. This launched them into a new era in which they helped to change the landscape of New Orleans. They took this opportunity to move away from Desire in the

Ninth Ward to Gentilly, a community in the Eighth Ward. Gentilly was slowly being integrated, and we were only the second Black family to have moved there. It was, and still remains, a desired community in which to live.

I was five years old when we moved to this new place. I had been happy in the Ninth Ward, with close connections to neighbors and the community at large. However, Gentilly was a place ripe for integration in a post-civil-rights era. At first, I found it awkward to adjust to a new place, but overall, the community was welcoming, and I made friends. Although our residence changed, the commitment to our old community remained. We maintained ties to Desire; I finished elementary school there, and my parents worked and provided support to the community in many ways.

Finding My Path to Dentistry

Growing up, I learned from leaders, teachers, and members in my community. In my family, I took notes from my parents and other family members who worked in social work, education, arts, and mechanics. These observations greatly influenced my quest for identifying the path that would lead to serving others, fit my interests, and support my motivation to enhance my skills in the sciences.

My college education started in state-supported universities. However, a sociology instructor advised me to transfer to Xavier University. He was aware that studying at Xavier University would increase the likelihood of an African American woman from the Deep South succeeding in achieving a career in medicine or dentistry. At first, I fought against going to Xavier University because I wanted to experience some independence at a school away from home. However, after I transferred, I realized that being educated in a historically Black college/university (HBCU) was a good decision because it was a nurturing environment for African American students. I received sound instruction and guidance, and I felt a sense of belonging and purpose. It was there that I was encouraged by my advisor to look into dentistry. In a strange way, dentistry fulfilled that need in me to marry my love of science and art. During a visit to an open house at a dental school, I caught a glimpse of dentistry as a profession. I was intrigued/impressed to see dental students carving chalk structures. Sculpting shapes helps students to develop the skills needed to use hand instruments to shape restorations and maneuver around the anatomical structure of teeth and the periodontium. So, I applied and was admitted to Meharry Medical College of Dentistry.

Becoming a Professional

After graduating from dental school, I moved to Rochester for my postdoctoral training. I made friends through connections I had with a high school friend who had moved to Rochester for work. The African American community was tightly knit and relatively small. At that time, corporations such as Eastman Kodak and Xerox had a large footprint in the area, and most of my friends had moved there for jobs. They welcomed me as a new transient resident, and in very little time I surrounded myself with a circle of women that I called my "Sister Circle." All of us were around the same age and at similar points in our lives. We juggled jump-starting our careers; maintaining good mental, spiritual, and physical health; and managing meaningful relationships. We searched for the careers of a lifetime and the men of our dreams—and/or what our parents dreamed for us.

Our commonalities created bonds while we struggled to move up the rungs of the ladder of success. In the Sister Circle, we shared our hopes and dreams and considered nuggets of wisdom we received from those who mentored us individually. One conversation with one of my good friends from this circle has stayed with me throughout the years. We lamented about how difficult it was for us to find a position that was the right fit for us and to find the place where we could make our marks. My friend shared this conversation with her mentor. This woman told my friend that we should rethink our perspective by accepting that we may not be able to find a place for us; instead, we would have to create our place in the world.

That message was a point of reckoning for me. I realized that my African American heritage was village oriented. We come from villages that nurtured us, cared for us, and embraced and admonished us. However, the larger society outside of that village was not at all like the village. Our social norms, the ease of relationship building, and the customs experienced through that lived experience did not always translate into societal norms. In fact, societal norms were often contradictory to the ways I was used to, how I functioned, and how I was supported and embraced. I was not well prepared to maneuver in a white-male-dominated profession that did not emphasize dental public health as a specialty. I started to call myself a triple minority because I was Black, female, and a dentist in public health. Some might consider it even a quadruple minority because they think of dentistry as the unwanted stepchild to medicine. This realization helped adapt to a system that was different from what felt natural and customized to fit my character and credentials. I also realized that my residency program was supportive and helped in my development as a public health professional in dentistry. However, there was less support for me as a person who was an African American woman from the South, with strong family ties and a will to contribute to society. Understanding how my background and professional preparation had shaped me helped me create a space for my contribution to society.

My Mentoring Relationships

Through her work, Dr. Jeanne Sinkford understood how to create space for minority dentists. Through her ability to network and share resources with young dental professionals, I was offered an outstanding opportunity to submit my research to what would be my first professional presentation at the ADEA Women's Leadership Conference in Nice, France. She was an influencer in my early career who helped me to create my space in the world.

Mentoring provides bridges that connect us to the pathway that leads us to success. I am fortunate that I had mentors who pointed me in the right direction. Their guidance helped me to prevent wasting time with exploring paths that would not have been right for me. Mentors, who have journeyed to places we hope to travel to, can advise us about how to best navigate our paths to reach our goals. Parents often know their children's needs and can assist them with identifying appropriate mentors. After I completed dental school, my mother found an African American female dentist with a background in public health who she felt might be a positive influence on me. I remember being amazed and excited that she'd found someone who had walked on the path that I was starting on and who was engaged in the work I wanted to pursue for my career. Dr. Blache was a fellow Meharrian and public health dental professional; she was a rare gem, hidden in the trenches, always behind her mask, yet addressing the oral health-care needs of vulnerable populations in the urban centers of New Orleans. Observing her work and taking her advice helped me to understand the mission of my work to come.

Along my journey, through my postgraduate training and my master's in public health program, I had several great mentors. They were creative, analytical, academic, business savvy, clinically oriented, or focused on research. I carried the lessons I learned from each of them with me through my career, and these lessons influence my perspective of the work even today. Collectively, they help me to operate with compassion and purpose.

Becoming a Woman Leader

In addition to my mentors, my postdoctoral training as a resident helped me to get a better understanding of the world. Specifically, it helped me to understand diversity in a broader context. The Eastman Dental Center at the University of Rochester attracts dentists from across the globe. This allowed me to interact with individuals from many different countries and to establish friendships that I still maintain. As residents, we had a bond that was richer because of our diversity. While we did not always agree, we discussed our different ideas, solved problems together, and presented plans collectively to make a difference in dentistry. Diversity ushers in progress, and it is the prerequisite for success.

When I was married and had two small children, we decided to move our family from the Northeast to New Orleans to be closer to my parents. I wanted my children to enjoy some of the nurturing that I had received growing up in my hometown. Therefore, my husband and I would search through the classifieds to seek employment until he found an ad for a dental director position with the state's department of health. I applied, and after all the years of education and training, I finally landed a position in public health as the state dental director in Louisiana. Four months into this new role, Hurricane Katrina hit. I had finally found a position after a long preparatory period when this storm completely displaced and dismantled the infrastructure of New Orleans. Strength and resilience had to be added as new dimensions to my character as a public-health leader. I did not know the extent of my God-given strength to endure. Emergency operations had to begin. I called upon my friends, established new professional relationships, and found a temporary post graciously offered by public health colleagues in Atlanta. The Division of Oral Health at the Centers for Disease Control and Prevention (CDC) took me in and offered me a space to work, so I learned to work remotely during this state of emergency. As it was not possible to implement federally funded programs, I worked with federal, state, and local partners to redevelop a school-based prevention program at a time when the children were scattered all across the state and beyond. The Federal Emergency Management Agency (FEMA) provided trailers that offered a community space to engage displaced community members. These New Orleans citizens were happy to see familiar faces supporting them. We assured them that even though their lives were turned upside down, we were there to reconnect and offer something familiar through our oral health program efforts.

Words of Wisdom for Future Leaders

I am most proud of my resilience—my ability to bounce back from calamity, adversity, uncertainty, and unrest. Along my journey, I have developed a greater sense of purpose and of knowing who I am, why I am here, and what I have to offer to the world, my community, and the individuals who need us most. My advice to you is to embrace all of who you are and use that to tear down walls, barriers, and obstacles that may block your path. Search for mentors who may not always look like you on the outside but resemble who you are on the inside. Have an unrelenting commitment to the work at hand and be willing to use your gifts, talents, and expertise to make meaningful contributions to your profession by serving the individuals in your path.

Jessica A. Rickert, DDS

◆ ◆ ◆

My Family Background

As a member of the Prairie Band Potawatomi Nation, I am the first American Indian female dentist. The Prairie Band Potawatomi Nation is my grandmother's tribe, and I am proud to be a member. My grandfather Whitepigeon is a member of the Saginaw Chippewa Indian Tribe. Both tribes are indigenous to Michigan (Michiganong). In 1837, President Andrew Jackson forced the Potawatomi to walk all the way from Western Michigan to Kansas to live on reservation lands completely unlike Michigan. My fifth great-grandmother Angeline marched that distance. My grandparents met as young teens on the Kansas reservation.

My grandfather's family had traveled there from Michigan to attend a powwow and some weddings. Grandfather was smitten with Grandmother, and he promised to return and bring her back to Michigan. She insisted that he wait until after her graduation from high school. During that time, he worked several jobs and saved all his money. After he had purchased a densely wooded property south of the Grand River in Michigan, he rode the family horse to Kansas to marry her. On the way back to Michigan, she rode the horse and he walked.

When they arrived, they lived in a tent on that property and planned their farm. On a hilltop, they paced the dimensions of the house; he pounded stakes into the ground at the four corners and tied sturdy rope to make straight lines. He started digging with a shovel and a wheelbarrow, walking the dirt up and out on wooden boards. They were both working, and they raised a vegetable garden, along with chickens and a pig, while they built the house. The family was never hungry. Fourteen children were born there, including two who died as infants. My grandparents finished the house, a red-brick two-story house with a cinder-block basement, and my aunts still live there today.

My Early Years

I was the oldest of seven children. We all attended public schools in Wyoming, Michigan. My graduating class was about 112 students. I enjoyed math and science as a student. Once, we dissected a cat in biology, and I brought home the cat's skeleton and glued it back together as a walking feline. Someone in my family made the comment, "Oh, that's just Jessica. Leave her alone."

As foreshadowed by my cat-skeleton stunt, human anatomy and physiology intrigued me. My family doctor had encouraged me to consider nursing, and I spent some hours in his office while he cared for his patients. As I peered over his medical books, he said, "You know, Jessica! Uh, I think ... um ... you could be a doctor." With this sentence, he had seeded a thought in my preteen brain. "Oh, that's just Jessica," members of my family said, with a sigh, when I started writing "Dr. Rickert" all over my notebook paper.

Sometimes, all nine of us left our small two-bed, one-bath home at dawn, and our parents piled us into the car and drove to East Lansing and Ann Arbor to walk around the campuses. We just wandered around, not even knowing what we were looking at. I had no idea how to apply to college; I did not even know what "college board exams" were. When I told my high school counselor I would be a doctor, he swallowed his shock to reply, "The University of Michigan has a medical school. You could apply there. Good luck." However, then he did walk me through the college boards process. It was a big surprise to me that the boards cost money. But because I had worked from the age of fourteen years on, I could pay for them with my own savings. Still, I did not even know that I should prepare for the exam. My aunt dropped me off at the test center, and I just took the test.

Becoming a Dentist

The same high school counselor who suggested medical school then helped me to apply to the University of Michigan. I was the only student from Wyoming Public Schools with an acceptance to the University of Michigan that year. I therefore went to Ann Arbor alone, into the great unknown. Regents scholarships, a National Merit Scholarship, and other scholarships covered the undergraduate expenses. In addition, I worked every summer and over all holidays. I lived in a co-op called Henderson House. This meant that residents there worked off one-half of the housing expenses.

Once I was on campus, I visited the University of Michigan's medical, dental, pharmacy, and nursing schools. I was most intrigued by the medical and dental schools and returned to visit them several times. Once, while I was at the dental school, I watched a student casting a gold crown. I was amazed at the complicated process and that dentists could use this beautiful, precious metal to restore a patient's dentition to function, form, and health for many years. It is a bioengineering marvel.

In the 1960s, all dental professors were white, privileged males, and all the professional students were white, privileged males. The University of Michigan, like all universities at that time, was monolithic. When I walked into a brand-new dental school building in the fall of 1971, there were still over 140 white, privileged male students and only five other women, a smattering of Black students, and several Jewish men. These students became my cohorts, and they are still my friends today. Being a dental student was fascinating. It opened up a new world for me. Dental school studies were challenging, difficult, and very exhausting. I graduated from the University of Michigan School of Dentistry in 1975 and felt blessed, excited, and relieved.

The first American Indian dentist, Dr. George Blue Spruce, had graduated in 1958. I was the second American Indian dentist in the world and the first female American Indian dentist. As of this writing, there are about three hundred American Indian dentists in the United States. In order to have parity with the population in the United States, there should be three thousand of us.

Dentistry has been extremely good to me. Every morning I sing, "Rejoice, be glad! Blessed am I!" Dentistry has opened many doors for me, but success demands mastering difficult skills. Dentistry is the profession that allowed me to achieve greatness; "greatness" is measured by how we use the talents our Creator has bestowed on us to benefit others. For forty years, I owned a private dental practice while raising three children with my husband. We are truly grateful for our three wonderful kids-in-law and eleven grandchildren.

Becoming an Advocate and Leader

Along the way, I directed the dental clinic and provided general dentistry for the Children's Aid Society, the Michigan Department of Corrections, the Family Health Care organization, and for Reach Out Healthcare America, providing dental services to military reserve units. Currently, I am the Anishinaabe dental outreach consultant for all Michigan Indians.

My professional service includes being a member of the board of directors of the Michigan Urban Indian Health Council, chairing the speakers' bureau of the Oakland County Dental Society, being a member of the Michigan Dental Association's Public Relations Committee and president of the Resort District Dental Society, and a member of the board of directors of the Society of American Indian Dentists. Being a private practitioner has afforded me the privilege to serve my community in many roles including leading youth groups.

In addition, I wrote a book entitled *Exploring Careers in Dentistry* that was published by the Rosen Publishing Company in New York. It is available in libraries and schools. Many national journals, magazines, and books have published my articles and reports. The American Dental Association presented me with its Access Award for writing dental advice columns for tribal newspapers across the country for seven years. Reprints of these columns are available in tribal clinics.

The University of Nebraska developed the "Power of Role Models" series for the National Science, Technology, Engineering, and Math (STEM) educational program, and I am featured in the dentistry section. While this series is excellent for all students, it focuses especially on reaching American Indian students. This program is now available for a free download at https://nativeamericanrole.wixsite.com/rolemodels.

For anybody interested in increasing the numbers of dentists from historically underrepresented, especially American Indian, backgrounds, information can be found at the following link: https://www.9and-10news.com/2020/07/29/breaking-barriers-and-making-history-dr-jessica-rickerts-inspiring-story/.

It features my story as a pathfinder to life, and I hope it will inspire more American Indian students to consider the health professions, particularly dentistry, as their careers.

My own efforts to recruit American Indian students into the health professions and dentistry include traveling to speaking engagements in many venues across the United States. My presentation entitled "Changing Perceptions and Exceeding Expectations" aims to expand the cultural competence of the attendees and enable them to work effectively in cross-cultural situations. For many audience members, attending my presentation is the first time they hear accurate information about American Indian history.

Finally, I want to share with you the following lines I spoke in my acceptance speech when I was inducted into the Michigan Women's Hall of Fame:

> As I stand here, I stand on the shoulders of all who have gone before me.
> I stand on the shoulders of Wahbememe.

I stand on the shoulders of Angeline.
I stand on the shoulders of cherished grandparents Whitepigeon.
I stand on the shoulders of my own parents, Carl and Jennie Wicker.
I am humbled by their courage. Here is how they treated each of their three daughters:
Because they listened to her, She knew she had something important to say.
Because they believed in her, She believed in herself.
Because they said she could do anything, She did.

I thank them.

Rochelle L. Rollins, PhD, MPH

◆ ◆ ◆

Family Influences

I grew up with parents who were strong believers in the importance of education, public service, and quality health care. My father was a dentist who ran public health dental clinics in Washington, DC. Two childhood memories that fueled my interest in oral health came from being with him at the clinics. The first memory was playing in the Hunt Place Clinic's waiting room with the children who were waiting to be seen. I remember asking a lot of questions about the Women, Infant, and Children clinic that was upstairs. This was my first exposure to coordinated health care for low-income families.

My second fond childhood memory related to oral health was going with my family to the National Dental Association conventions. From an early age, I understood that oral health is integral to overall health because of my exposure to the conversations of dentists, dental hygienists, and dental technicians. I also learned that the dental clinic staff members were a team and that good patient service was expected from everyone, beginning with the receptionist. Thinking back to my childhood, I realize that while I did not directly follow in the footsteps of my parents, the messages I heard as a child stayed with me and informed my life choices.

Starting My Professional Education and Life

In college, I majored in sociology because I was fascinated by group dynamics and the processes that groups go through to either keep the status quo or change. Since I wanted to improve the population health of low-income populations, especially from racial and ethnic minority backgrounds, I also got academic degrees in public health and health policy. These degrees allowed me to begin my career in the US Department of Health and Human Services (HHS). From 1999 to 2008, my work focused on HIV/AIDS, workforce shortages, cancer health disparities, and the collection of racial and ethnic data.

The year 2009 was an important year for me because I began a collaboration with two HHS dentists and shifted my focus to oral health disparities. These colleagues, Dr. Gina Thornton Evans, an epidemiologist in the Centers for Disease Control and Prevention, and Dr. Arlene Lester, a regional expert and clinician based in Atlanta, Georgia, showed me how to take my childhood observations about oral health inequities and connect them to my public service work. With critical support from Dr. Garth Graham, the director of the Office of Minority Health, we encouraged the HHS Oral Health Coordinating Committee (OHCC) to meet more often and add more offices and agencies focused on women, children, people with disabilities, and older adults. Specifically, we suggested adding staff to the committee from the Office on Women's Health, the Administration for Children and Families, and the Administration for Community Living, formerly known as the Administration on Aging. This expansion of the oral health dialogue within HHS led to a more robust federal conversation and a deeper understanding of oral health issues by offices that did not have chief dental officers.

Later that year, we presented evidence concerning the importance of oral health and succeeded in making oral health one of a dozen "Leading Health Indicators" in the Healthy People 2020 Initiative.

This was a milestone for oral health because the Healthy People Initiative is a ten-year framework for public health prevention priorities and actions across the United States. This inclusion put the spotlight on oral health from 2010 to 2020 and supported measuring the number of children, adolescents, and adults who visited the dentist in the past year. This successful inclusion of oral health as a Healthy People Leading Health Indicator continues in the Healthy People 2030 Initiative: https://healthypeople.gov.

The HHS Oral Health Coordinating Committee continues to be a strong group that discusses oral health topics such as fluoride and plans seminal documents such as the second Surgeon General's Report on Oral Health. As we serve the public, I am reminded of Margaret Mead's quote: "Never doubt that a small group of thoughtful committed citizens can change the world. Indeed, it's the only thing that ever has."

Leadership Considerations

I believe that key attributes for attaining and sustaining success as a woman leader are to be bold, strategic, and listen well. A poem by Edward Sanford Martin (http://www.greatthoughtstreasury.com/author/edward-sanford-martin) that was quoted in the *Washington Post* in 1983 guides my thinking every day:

Will the Real You Please Stand Up?!

Submit to pressure and you move down to their level.

Speak up for your own beliefs and you invite them up to your level.

If you move with the crowd you'll get no further than the crowd.

When 40 million people believe in a dumb idea it's still a dumb idea.

Simple swimming with the tide leaves you nowhere.

So, if you believe in something that's good, honest, and bright stand up for it.

Maybe your peers will get smart and drift your way.

In 2006, when I was a senior executive fellow at the Harvard University John F. Kennedy School of Government, I put this quote to the test. For a month, I lived on campus and analyzed case studies with seventy federal leaders from mostly military and intelligence backgrounds. There were a couple of fellows from NASA and the US Forest Service, but I was the only person from a health department. I enjoyed the experience until the conversation turned to a discussion of the lessons learned from the government's response to Hurricane Katrina. Specifically, our objective was to contribute to drafting a new case study on the government's response to the hurricane for Harvard. My military classmates praised each other for their rescue missions, while I became increasingly more uncomfortable with what was not being said. When I voiced my belief that there were some failures in the response to Hurricane Katrina and that the case study being developed should highlight the failures as well as the successes, the room fell silent. It seemed to me as if most people thought I was unpatriotic. Fortunately, a handful of my classmates joined with me in submitting two recommendations to the university: first, to incorporate a race and equity perspective in the case study of Hurricane Katrina, and second, to design a class on race matters at the executive level for future fellows in the program.

Being a Mentee and a Mentor

Being bold and strategic are not usually skills we are born with. Instead, we learn them through observation and life experiences. I have sought the advice of mentors throughout my career, and I have learned the art of leading and following. I used to think leading was the most important skill, but actually both talents are needed in the workplace.

Several of my mentors set aspirational goals for the programs they led. For example, retired RADM Marilyn Gaston set the goal of "100% Access and 0% Health Disparities" for the bureau she led within the HHS Health Resources and Services Administration. Every time I work on eliminating health disparities instead of just reducing them, I am reminded of the power of aspirational goals for motivating people and changing systems.

My mentors helped me to stay on the path of doing impactful work for improving the health of racial and ethnic minorities. The secret to a successful career is to find the connection between your work and your core values and passions, and then be strategic. I encourage young professionals to be like a sponge no matter what their job assignment might be. Their tasks should always be to soak up the knowledge, make new contacts, and be prepared for career detours, because straight lines are as rare as unicorns.

Coping with Challenges—Lessons Learned

The challenges I faced have been threefold. First, as an African American woman, I often have to claim and protect my ideas when a male colleague makes the exact same point in a meeting, explains to a group what I mean, or interrupts or speaks over me. Second, as someone who is dedicated to the value of equity, I require racial and ethnic and gender diversity on every team that I participate in and every project that has my fingerprints. This frustrates some colleagues, but fortunately, fewer are frustrated over time.

The third challenge that I face is that my passion is to eliminate oral health disparities. Individuals often struggle to understand a disparity if they have never experienced it nor know anyone who has experienced it. This means that you have to explain that a toothache is more than just a missed day of work for people who lack access to care and that diseased teeth impact school performance and employment. I learned these lessons watching my father provide dental care for low-income families in public health clinics. These lessons about pain and need are as familiar to me as my name.

To the women and girls who aspire to be future leaders, my advice is to not try to do it alone. Building a broad professional and personal network of advisors and supporters is important because you will need them along the way. Don't be myopic in considering your options. For example, if you want to be a dentist or dental hygienist, consider joining the Public Health Service Commission Corps. The rewards of federal service are immense. And do not think you have to be in charge to have influence. There are different types of power: position power, budget power, personal power, and network power. I cherish my network power the most because long after I will have left the federal service, I will still remember the people I worked with and the people whom I served.

Frances Emelia Sam, DDS

◆ ◆ ◆

Not Like the Others

"One of these things is not like the others. One of these things doesn't belong. Can you tell which thing is not like the other by the time I finish this song?"

If my life had a soundtrack, this *Sesame Street* tune would undoubtedly be the theme song. While my story is unique, the feeling of non-belonging is common to all journeys. Mine began in a small Canadian town of Ukrainian influence named Smoky Lake. My parents emigrated from Ghana, West Africa, to Alberta, Canada, for my father's teaching job. It was culture shock in every way imaginable. Never having seen snow, they experienced a record-breaking brutal winter. In addition, living in a small trailer after leaving the comforts of a spacious home (with attendants) proved to be a difficult transition. My parents assumed that preparations for their arrival had been made, because this was the case when visiting professionals arrived in their home country. They were sorely mistaken and had to improvise. They, along with my older sister, made the best of what they had and proceeded to make a new life in Canada.

Early Childhood

A year later, I was born at the regional hospital. As far as we know, I was the first Black newborn. Some of the locals would come in groups each afternoon to see the African baby with the pierced ears. I suppose the peculiarity of my birth foreshadowed much of the way I was to experience my life.

Three years later, we moved seventy miles away, to the capital city of Edmonton. My mother had attended a teaching college in Ghana and continued to pursue her degree in education at the University of Alberta. My father continued to commute daily to the county of Smoky Lake, where he taught math and science.

Not surprisingly, education was of prime importance in our household. This suited me just fine, as I was an introvert content with reading books in my spare time. The encyclopedia offered endless content for my perusal. By six years old, I remember taking notes and writing reports no one had assigned.

The next year, my parents bought a home on the north edge of the city. Castledowns was idyllic in many ways. Before our fence was built, the backyard was contiguous with the brush. We occasionally spotted deer running through the area until more development took place.

One by one, young families moved in, and I soon found playmates. We played all day long until one of our mothers would call out from a doorstep, reminding us that the concept of indoors existed. Seemingly carefree, I was acutely aware of being "the only one." I could easily go days without seeing another Black person outside of my family or on the TV. Without being told, I knew why I was not invited to the neighbor's swimming pool, four houses down. While the other kids screamed and splashed around, I would silently return indoors, out of earshot.

Over the years, two other Black families and one interracial family moved into the neighborhood. However, none had children around my age, so I still felt isolated in that regard. Until university, I was "the only one" in classrooms. From grades seven through nine, I was one of four out of approximately five hundred. In high school, there could not have been more than fifteen of us out of 1,500. Simultaneously feeling invisible and conspicuous was unnerving. Where I did feel some confidence was in my scholastic ability. After a careerday event in junior high school, I declared I would pursue dentistry.

Becoming a Dentist

Toward the end of high school, a friend and I decided to visit the campus of the University of Alberta. We wanted to speak with an advisor who could elaborate on the prerequisites for our chosen career paths. When my friend asked about requirements for optometry, the advisor cheerily gave her a lengthy explanation of expectations. When I inquired about dentistry, her expression flattened. Looking squarely at me, she coldly stated, "Dentistry is hard." The conversation was decidedly finished. It was the pool all over again. I was not invited.

Despite that encounter, I completed my undergraduate degree with a specialization in genetics and then applied for dental school. Unsuccessful in my initial attempts, I was disheartened. It was the first time in my life that I was rejected in an academic setting. Later that year, I ran into a fellow student on the bus. He was one of the "conscious crew." He seemed to know everything about all aspects of Black history. He also knew the latest on a former student who was in dental school at Howard University. Howard was mythical. My only experience with Historically Black colleges and universities (HBCUs) was watching *A Different World* and Spike Lee's *School Daze*. The idea of not being "the only one" held unfathomable appeal. I eventually made a terrified call to the admissions office for an application.

Several months later, I was accepted into the program. Excited for a preview, my cousin and I traveled to Washington, DC, in advance of my move. When we entered the city limits, a palpable rhythm engulfed us. A crescendo was reached as we turned onto Georgia Avenue. The energy was foreign and exhilarating. We stayed at the Howard University Hotel. On Monday morning, we visited the school. The women in the admissions office welcomed me in a way I had never experienced at a postsecondary institution. Six months later, I returned to start a new life in "a different world."

The advisor at the University of Alberta was right, but not in the way she'd assumed. Dental school was hard, but not because of the academic demands. Being homesick was hard. Not having my best friends around was hard. Trying to fit in was still hard. Though my skin color no longer differentiated me, my experiences did. Being Canadian made me a different kind of other. There were small things, such as the variations on fast-food menus, which I once assumed were universal. There was slang with which I had to become familiar. Black Canadian history had some overlap but was distinctly different from African American history. The minute I opened my mouth, my accent made me an oddity.

Despite having physical reflections of myself around me, I still felt the pangs of not quite belonging. Thankfully, the newness of things overshadowed all else. Though I was busy with studying, examinations, and cadaver labs, I found time to partake in happy hours, occasional house parties, and homecomings. The Notorious B.I.G. and Tupac provided the soundtrack of those years, along with my ever-present *Sesame Street* theme.

Becoming a Surgeon

Meanwhile, I was uncertain which direction I wanted to take in dentistry. In second year, we had our first surgery course. I found the subject extremely interesting, but an additional four years of residency sounded appalling. Besides, most of the surgeons I had encountered were old-school and somewhat unfriendly men. That was true until the day Dr. Karyn Mygil lectured to our class. She was young, intelligent, and vibrant, with an air of confidence I immediately envied. Here was a woman who was certainly a rarity in that world. Suddenly, surgery was on my radar.

I maintained top-of-the-class standing throughout dental school, which certainly helped my acceptance into the maxillofacial surgery residency. Unlike most institutions, Howard had a history of accepting qualified female candidates, thanks to the foresight of former dean Dr. Jeanne Sinkford.

I interviewed at only one other oral maxillofacial surgery residency program, which had just accepted their first female resident, "Jane." I was under no illusion that they would choose a Black female resident a year later. However, I used their interview as a practice run for Howard, since that was where I wanted to be. Every man who interviewed me at this other institution said, in a hushed, concerned tone, "You should really talk to Jane." I would smile tightly in response and move on to my next interview. Eventually, I met her, and the unhappiness was apparent. Perhaps she was post-call or just an overworked intern, but my gut instinct told me that the condescending environment was suffocating her.

Thankfully, Howard was different. Out of twelve residents, four were women, two of us in our first year. In addition, our program director was Dr. Andrea Bonnick. I had not been familiar with her during dental school, but I soon became acquainted with her keen eye; quick, dry wit; and straightforward manner. Besides her unquestionable competence, she expressed a compassion for patients that was rare. She was extremely insightful when dealing with people and became a role model for me inside and outside of surgery. Years later, she would become a dear friend and a well of infinite support.

Finding My Calling—Becoming Emelia Sam

For years, I watched closely and noticed a dearth of compassion within health care at large. The unspoken rule, referred to as the "hidden curriculum" in medicine, was to put anything emotional aside. Professionals treated cases. Human connection was secondary, if considered at all. Remaining somewhat detached from patients was once considered a hallmark of professionalism. However, detachment from others goes hand in hand with detachment from self. Throughout my residency, I felt a remote longing. Though the days were busy and interesting, my soul felt starved. When I entered the doors of the building, I left much of myself at the threshold.

This habit of compartmentalization carried into my professional life. After a few years of part-time private practice, I chose academia full-time. With its structured expectations, the traditional environment left little room for self-expression.

My creative self—the writer, the meditator, the voracious reader of spirituality and self-help books—was hidden from my colleagues, students, and patients. Most of the people who knew Dr. Frances Sam had no idea that Emelia Sam was a blogger and author. I felt out of place in my dental community. When comparing myself to committed creatives, I felt similarly. I could not inhabit either space without feeling like an imposter.

In the spring of 2011, I spoke at an American Association for Women Dentists (AAWD) chapter event. Fortuitously, the theme of my presentation centered on self-care. Also scheduled to speak was the esteemed Dr. Jeanne Sinkford. I had made her acquaintance during my years as a faculty member in the College of Dentistry. Briefly chatting that morning, the topic of my book came up. She asked, "Where is it?" I had no answer. She said that if a man was presenting, he would have copies on hand for self-promotion. She then insisted on purchasing forty copies for distribution to attendees later that week.

Her words reverberated in my thoughts. Why did I not bring my books? Did the concept of self-promotion conflict with my notion of humility? Was I afraid to put myself out there and risk judgment? The answer was clear. By choosing to share that aspect of my life in a professional setting, I would have chosen to expose my otherness. That was something with which I had never been comfortable. Dr. Sinkford's inquiry and generous action changed something that day. So did Dr. Bonnick's presence in the audience—and her enthusiasm. So did the faculty members and students who thanked me while sharing their own challenges in achieving work-life harmony. This community of women helped me to shift my trajectory.

Over the next several years, my voice strengthened while writing articles for major platforms, including the Huffington Post. My words were reaching tens of thousands of readers to whom I felt great responsibility.

The reward of adding value to the lives of others while honoring my soul's intentions far outweighed any risk of judgment.

I eventually came to understand that what I hid in my professional life was precisely what it needed. In writing *Compassionate Competency: Healing the Heart of Healthcare*, I was able to bridge my professional experiences with my longtime interests in personal development. Consequently, I have the honor of being an early voice in the burgeoning area of wellness for health-care professionals. Being on the leading edge of new terrain holds many lessons.

Leadership transcends official titles and positions. It is not a role to play but rather an ideal to embody wherever one finds oneself. It is an art requiring the balance of self-assuredness alongside vulnerability. It is a natural outgrowth of authenticity combined with intention.

Contrary to the *Sesame Street* premise that the other does not belong, it asserts that differences are exactly why one belongs in any given space. I learned that leadership emerges from the courage to share one's otherness.

Jeanne C. Sinkford, DDS, MS, PhD, DSc, FACD, FICD

◆ ◆ ◆

Preface

I have been called a "Black pioneer," "Renaissance woman," and a "modern Candace" because I dedicated my life to the cause of overcoming social, cultural, and educational inequities in our society by forceful leadership and in constant support of equal opportunities and civil liberty. As an octogenarian and scholar, I continue to learn, lead, and serve.

Growing Up

I was born on Capitol Hill in the shadow of the nation's capital on January 30, 1933. My parents, Richard Edward and Geneva Jefferson Craig, were both native Marylanders and federal government employees. My mother taught elementary school for a brief period but then accepted a government job that became available to women to support the war effort. My family had four daughters. My father said he "gave up for a son after the fourth." I became his "son" because he had a passion for teaching others what he knew. He taught me to fish, paint, wire circuits, build furniture, interpret the news, and to manage and save money. I often wondered how a man who made seventeen dollars a week could save money and provide for the family. But he and my mother were a team who valued education and had decided early on that all of their children would graduate from college. He was a happy man when his last daughter graduated. Two of us became teachers, one a pharmacist, and I became a dentist.

My education was a mixture of public and private schools. I went to public school for elementary education, Catholic school for middle school, and Dunbar High for public high school. Dunbar was the college preparatory school for "colored" students in DC. At Dunbar, we had teachers with master's degrees who mentored us and encouraged academic achievement. My first leadership position was as a captain in the girl cadet corps at Dunbar, where I learned military protocol, ethics, and drill exercises. Winning the citywide competition was an honor for the school and the girls in Company D.

Becoming a Dentist

The Sinkford family was not well off. But my parents worked out a "family" plan whereby the older sister would help the next in line after finishing college. I, of course, was in school the longest: four years of college, four years of dental school, and three years of graduate school. I was fortunate to receive fellowships for both undergraduate and postdoctoral studies.

After "skipping" my fifth and eighth academic years, I started as an undergraduate at Howard. My undergraduate major was in psychology and chemistry. I graduated with honors and was awarded Phi Beta Kappa. At Howard, I met and married Stanley M. Sinkford, who was a medical student from Bluefield, West Virginia. My best friend introduced us after meeting him at her relative's home in West Virginia. I always thought that our marriage of sixty-two years was made in heaven. I gave up all ideas of becoming a ballerina, for which I had studied intensely during my high school years.

Jeanne C. Sinkford, DDS, MS, PhD, DSc, FACD, FICD

I graduated from Howard with my bachelor of science degree and decided to pursue dentistry instead of medicine because I wanted to avoid any competition with my husband, who was a medical student. My family dentist suggested dentistry because of my sincere interest in science and my manual dexterity. I was awarded a full-tuition scholarship to the College of Dentistry, where I graduated first in my class with the doctor of dental surgery degree in 1958. I accepted a position in the Department of Prosthodontics at Howard University and taught both crown and bridge prosthodontics and dental materials. After two years, I left this position to pursue a postdoctoral degree in physiology and crown and bridge prosthodontics. My postgraduate study was funded by the Louise C. Ball Graduate Fellowship for Graduate Study in Dentistry. This funding required me to return to Howard. But I was able to complete both my master of science (1962) and PhD degree (1963) at Northwestern, while my husband completed his residency in pediatrics at the University of Chicago. Both of my daughters were born while I was in school at Howard and Northwestern Universities. My son was born much later in 1970, after I had returned to Howard to pursue my academic career in teaching and research in inflammation and dental implantology.

Taking On Leadership Responsibilities

When I returned to Howard in 1964, I was appointed chair of the Department of Prosthodontics, the college's largest department. I was the first woman to head such a department in this country. Dean Russell Dixon, the school's long-term dean, selected me for this administrative post because I was fully qualified. My predecessor was scheduled to retire, and the department needed new leadership. For me, the appointment was a significant shift in responsibilities and an opportunity for visionary and courageous leadership. The department was full of older men who had been my teachers. They accepted my collaborative leadership style and my quest for both excellence and service. We instituted a faculty evaluation program that linked merit pay increases with performance and introduced collaborative teaching with total-patient-care concepts.

Under the leadership of the new dean, Dr. Joseph L. Henry, I became the associate dean for advanced education research and special programs from 1967 to 1974. The scope of my leadership expanded, and I became responsible for academic policy development and implementation, collaboration across departments and divisions, intramural and extramural research, and community outreach programs. The dean often traveled, and during those times, his leadership responsibilities were delegated to me. By that time, I had obtained leadership training at both Harvard University and the Research Triangle in North Carolina. In 1974, I was granted a sabbatical leave, which I spent at Children's Hospital Medical Center in Washington, DC. At that time, I was interested in developing the foundation for a postdoctoral program in adolescent dentistry. My interest was to study behavioral and developmental changes in adolescent patients that influence long-term outcomes and therapies.

In 1975, I returned to Howard University as the dean of the College of Dentistry. This appointment as the dean of a dental school was the first for a woman in the United States. I have been asked many times why I became dean. My answer is that I was recruited to the position after a long search. I did not want to be a dean. My interest at that time was to continue my research and develop the program in adolescent dentistry. My decision to accept the position was based on the fact that I was more than qualified to do the job, and I did not want to work for a lesser-qualified individual. In other words, I would rather be known as the "SOB" than have to work for him. At that time, there were no other women candidates for the position, and only 12 percent of dentists were women. The year 1975 was an interesting year worldwide! It was known as the International Women's Year. I turned down job offers from Stony Brook University and the University of Washington to accept the position at Howard. That decision was an impactful moment for my family and me. I firmly believed that other institutions had choices for leadership at that time, while I was needed at Howard.

After sixteen years as a dean, I retired in 1991. I became a professor and dean emeritus in recognition of the college's innovative programs in academic/community partnerships; dental auxiliary utilization;

management of chronically ill and aged patients; infection control; implant research; faculty development and evaluation; and underrepresented minority recruitment, reinforcement, and retention. At the time of my retirement, all of the academic programs at the dental college were fully accredited by the Commission on Dental Accreditation.

On November 4, 1991, I was recruited to the American Association of Dental Schools, which later changed its name to American Dental Education Association (ADEA). I was the first director of the Office of Women and Minority Affairs and later became the associate executive director and director of the Center for Equity and Diversity. My challenge there was to increase diversity in the applicant pool for US and Canadian dental schools, to secure funding for diversity programs, and to create a culture of diversity at the association. My efforts were supported by the Minority Affairs Advisory Committee and the Women's Affairs Advisory Committee. In my leadership role at ADEA, I was able to create academic/community partnerships, establish minority leadership programs, support the pipeline for minority student recruitment, and create leadership opportunities for the advancement of both women and minorities. While at ADEA, I created both the Enid A. Neidle Scholar-in-Residence Program for women faculty and the First International Women's Leadership Conference, which convened in France in 1998. I retired from ADEA in 2018 after twenty-seven years of service and am now a senior in residence emerita. My motto of continued vigilance is a matter of record.

My Mentors

My early mentors were my parents, teachers, and family members. Most of my professional mentors were males because I was in a male-dominated profession with men holding the leadership positions. Howard University's president, James Cheek, was a dynamic academic mentor and leader for me, as were dental deans Russel Dixon and Joseph Henry at Howard and Dean Clifton Dunmett at Meharry Medical College. My corporate and foundation mentors were Michael Sudzina from Proctor

& Gamble and Henrie Treadwell and Barbara Sabol from the W. K. Kellogg Foundation. When Dr. Richard Valochovic became ADEA's president, he became a mentor to our leadership team.

One of my most impactful moments was in August 1972, when I served on the nine-member panel to study a US Public Health Service experiment that had begun in 1932. This study, known as the Tuskegee Syphilis Study, included four hundred African American men with syphilis who went without medical aid for forty years to determine the effects of the disease on the human body. The inhumane treatment of the men and lack of consideration for the spread of the disease in their communities is still unbelievable to me! As a research member on the panel, I condemned the research value of the study because of its methodology and lack of calibration of the investigators. I felt sympathy for Nurse Rivers, who was depended upon for her contact with patients during the entire study period. I learned about "man's inhumanity to man" during the Tuskegee study, and it still lingers with me today. It created my proactive role in the protection of human subjects throughout my research and professional career. Thinking of the Tuskegee Syphilis Study reminds me of the Nuremberg trials at the end of World War II.

Overcoming Challenges

As the dean of Howard University, my biggest challenge was the competition with other schools for underrepresented minority students. The underrepresented student applicant pool was small, and recruitment consisted of a combination of academic preparation, active recruitment of qualified students, and the creation of a financial aid package that was acceptable for both the student and parents. Dental student debt has been and still is a significant challenge for the profession. It is now in excess of $285,000!

My second greatest challenge as dean was the traditional mission of Howard University, which was founded two years after the Civil War ended in 1867. It is now one of the historically Black colleges and universities (HBCUs) in America. These academic institutions are committed to the enrollment and education of minority students. Balancing tradition, innovation, and change are still major challenges for HBCUs as they continue to strive for excellence in a highly competitive environment.

Another major challenge for me as a woman leader and dean was balancing a career and my family. Supporting working mothers has not been a strong suit in America. Fortunately, my husband and I shared responsibilities. I was blessed through prayer and with the help I needed so that my support team worked in harmony with my professional and personal responsibilities.

My sense of pride and joy is found in my family—especially my three children, now proud citizens who love me—and in Howard dental graduates who serve throughout the world and still respect me and refer to me as "my dean."

When asked for a word of wisdom to pass on to future leaders, I think of Dean Dixon and his advice to me and to classmates when we struggled with the curriculum load during the first year of dental school. He told us, "You all had better work as well as pray." Above all, it is important to remember that great leaders prepare and pave the way for their successors.

Janet H. Southerland, DDS, MPH, PhD, FACD, FICD

◆ ◆ ◆

Early Years

When I was growing up, there was a great deal of uncertainty around my survival because I suffered from severe allergies and asthma. I was born as one of twelve children; my mother was one of seven, and my father one of thirteen. My mother had a ninth-grade education, and my father had a third-grade education. My father was a long-distance truck driver, and my mother stayed at home until all younger siblings were in school and the older ones could look after them. We lived on the west side of Charlotte, North Carolina. I recall that the community was close knit. However, differences existed between neighborhoods and because of economic differentials. When I was a young child, my family did not emphasize education, and no one ever asked about homework or could help with it. The focus was more on survival.

Despite those circumstances, I have some very fond memories of growing up and having picnics in the park, going to the local swimming pool and staying all day, having family reunions, or just sitting and reading. The first people who took an interest in me were a group of women in my community who were retired educators and/or widows and had a garden club. They took my older sister, my two younger sisters, and me under their tutelage. They introduced us to religion, sewing, proper etiquette and manners, Girl Scouts, polite conversations, and 4-H. Eventually, we moved a couple of streets over in the same neighborhood and lost touch with most of them except one. I believe these women gave me a glimpse of how knowledge and exposure could lead to a better life. As I think back, I am sure I had no idea of what effect the things they were saying or doing would have on my future. In addition, teachers and health professionals in the neighborhood were also role models for me.

My Mentors

The person who influenced me to think about dentistry was my dentist, Dr. Thomas Mack. I did not regularly go to the dentist or doctor as a child. I recall that Dr. Mack talked to me about what I wanted to do when I grew up. During the appointments, he would comment on my straight teeth and tell me about dentistry. I became fascinated with teeth and started observing the teeth and smiles of others. This became somewhat of an obsession. When I attended a health fair in middle school and spoke with a dental hygiene program representative, I decided that after high school I would attend a dental hygiene program at our local community college. Most individuals in my immediate family had not finished high school or had dropped out. Becoming a dental hygienist seemed like a decent choice.

During high school, there were two transformational moments in my life. The first was that I joined a Christian-based student group called Young Life and discovered my spiritual self. The second came in the form of my high school counselor, Ms. Reid. I was bused from the "west side" of town to a majority high school on the "east side" of town that had been integrated the year before. There had been many riots and fighting between white and Black students as a by-product of the integration of the public schools in Charlotte. By the time I attended high school, everyone had pretty much settled into a desegregated school system. Ms.

Janet H. Southerland, DDS, MPH, PhD, FACD, FICD

Reid, an African American woman, was my guidance counselor. She refused to allow me to consider community college after high school. She enrolled me in advanced classes, signed me up for the PSAT and SAT, and made sure the cost was covered or found exemptions. She also made sure that I participated in programs that would challenge me educationally beyond my experiences at home or in school. She provided nominations for programs and awards, and she helped me with essays.

Additionally, my dentist, Dr. Mack, helped me during this time by providing money for application fees and sponsoring me on trips. He also wrote my letters of recommendation for undergraduate and graduate training. Both individuals did not only serve as my role models, they were also my advocates and sponsors. I did not recognize that fact until well into my career, when I realized that there are people in our lives who can see our potential and are interested in our success. In turn, when we receive those opportunities, it becomes our responsibility to help others to find similar successes.

Once I completed my undergraduate studies, many of my mentors chose me versus the other way around. I was not aware enough to seek out mentors intentionally. Instead, these mentors saw something in me that I did not see in myself at that time. While I was an undergraduate student, a first memorable experience happened at one of the orientations with Dean Hayden B. Renwick, who became a mentor and friend. The orientation focused on African American students admitted to the University of North Carolina at Chapel Hill. Dean Renwick asked everyone in the auditorium to first "look to your left and then look to your right," and then he told us that those individuals on either side of us would not make it through their first year. As a first-generation college student, I struggled my first two years and at times thought I might be one of those students Dean Renwick had been talking about.

I managed to get my bearings, and in the fall of my senior year, I found out that there was a dental hygiene program on campus. I met with the program director, Ms. Moore, and she asked me to send in my information. I was accepted into the program before graduation. Before matriculation, I met Dr. Lavonia Allison, another African American woman. She was the director of the summer health careers program. I told her about my acceptance into the dental hygiene school. She looked at me and said, "Why not a dental school?" I did not have an answer to her question. Dr. Allison was an educator and a fierce advocate for minority students, particularly those who came from disadvantaged and underserved communities. I admired her passion and dedication to help others. She was strong, articulate, and a great role model and mentor.

Prior to graduating from dental hygiene school, all senior hygiene students received a letter from the dean of admissions to apply to the dental program. I had heard a lot about burnout of hygienists from various faculty members. This prompted me to make an appointment with the dental school admissions dean. Our meeting went almost identically to that in the application process to the dental hygiene program. I was accepted as one of eighty-two students and one of four African American students into the dental class of 1989. The faculty was comprised of white males, with white women educators in the dental assisting and hygiene programs. It was apparent that no more than four or less African American students would be admitted during any given year and that all of them probably would not graduate on time. I observed that the Black males were often targets for failure of not progressing. While I enjoyed my time in dental school immensely, I was not oblivious to the racial challenges that prevailed.

In addition to my earlier mentors, other memorable individuals emerged during my predoctoral and graduate training. While a PhD student, Drs. Steven Offenbacher and Jim Beck, as well as Dr. Jane Weintraub, were central to my success. They were all accomplished faculty members and taught me how to become a scientist and apply my knowledge to approach scientific discovery. Dr. Offenbacher became my PhD mentor and saw more in me than I saw in myself. He asked what I wanted in a career, and I told him I wanted to be an academician. He told me that if I wanted to have any longevity as a Black female in a white-male-dominated profession, then I would need a PhD, and he would help me. He also said that he was part of the majority, but he would make sure I had what I needed to be successful. He turned out to be a sponsor, advocate, mentor, and, most importantly, a dear friend. Near the completion of my training, he asked what my plans were, and I told him they were to become tenure-track faculty and teach. In response, he asked me why I did not want to become a dean. I laughed at the suggestion. Turns out he was not only a brilliant man but also a prophetic one.

Leadership Characteristics

Characteristics that I perceive as most critical to attaining and sustaining success as a woman leader are: first, to not let others define who you are; second, be open to opportunities; third, lead with humility and gratitude; and fourth, always see the value in others, no matter their circumstances.

A very important moment for me as a leader was when I became the dean at Meharry Medical College School of Dentistry in 2011. I realized that only two other African American women had served as deans of dental schools in the United States. Dr. Jeanne Sinkford was the first, and Dr. Eugenia Mobley McGinnis was the second. I was the third dean of a dental school in the United States and the second female dean at Meharry. Dr. Mobley-Singleton passed away shortly after I arrived in Nashville. Giving remarks at her funeral was a very humbling experience for me. I realized that while there had been some gains in increasing the number of women as leaders in dentistry, the level of diversity among deans still left much to be desired.

Overcoming Challenges

The two major challenges I faced as a woman leader were being in a profession that was male dominated and having no access to women role models in leadership positions. Immediately after successfully defending my dissertation, I became the chair of the department of dentistry, chief of oral medicine, director of the hospital dental clinic, and director of a GPR program while also being a tenure-track assistant professor. I maintained an active outpatient faculty and operating room practice. Challenges included lack of leadership; resistance to change; low morale among staff, residents, and faculty; a lack of communication across all entities; and a financial deficit in the clinic. The expectations were that I would improve the training program, develop collegial relationships across professions, provide better customer service, lift morale, and improve the financial base of the entire department and clinic. I was able to overcome the challenges by listening to all stakeholders involved across the leadership of schools, departments, faculty, residents, staff, and students. After hearing all concerns, I was able to develop and implement a strategic plan that helped resolve major issues and bring in revenue at $1.2 million.

Looking back, I am most proud of the numerous students, trainees, and mentees whom I have had the immense privilege to help along their journey and who became outstanding professionals. I have been abundantly blessed to serve in leadership roles that have allowed me to leverage all of the knowledge and skills I have acquired over my career to be a change agent, to innovate, and create improved educational experiences for students and, ultimately, better patient outcomes. Last and most importantly, I am proud to have had the pleasure of serving those most vulnerable and least considered in our communities.

Carol G. Summerhays, DDS, FACD

◆ ◆ ◆

My Early Years

As a little girl, I would sit until late into the evening with my father whenever he was home from his long deployments in the US Navy. He spoke of his dreams as a child growing up in the Philippines and how he'd imagined the streets of America were paved with gold. Throughout his life, my father believed anything was possible in America. He told me about getting an education at the best universities in the world. I tried to calculate how much we would need to save to attend one. My father had wanted to be a physician. However, the only way he could get to the United States was by enlisting in the US Navy. At that time, Filipinos could only enlist to work on ships as stewards, even if they had a college education. It was the price he was willing to pay for a better future for himself and his future family. My father was the eternal optimist and enthusiast.

My maternal grandfather took a similar path to immigrate to America by joining the US Army. My mother was a teacher who insisted on excellence at school. Education was the foundation to success. She taught me to read, write, and do simple math before I entered elementary school. It gave me a head start in my education. Perhaps the greatest lesson she taught me was to be self-reliant in life. My mother was disciplined and a pragmatist.

One summer during high school, I traveled with my father to the Philippines. Poverty was everywhere. Shanty homes made of cardboard lined the rivers. Too many children were begging in the streets. It was the first time I witnessed such poverty firsthand. It was heartbreaking, and I thought, "There but for the grace of God go I." I returned home determined to do something to make a difference in people's lives. I decided to go into medicine, and this decision made my father very happy.

Becoming a Dentist

I completed high school at the age of seventeen and began premed courses at the University of San Francisco. In the summer of 1972, I did a program in Guadalajara, Mexico, and lived with a Mexican family. This would be a turning point in my life and career. In Mexico City, a friend's cousin gave us a tour of the Universidad Nacional Autonoma de Mexico, the oldest dental school in Mexico, which he attended. The dental students were very engaged in their studies and shared their experiences. Half of the students were women. On return to USF, I became involved in the premed/predent club to learn more about the profession of dentistry. It was the path I chose to take.

A university education cost more than what a family of modest income could afford. Throughout my university studies, I worked part-time as a sales girl at Macy's and for a professor at USF. I was fortunate to receive a California State scholarship for each of my undergraduate years and smaller scholarships from the Rotary Club and Filipino organizations. My mother saved enough to contribute $1,000 per year. My parents had three more children to put through college, so I had to find another way to finance my postgraduate education.

Through his research, my father found government scholarships for dental school. Receiving those would make it possible for me to pursue this avenue if accepted. While I had been a navy dependent my whole life, a fifteen-year commitment in return for a scholarship seemed like an eternity. It would mean that for four years of dental school, I would have to do four years of active duty in the navy. This was during the Vietnam War, and the military was not well respected. In spite of all this, I applied for the scholarship. It would give me the means to become a dentist. In my senior year at USF, I was commissioned an ensign in the US Navy.

Just before commencement at the University of San Francisco, the chairman of the biology department, Dr. Stevens, called me into his office and said, "Carol, you are taking the road of least resistance by going into dentistry and joining the navy. You should be going to medical school!" My father also felt I should be going into medicine. These conversations put some doubt in my decision for the next ten years.

The Armed Forces Health Professions Scholarship covered tuition and supplies for all four years of dental school at the University of Southern California, along with a small stipend for living expenses. The scholarship made it possible for me to attend USC, my first choice.

Attending dental school was the hardest thing I had ever done. We had to attend classes or clinic all day, perform lab work late into the evenings, and engage in more studying at home. However, I loved it!

I became involved in many school activities, such as the USC Mobile Dental Clinic, which served children of migrant farm workers. I also became the student body treasurer and the founding editor of the student newsletter. Dr. Charlie Goldstein, director of the mobile clinic, mentored the student volunteers in our clinics. He told us we were there to do more than treat patients' dental problems. We were there to be role models for those children and plant the seeds that they, too, could be dentists.

Dr. Clifton Dummett—a professor of community dentistry, historian, and author—became my mentor after I interviewed him for our student paper. He had emigrated to the United States from British Guyana and had served in the US Army. He became a lifelong mentor to me, as he was to so many other dentists.

After graduation, I reported to the 32nd Street Naval Station, the largest naval dental facility in the world. I had come full circle from being born at the navy's Balboa Hospital in San Diego and receiving my naval orientation there. My parents were as proud of me being a naval officer as a dentist. Few Filipinos were officers in those times.

There had only been one female dental officer before I arrived with two other female colleagues in San Diego. No facilities were allocated for female officers, so we used the smallest women's bathroom to serve as our "locker room." In the beginning, some male dental officers made occasional comments that the "skirts"—as they would call female dentists—received all of the "easy" duty. I would have none of that and offered to exchange my schedule with anyone who believed that. We were determined and did not show any weakness, so the comments stopped. During my four years on active duty, I had the opportunity to serve at 32nd Street, with the US Marine Corps (USMC), and with antisubmarine warfare in San Diego. I am proud to have served our country.

The years following military service were some of the happiest and saddest of my life. I was happily married, became mother to two sons, and built a successful private practice. At the same time, my mother began to experience unexplained behavioral changes. Shortly after my first son was born, I took my mother for an evaluation for Alzheimer's disease. The physician confirmed the diagnosis but offered little guidance. The tragic years of seeing my mother slip away slowly and painfully overshadowed the magic moments of watching my sons grow up.

Luckily, I had my work to occupy my thoughts. My professional goal was to be the finest clinician I could be for my patients. I therefore decided I would earn a master's degree from the Academy of General Dentistry because it would be a pathway to excellence by studying with some of the best teachers in dentistry. Among them were Dr. Gordon Christensen, Dr. Pete Dawson, and Dr. Irwin Becker, who each became my mentors.

Taking On Leadership Positions

My first position at the San Diego County Dental Society (SDCDS) was chair of member services. This position soon led to becoming a board member. After my first term on the board, the president of the SDCDS called to ask me to move up the ladder toward SDCDS president. When I told him that it was not the right time for me to take on that level of commitment with two young children and an ill mother, I was not given another term on the board. It deeply shocked and disappointed me. I could see that there was lack of understanding for female dentists with family obligations who still wanted to serve. I planned to never volunteer there again.

For the next ten years, my volunteer service was focused elsewhere. It led me to become the president of the San Diego Academy of General Dentistry (AGD), board member of the California AGD, spokesperson for the AGD, and a member of the AGD Dental Care Council. As secretary of the Thousand Smiles Foundation of the Rotary Club, I was involved with building a dental clinic for underserved children in Ensenada, Mexico. Community service included chairing fundraising events for the Salvation Army and the La Jolla Cancer Society.

Throughout the years following dental school, Dr. Dummett called every few months to catch up on life. After a decade of not being involved in organized dentistry, Dr. Dummett said it was time for me to reengage the SDCDS and the California Dental Association. Unbeknownst to me, he even wrote a letter to the executive director of SDCDS to get me involved. I decided then to focus on two passions: community service and excellent continuing education (CE). At the local dental society, I chaired the CE committee and the philanthropy committee. My first position at the California Dental Association (CDA) was on the Council on Scientific Sessions. Within two years, I was vice chair, followed by two years as chair. Encouragement to run for CDA's executive committee first came from the executive director, followed by two CDA presidents. Dr. Dummett was thrilled. It was something I had never considered. Mentors show us the potential and possibilities we cannot see ourselves.

By the time I was installed as president of the California Dental Association, Dr. Dummett's health was declining to the point that he could not attend. We spoke by phone. He said, "Congratulations, Carol, now just one more . . ." I knew exactly what he meant by "one more." It would be a huge leap to becoming president of the American Dental Association (ADA).

Volunteer service was never about "position" but about what could be done to improve the profession and the public's health. The ability to make changes at the national level, as Dr. Dummett had done throughout his professional career, was paramount. Sadly, he passed away shortly after I was installed as an ADA trustee. Nonetheless, his words of "just one more" would stay with me.

The ADA Board was not diverse in 2012. In my final year as a trustee, I was the only female out of seventeen trustees. We seemed to be going backward. Dr. Maxine Feinberg had been installed as president-elect. She would serve as the third female ADA president in its 150-year-plus history. Some of the "word on the street" was that the ADA House of Delegates, predominantly older white males, would never elect two women in a row, and that if Dr. Feinberg failed then all women would fail. Negative messages would not deter me. They made me work harder to stay focused on my message for the future of the profession and the public.

With the help of many friends and colleagues throughout the country, I won the election and became the 152nd president of the ADA. How I wished my parents and Dr. Dummett had been alive to attend the installation. I would honor them whenever possible. Dr. Jeanne Sinkford, the first female dean of a dental school and another mentee of Dr. Clifton Dummett, received the ADA's Distinguished Service Award. On accepting the award, she said she never thought she would live to see two female ADA presidents in a row.

I think back to Dr. Stevens, the chairman of the biology department at USF, who thought it was a mistake for me to go into dentistry instead of medicine. We spoke on the phone just after he had retired and laughed at how well everything turned out for me after all.

Machelle Fleming Thompson, RDH, HCAP, MPH

◆ ◆ ◆

My Educational Journey

My life story began in the small town of Franklin, Tennessee. I was the oldest of four children. We grew up in the single three-story frame house we shared with our parents, grandmother, and cousins. It was a place filled with love. I will always cherish the time my grandmother took the girls on a shopping trip to Nashville. It was an experience of a lifetime. My grandmother treated us to doughnuts at the bakery, and we each got navy and green plaid dresses for back to school, which were later lost when our home was destroyed by fire.

My mother was the daughter of a schoolteacher, and this fact might explain why she always stressed the importance of education. When it was time for me to decide which college I would attend, my dentist encouraged me to pursue a degree at Meharry. *Wow, Meharry*, I thought. Me, with a degree from Meharry! The excitement came to a screeching halt when I experienced comments that I would not be able to get into Meharry because the color of my skin was too dark. I was devastated and at first did not understand the comment. But my mother and godmother said, "Yes you can and yes you will!" So I submitted my application and was accepted with a full scholarship award. I became one of only ten students in my class. My mother stressed that I had to work hard, stay focused, and do my absolute best. She made sure I realized that if I lost my scholarship, she would not be financially able to pay my tuition. Determined not to disappoint my mother, I completed my degree in dental hygiene as a member of the one hundredth graduating class of Meharry Medical College, with honors.

My degree came with many sacrifices. At that time, the dental hygiene program was a dual degree program between Tennessee State University and Meharry Medical College, and classes were held on both campuses. I decided to live in the dormitory at Tennessee State University (TSU) to be closer to my high school friends. But it was difficult to see my friends and other students attend campus activities or pledge a sorority when I was walking approximately 1.5 miles from one school to the other for classes and was studying for tests. I felt isolated. But my mother often reminded me why I was there with the words: "It's delayed gratification . . . stay focused."

After receiving my degree, I married my first-grade classmate and high school boyfriend. He enlisted in the US Army, and we had to move to Savannah, Georgia, where I worked for two years in the office of a Meharry dental alumnus. Then I returned to Meharry and worked as a registered dental hygienist in the Comprehensive Health Center. After being employed for two years, I was laid off from work.

While wondering what I would do next, one of my colleagues, Ms. Rosalyn Word, RDH, MS, informed me that she had decided not to take a job in the General Practice Residency Clinic (formerly the Hospital Dentistry Clinic) but had completed an application for this job in my name. I will never be able to repay this act of kindness that laid the foundation for my successful career. Ms. Word remains one of my mentors to this day.

I was always passionate about serving those who needed me the most, so I returned to school to pursue a bachelor's degree in healthcare administration and planning. I used my student project to explore ways to decrease bottlenecking at the patient registration desk in the student clinic. The proposed changes impressed the administration so much that they created the new position of director of patient resources in the School of Dentistry and offered me this position. After graduating with honors, I accepted it and immediately began to identify ways to modify the existing protocols. My changes clearly improved the workflow but were not readily accepted by the involved faculty, staff, and students. I spent long hours working on the front line and talking to them to understand their concerns. But I was met with passive-aggressiveness. Many would agree that changes were needed, but they resisted their implementation. I remained steadfast, trying to understand why they responded in particular ways and how I could coach them into realizing the benefits of change.

At this time, I was married, had two children, and was employed full-time. Nevertheless, I became convinced that I needed to increase my skill set to be more effective. So, I decided to pursue a master's degree in public health. I knew it would be a huge challenge, but my deceased mother's mantra, "stay focused," was loud and clear in my mind. I was able to receive an employee discount and a scholarship, which helped me to stay focused to make it through this program. My colleague, who was also my mentor, never allowed me to complain. She would always say, "Is it in the book?" I knew I had to work hard if I wanted to make a difference. I completed my master's in public health from Meharry Medical College with a 4.0 grade point average. I was more than excited. The fact that I was the number one graduating student in my class but was overlooked and not recognized during the commencement exercise dampened this excitement. Even the apology that had been extended later could not change that.

Coping with Professional Challenges and Taking On Leadership Roles

Becoming the first female non-dentist to serve as the assistant dean for clinical affairs in the over one hundred years of history of our school was the culmination of my dream as an administrator. I did not have a doctorate of dental surgery degree, but I knew I could make a difference for our patients. I realized that my efforts would be going against the established practices and that building trust would be critical to my success. I worked hard, utilizing what I knew from the bottom to get to the top. I was walking the walk, not in the moccasins of those on the front line who reported directly to me, but in my own shoes.

It was important to me to ensure that I maintained balance between life challenges, home, and work—doing it my way while trying to listen to my mentor. Many times, I put my professional goals on hold for my family. But I never gave up on my goals; I continued to work my plan until it worked for me. As another mentor often reminds me, "When you are at the table, you always have something of value to share." It is not about black and white but being able to add color to any situation. While working with mind, body, and soul to achieve optimal care for patients who put their faith and trust in us when they come to our offices, I always remember that my higher power will not forget my labor of love. He will reward you and me with loads of blessings. Listen, learn, stay green, and grow—these are words that I live by.

One defining moment in my leadership career was a statement from a former supervisor, who said, "You have high expectations. Remember who they are." The comment was in reference to the team I supervised at that time, the people working the front desk. These words affected me as I reflected on the backgrounds of the members of my team and how my own personal journey paralleled theirs. I believe it was the turning point of my career. I became more determined than ever to be a leader who would inspire and show them the way to move to the next level, overcoming whatever odds. I was committed to understanding the "why" and was always honest in my communication with them and in holding them accountable for their assigned tasks. It was a partnership. When a challenge arose, my philosophy was to work together as a team to fix it. I believe that developing trust keeps people on the team. More importantly, it was the team's trust in my ability to "walk the talk" that validated the genuineness of the relationship.

The team was the face of the organization. Their role was one of the hardest jobs in the clinic and critical to the overall success of the program. I have a passion for doing things better and striving for excellence. Working with a diverse team has afforded me the opportunity to help them become their best selves and excel in their performance. I used each opportunity to do just that.

As I reflect on my journey, I am most proud to have been selected by ADEA as an Enid A. Neidle Scholar-in-Residence and mentored by the eminent Dr. Jeanne C. Sinkford. The coaching and mentoring I received propelled my career as I went on to serve as the first non-dentist and first female assistant dean for clinical affairs at Meharry School of Dentistry. I now serve as associate dean for compliance. My career path has allowed me to also be engaged in research; publish in peer-reviewed journals; and to make presentations at local, state, national, and international conferences. Additionally, I have been blessed to serve as a core faculty member for the Vanderbilt University Leadership Education in Neurodevelopmental Disabilities (LEND) program, which focuses on preparing health professionals to assume leadership roles and develop interprofessional team skills to meet the complex needs of the patients receiving care.

Lessons Learned

I was most effective when I trusted my inner voice. I had to find out who I was and then be that. I had to believe I could make a difference in life and find my purpose, which was to be a servant. The secret of achieving my goal has been love. Love keeps me grounded and sustains me. It gives me the strength to get things done and to inspire others to do the same. Nothing in life is more exciting and positive than the feeling of love. Summarizing my life, I would describe it as a journey toward a greater faith: a daughter, a sister, a wife, a mother, a mentee, a mentor, a leader, a servant.

Jennifer Webster-Cyriaque, DDS, PhD

◆ ◆ ◆

Growing Up

I grew up in an area of Long Island that was a largely physically segregated suburb of New York City. Our neighborhood was a paradox, a place with people who looked after you as if you were their own and at the same time a place with an unsavory undercurrent. I was the beneficiary of unconditional parental love and the fierce belief that my two sisters and I could become anything we wanted to be. Like many others, my parents migrated to New York from the South in search of better opportunities. My father, who once introduced me to his friend as his "resident genius," made it clear that we would "never have everything we wanted" but that he and my mother would make sure that we would "always have what we needed." Our parents encouraged us to read a lot and to play outdoors instead of watching too much of the "idiot box." My mother made it clear to us that we should become involved in our community. Like the others in our local neighborhood, we were bused to majority schools with some great educators—and some teachers who did not expect much from us. However, in our home, the pursuit of higher education was an expectation, and our parents were great advocates for us. Likewise, it was expected that we would do our best in whatever we did. As a tween, I wrote a poem focused on "Being Me," which contained a line that read, "being Black won't hold me back." I received thunderous applause and won the Long Island NAACP youth award for my recitation. I am proud that I remain true to my younger self.

Becoming a Dentist and Dental Scientist

My interest in health science has been evident since high school, when I wrote an essay about wanting to be a doctor, and when I attended the University of Buffalo and my goal was to become a health-care professional. My older sister had inspired me because she had become a nurse. I was always curious and found science very interesting. But while growing up, I had not seen people of color in science, and it was never presented to me as a potential career path. While I was in college, I had the opportunity to do undergraduate research, to work at the dental school, and to be a dental assistant for a local dentist. I had also explored the option of becoming a dentist when I participated in a six-week course for students who wanted to pursue dentistry at the University of Maryland. In the end, when I graduated with a double major in biology and interdisciplinary social science, all these experiences had convinced me that becoming a dentist was a good fit with my skills and interests.

But I did not receive much support for this decision. My pre-health advisor in college suggested that I focus on a social science career and not a career in the health professions. A dean-level administrator laughed when I told him I was pursuing dentistry until he heard what my score on the Dental Admission Test (DAT) had been. Above all, my father, whom I adored and highly respected, said, "Whoever heard of a woman dentist?" because it was likely that he had never seen one. But the lesson I learned in this situation was to listen to my inner voice instead of paying attention to the "learned" external voice. My advice to future women leaders therefore would be to persist if you feel you are on the right track. At that time, I strongly felt that I was on the right track because becoming a dentist would allow me to work with people and use my manual dexterity. Additionally, it would satisfy my interest in science and my inquisitiveness and would let me enjoy artistic expression.

So, I applied to the dental school at the University of Buffalo in New York and was accepted. I had become interested in research in college when I worked in microbiology and genetics labs. I had also worked in dental research labs for two summers during dental school. During dental school, I became fascinated with oral soft tissue diseases and wanted to understand their origin. So, after I received my doctor of dental surgery (DDS) degree, I decided to enroll in the dental-scientist program at the University of North Carolina, Chapel Hill. My researchfocus areas were in microbiology and immunology. After I graduated with a PhD in these fields of study, I stayed on and did a postdoctoral fellowship in the pathogenesis of infectious disease. The challenge of remaining funded remains onerous to this day, but the potential to make a difference through the work makes the journey worthwhile.

The Importance of Mentoring Relationships

Mentoring has been exceptionally important for me. I have been fortunate to have wonderful mentors, irrespective of ethnicity and gender. They have been a part of a cheering squad that has been there for me at every major juncture/transition point—at my high school graduation, when I graduated from dental school and my PhD graduate program, and while looking for employment. These individuals gave of themselves to help me live up to my best potential and shared their love for science and their fields with me, and sometimes their personal lessons learned. They were an incredible gift for me. While moving forward, I have had new mentors cross my path. Collectively, they demonstrated the importance of modeling personal beliefs and advice. By sharing that they stayed in touch with their own mentors, my mentors demonstrated to me that this type of guidance is lifelong and does not end with a degree.

As I mentor my own students and junior faculty, it is clear to me that mentoring is a gift that keeps on giving, and I have worked to pass these lessons on to my own mentees. When I reflect on which characteristics are most important for having a successful career as a woman leader, I always think persistence, "stick-to-it-ness," is crucial. In addition, building community connections and being involved with the community are attributes that are key to attaining and sustaining success. In my opinion, the beauty of science is that the data should supersede both the dogma and who is delivering the message. However, multiple situations have showed me that this is not always true. Early on, this was a critical "aha" moment. I learned that it was crucial to "stick to it" if I knew that I was on the right track. Sharing these lessons learned with my mentees is important to me.

Overcoming Challenges and Becoming a Leader

Over the course of my life, I have experienced a recurring major challenge that centers around the question "Do you belong here?" It began in middle school and high school honors courses, when I was often asked, "Are you sure you are in this class?" While in dental school, an instructor questioned why I was there and told me that I was taking the seat of a man. In numerous clinical situations over the years, patients asked me if I was the doctor. And finally, when I attended national and international scientific meetings, I have been asked, "Whose lab are you in?" or "Who do you work for?" In response to these encounters, I learned that the key to overcoming such bias is demonstrating my competence and thus establishing my right to be there.

This lesson has served me well over the years, starting with my first leadership position as a tenure-track faculty member at UNC when leading my own research group, named "Viral Opportunistic Infections in Immunosuppression and Cancer" (VOIICE), and over time as I have become a leader in my field. Supportive mentors were critical to my attaining these positions.

Over the years, I have led a laboratory group that focuses on understanding viral molecular pathogenesis in oral disease in states of health and while immunocompromised. There are eight known human herpes viruses that cause persistent infections and are shed into the oral cavity during immunosuppression, causing increased morbidity. These DNA viruses are all marked by their ability to establish permanent, persistent infections where the viral infection may be latent, chronic, or transforming. They manipulate host immune recognition and response to allow for these continuous infections and affect specific cellular pathways to induce cell growth and death. Our laboratory seeks to understand the critical molecular interactions that occur between the virus and the host that govern the development of oral lesions and malignancies. In simple terms, my goal is to make a contribution to our knowledge base. I would like to add some of the missing pieces to the puzzle of infection and disease by understanding of the role of viral infection as it relates to oral infection and clinical disease.

In addition to leading my own laboratory research group, I have been involved in leadership roles in multiple scientific groups and networks of the International Association for Dental Research (IADR). I joined the Oral Medicine and Pathology Group, and I became an officer of the group and then its president. Over the years, I served as a review group program chair, helped organize symposia, and have been involved in the meet-a-mentor program. I became the chair of the newly formed American Association of Dental Research (AADR) Committee on Diversity and Inclusion because I firmly believe that it is important to have a diverse workforce. It allows us to increase the depth and breadth of our science and expand the pool of dental researchers and academics. It is also important to improve access to care and the type of care that underserved patient populations receive. In some way, this position is one of many ways that I followed my mother's advice to "be involved."

Looking back over my personal life, I am most proud of my children. Professionally, I am most proud that I, along with my team, ask scientific questions that make a clinical difference and that my trainees will continue to contribute to the field.

Thinking of students, I want to encourage them to go for whatever it is that they aspire to do, to build on their natural abilities and interests, and see where those lead them. I want to challenge them to not let others tell them that they cannot accomplish their goals and to realize that there are no mistakes, only life experiences. Thinking of future leaders in our field, I want to point out that in every leadership and research career, there are numerous challenges. For me, the key to overcoming challenges has been communication and finding creative ways to circumvent obstacles. In short: believe and persist.

Marilyn P. Woolfolk, MS, DDS, MPH, FACD

◆ ◆ ◆

My Early Years

I was born in Wilmington, Delaware. My parents were both college educated, and each had distinguished careers outside of the home. My mother, Gladys S. Porter, was an elementary school teacher, and my father, Winder L. Porter, was a pediatrician and medical director with the Delaware State Board of Health. They were both achievers and modeled strong spiritual faith and moral character. My mother is Nanticoke Indian, and my dad is African American. I have one sister, Jacquelyn, who is three years older. We had a compact family unit of four, with many relatives located in the same city.

I started kindergarten the first year that schools were being integrated. This meant that from elementary through high school, I attended schools where the students and teachers were predominantly Caucasian. I was comfortable being one of the few and, more often than not, the only person of color in the classroom and in various extracurricular activities, and I learned to thrive in those predominantly majority settings. I enjoyed robust academic, emotional, and financial support provided by my parents, who were crucial in my development. I took music lessons, attended music camps, attended National Medical Association conventions, and benefited from the village of people that came with my parents' circle of professional contacts and friends. At home, we played cerebral board and card games that invoked strategy, used mathematical calculations, and were taught financial principles related to property acquisition. Even my favorite relaxation activity of playing ping-pong evoked competitive rallies. I always looked forward to the next game, the next challenge, the next opportunity to advance to a higher level or improve my record of success. Fortunately, my sister and I were raised without gender limitations or specific roles. We had a healthy mindset from which we approached any challenge or obstacle and were unfettered by gender-defined boundaries. Empowered by this background—and girded by personal qualities of being fearless, relentless, and resilient—I could attack any problem, climb any mountain, and overcome any adversity. These assets would prove valuable on the playground, in the classroom, in the training program, at the table in department meetings, in executive committee sessions, and on the leadership team.

My parents were pillars in the community and were somewhat rare among the parents of our peer group as being dually college educated. As achievers, they set high standards for themselves and others. To be a product of that union was a blessing. When I considered careers, being a physician like my dad was appealing. I went to college and took pre-med courses. However, sometime during my junior year, I became disenchanted with the pursuit of medicine. I naively perceived the educational pathway to medicine as protracted in years (med school, plus residency, plus specialty) and therefore incompatible with marriage and having a family at an early age. I decided instead to pursue a major in microbiology and get a master's degree with an eye toward working in a research lab. After graduating from Cornell University, I was accepted at several prestigious schools and chose to attend the University of Michigan (UM).

Marilyn P. Woolfolk, MS, DDS, MPH, FACD

On the Way to a Career in Dentistry

I got married during the time I was earning my master's degree, and when I completed it, I accepted a job working in an oral biology laboratory in the UM School of Dentistry (SOD). I worked for two years as a research assistant, investigating the oral microflora linked to periodontal disease and dental caries. During that time, my lab supervisor, Dr. Walter Loesche—a Caucasian faculty member—and Dr. Emerson Robinson—an African American faculty member—continuously encouraged me to consider getting my dental degree. Both dentists were pivotal in my decision to go to dental school. I realized that there was no possibility for advancement in the research position I held, and in order to advance in responsibility and earning capacity, I needed either a PhD or a DDS. I weighed both options and decided to pursue dentistry. It was not a stretch because I had all the prerequisite courses. Besides, dentistry was then being pitched as a family-friendly health career for women. As I was applying to dental school, women were beginning to apply and become accepted in greater numbers nationwide. I was admitted to the SOD at the University of Michigan and was one of twenty-eight women in a class of 150.

Becoming a Faculty Member

As I was finishing my final year of dental school, Dr. Robinson again steered me to a different career path. This time, he told me about a clinical instructor position that was open in the Department of Community Dentistry. At that point, Dr. Robinson became my lifetime mentor, colleague, and treasured friend. I was delighted to explore and later accept that opportunity, because it meant that I did not have to move from Ann Arbor to find employment. My husband and I had established roots and friendships in the city, he had a fulfilling teaching job as a band director in the area, and it did not take much convincing to get me to stay local and work at the school. By now, the SOD was a comfort zone, and I had gotten to know many of the faculty and staff throughout my student role and previous employment in the building. I had not considered academia as a career path before and did not know much about the full scope of opportunity that dental education offered. I certainly had no idea that it would become my career passion and life's work.

I joined the SOD faculty as a full-time clinical instructor in the Department of Community Dentistry and worked some evenings as an associate in a local private practice. After working for a year, I met one of the professors in the School of Public Health, Dr. David Striffler. Many of the faculty in my department had earned their master of public health degree, and Dr. Striffler convinced me that if I continued to work with underserved populations, I would need to become more knowledgeable about dental public health and versed in population health. Pursuing that credential at the UM School of Public Health was a logical option; it was on campus, and it would be possible to take one or two classes per semester while I continued to work full-time. I earned my MPH within two years of starting it and thereby qualified for an appointment as an assistant professor to launch my tenure-track trajectory through the ranks to full professor.

Taking On Leadership Responsibilities

I accepted all my responsibilities at each level and performed to the best of my ability. My leadership skills developed as I organized and led students to provide dentistry for underserved populations in the community, in writing grant proposals that would support developing the pipeline of students applying to health professions from underrepresented and disadvantaged backgrounds, and in committees that I chaired. These skills were further honed in several national leadership-development programs that I was selected to attend. Ultimately, I became part of the SOD administrative team and finished my academic career as the assistant dean for student services.

My fondest childhood memory was of summer Sunday afternoons when our family and all our uncles, aunts, and cousins went to a county park for a picnic and to play baseball. The principles of fairness in competition and lessons on how to respond appropriately in victory and defeat became instilled in me in this environment. This framework would underpin the rest of my educational and career pursuits. The games among family were friendly but fierce and ignited my competitive fire. I discovered I had an innate athletic ability and could stand out as a star on a team, and I gained a sense of supreme confidence from those games that carried over into all my life endeavors!

Lessons Learned

My most impactful educational moment came as a revelation during a promotion discussion. I realized at the time that one's strongest advocate is one's self. There comes a point where you have to champion your own strengths and contributions and fend off your detractors or those who attempt to set boundaries for you. A few colleagues you encounter will genuinely push you up the hill, but others have your interest only as a secondary consideration. Therefore, one has to be the advocate for one's own talent and seize opportunities when they are presented. While seeking wise counsel and perspective along the way, use your preparation and instincts, and know that your aspirations and accomplishments cannot be limited.

Mentoring relationships were a crucial support system on my journey. As mentioned earlier, Dr. Emerson Robinson became my lifetime mentor, colleague, and treasured friend. He was my role model of success in the academy. He carried himself with dignity and provided a blueprint for how to negotiate the rigors and expectations at a research-intensive university. His skill set as a dentist and his stature as a professor inspired me to put forth my best effort. Later, I was introduced to Dr. Jeanne Sinkford, who became a mentor, role model, and special confidante. It is hard to distill and put into words the full extent of her influence on me. She is among an elite tier in the health-care arena as a phenomenal woman of achievement who coincidently is African American. She gave me opportunities to enhance my skills as a faculty member and administrator and to assume committee assignments and leadership positions on the national level. I am eternally grateful and indebted for her mentorship, friendship, and wise counsel.

Looking back, I am most proud of the fact that I was able to balance my professional aspirations with personal goals of having a career and family. My husband and I welcomed our first child at the end of my first year in dental school. I am reasonably sure that I was the first woman in the DDS program at the UM to bear a child while enrolled. To have had a healthy baby, navigate the challenges of parenting, and graduate on time with my entering class was a personal triumph. Similarly, to be blessed with two more children, go on to have a successful professional career in dentistry, and become the first African American woman full professor and assistant dean at the UM SOD is indeed a great source of pride.

I would be remiss, however, if I did not acknowledge the unrelenting support of my spouse, three children, and other family members and friends that enabled me to pursue my professional goals without interruption and encouraged me during times when the load seemed daunting. Additionally, I am compelled to praise with gratitude the three Black women who provided daycare for my infants/toddlers before they could attend preschool and the nurturing women who provided care for my mom when she was suffering from dementia. Ironically, these women were not educated beyond high school but were fully invested in my educational journey and success as a professional. My faith, family, and these angels on earth propelled my upward spiral.

Coping with Professional Challenges

Addressing this topic evokes considerable emotion because it is a reminder of how isolating it can be at times when you are a woman in a leadership position. Being one of a few women at the top of the organizational chart was often compounded by also being the only woman of color in a group. Most males are recognized for their contributions, expertise, and competence without having to demonstrate it. However, women, especially women of color, are rarely granted that same deference or instant credibility. It can be hard to get your voice heard. I have observed that women leaders are often perceived and treated differently than their male counterparts, both by male leaders and by the men or women who directly report to them. Sometimes this differential treatment is blatantly obvious, and sometimes it manifests itself in more subtle ways.

In many situations a woman leader's authority and decision-making are more likely to be challenged and questioned than those of a male leader. Some don't hesitate to tell you how to do your job or go around you if they can. That is overt behavior. However, some people elevate themselves in importance and give the impression that they are more knowledgeable than you are, even though they do not have the experience or the credentials. They are eager to call you by your first name, belying your title as a subtle expression of disrespect when they would never take such liberty with a male of equal or lesser accomplishment and influence.

Overcoming such challenges required me to summon my resilience and to acknowledge that achieving unanimous approval and respect is not possible or necessary. I developed professional boundaries and sought to understand the interpersonal dynamics of each situation. I had to realize that I could not fight every battle and thus had to decide which battles to fight and which ones to let go. The strategic steps that were useful in winning at board and card games—assess the task, make the best use of the cards you are dealt, and boldly execute your game plan—have always served me well. I approach each challenge as a play on the stage. The characters may change, but the behaviors remain the same. If you do your homework, establish allies, identify the resistance, and build relationships before you perform, you will be satisfied that you have done your best and will not be disappointed or dismayed when others do not act appropriately or according to your expectations.

This Sisterhood!!!

By Dr. Beverly Y. Murdock

Some say praises to Allah…
We worship and serve the omnipotent one!
We pray our prayers in our own way…
We express our love with generosity,
Feeling the warmth of the agape love
For all of our sisters…
We touch the notes of the highest highs descending
to the lowest low…
We understand the love for each other and…
Our abilities grow day by day!
We stand UNITED in our sisterhood…
Unrestrained by the negativity of those who
think our link to one another is not real…
We stand firmly connected by years of living…
Reaffirming our meeting on the foundation of the Mecca…
Or OUR OWN SPECIAL PLACE…
Our choirs' voices harmonize in unison…
We sing the sweet melodies of happy birthdays…
We joyously celebrate the happy times together…
We glory in raising our children and caring for families…
We understand each sister's sacrifices to be made…

We respect the choices of each member
and we know the song of unity gives us

Braided wisdom to add to our lives...
We sing the song of Hope in an effort
to make the accurate choices in our lives survive...
Reinforcing what has already been taught...
Keeping boundless beliefs intact...
We sing the song of Joy...
The Joy achieved by the satisfaction that our lives
are worthy to be lived in the space of this friendship...
And
We sing the song of peace...
A peace that passes all understanding beneath the umption
of He who is omnipresent...
Guiding us...
Giving us HOPE and rendering our souls to accept that
PEACE...
We sing THIS song!
We SING this song!
WE sing this song
Of the lives of Us
AND this sisterhood!!!

Dr. Murdock holds a dental hygiene certificate (1977) and doctor of dental surgery degree (1983) from Howard University College of Dentistry. Permission to publish granted September 28, 2020.

BIO SKETCHES

◆ ◆ ◆

The bio sketches were submitted by the contributing authors and therefore vary in length and style.

Canise Y. Bean, DMD, MPH

◆ ◆ ◆

*Without community service, we would not have
a strong quality of life . . .*

—Dr. Dorothy I. Height

Dr. Canise Y. Bean is a clinical professor at the Ohio State University College of Dentistry in the Division of Restorative and Prosthetic Dentistry. She is currently director of community education and oversees the major outreach program for the college, the OHIO (Oral Health Improvement through Outreach) Project, which includes a three-chair mobile dental coach that serves children of the Columbus City Schools. The OHIO Project has expanded dental education so that students spend fifty days of their clinical education in community-based sites, thereby addressing the number-one unmet health-care need in the state: access to oral health care.

Upon attaining her doctor of dental medicine (DMD) degree from the University of Kentucky in her hometown of Lexington, she moved to Cleveland, Ohio, where she completed a General Practice Residency at Cleveland Metropolitan General Hospital.

Bean then became a founding member of Shaker Dental Associates, the first African American private dental group practice in Cleveland. Fulfilling a desire to impart knowledge to others, she became a part-time faculty member at Case Western Reserve University School of Dental Medicine. She was also an instructor at Shaker Dental Institute, a dental assisting training program managed by Shaker Dental Associates and the first of its kind to be state certified. Dr. Bean was elected to serve as the first female president of Forest City Dental Society, an organization comprised of sixty minority dentists in the Cleveland area.

Bean relocated to Columbus and received a master of public health degree from the Ohio State University (OSU). She was in private practice for five years before joining the faculty at the Ohio State University College of Dentistry in the Section of Restorative and Prosthetic Dentistry. Her duties included instruction in preclinical courses and student supervision in the clinic.

Bean is a Fellow of the International College of Dentists, American College of Dentists, and the Pierre Fauchard Academy. She is active with the Ohio Dental Association and serves as chair of the Diversity and Inclusion taskforce. Additionally, she is the current vice president of the Ohio State Dental Board. She is a life member of Delta Sigma Theta Sorority, Inc., and a member of the Twin Rivers Chapter of the Links, Incorporated.

Winifred J. Booker, DDS, FAAPD

◆ ◆ ◆

Dr. Booker earned a BS degree in biology from Tennessee State University in 1980 and earned a DDS degree from Meharry Medical College School of Dentistry in 1987. She earned the certificate in pediatric dentistry from the Children's National Medical Center in Washington, DC, in 1994. She is a board-certificated pediatric dentist, a member of the American Board of Pediatric Dentistry (ABPD), and a Fellow of the American Academy of Pediatric Dentistry (FAAPD). In private practice since 1988, Dr. Booker is the principal owner of Valley Dental Pediatrics. In 1997, she founded the Children's Oral Health Institute, a nonprofit organization dedicated to the oral health education of children and families.

In addition, she is the owner of Brushtime Enterprises, an oral hygiene products company that she opened in the 1990s. She is a past president of the Maryland Dental Society (MDS) and an immediate-past president of the Society of American Indian Dentists (SAID). Dr. Booker served on the 1999 and 2020 Oral Health Committees for the Surgeon General's Commission on Oral Health in America and is currently serving a third four-year appointment on the Maryland Medicaid Advisory Committee for the Maryland Department of Health and Mental Hygiene. She has also served on the American Dental Association Medicaid Provider Advisory Committee since 2015 and is the recipient of numerous awards.

Sheila R. Brown, MEd, DDS, FACD

♦ ♦ ♦

Always make a difference.

Dr. Sheila has succeeded in her goals by building consensus, by showing up, speaking up, and standing up to make a difference. Dr. Sheila has a dental practice in the South Loop of Downtown Chicago, Illinois. The practice focuses on comprehensive care.

Dr. Sheila graduated with a bachelor of science degree from Johnson C. Smith University, a master of education degree with a concentration in science from the University of Houston, and a doctorate of dental surgery degree from the University of Michigan School of Dentistry.

Marsha E. Butler, DDS, FACD

♦ ♦ ♦

Dr. Marsha Butler, DDS, is currently vice president of Global Oral Health and Professional Relations at Colgate-Palmolive Company, responsible for global strategies, programs, and policies that support Colgate's professional and oral health initiatives around the world. Dr. Butler interfaces with numerous international governments, dental and health organizations, academia, and NGO groups to promote programs aimed at the prevention of oral disease and the improvement of general and oral health.

In 1990, Dr. Butler conceptualized, designed, and implemented a comprehensive oral health education program called Bright Smiles, Bright Futures. This initiative is directed toward high-risk youth populations and utilizes public-private partnerships, community-based outreach, and parent involvement to improve the oral health of underserved youth in the United States. Under Dr. Butler's leadership, Bright Smiles, Bright Futures has been implemented in over eighty countries around the world, reaching over one billion children in thirty languages. Dr. Butler has authored and presented results from several publications that study the oral health habits, knowledge, and clinical status of young children in the United States and other regions around the world.

She has outlined a global public health strategy that has fostered several school-based oral health initiatives, working with Colgate subsidiaries and multiple stakeholders to significantly reduce caries among school-aged children. An example of such strategy is the Mexican mandatory tooth-brushing program/law that now requires in-school tooth brushing for school-age children in Mexico City by the Mexico City Legislative Congress.

Dr. Butler has been an advocate globally of leadership-development and scholarship programs, working with numerous dental, health, and NGO groups to provide aspiring students and rising dental leaders an opportunity to advance their careers through innovative leadership programs and scholarship awards. Most notably, she has worked diligently with the National Dental Association Foundation to provide more than three thousand Colgate scholarships for African American dental and dental hygiene students since 1990.

A graduate of the Howard University College of Dentistry, Dr. Butler is a member of the American Dental Association, the National Dental Association, the International Association of Dental Researchers, the American Association of Dental Researchers, and the American College of Dentists. She has received numerous awards for her oral health improvement activities, including the Howard University College of Dentistry Distinguished Alumni of the Year award, an advocacy award from the World Organization for Early Childhood Education, a Silver Screen Award from the US International Film Festival, a 2013 Telly Award, an Ebony Outstanding Women in Marketing and Communications Award, a Council Choice award from the American Dental Association, and other awards.

Gail Cherry-Peppers, DDS, MS

♦ ♦ ♦

Dr. Cherry-Peppers retired as a captain from the US Public Health Service, where she worked at several HHS Agencies (NIH, HRSA, FDA) as a dental clinical consultant, with focus on the oral manifestations of chronic disease and population sciences. Dr. Cherry-Peppers has been the lead oral medicine specialist on the AIDS Education and Training Center (AETC) dental section. She has led numerous initiatives, such as the dental component of the Baltimore Longitudinal Study on Aging (BLSA), Million Hearts dental component, and the dental component of the FDA and NIH's $40 million PATH (Population Assessment of Tobacco and Health Study) in 2017. Dr. Cherry-Peppers has been a pioneer in the efforts to formulate dental treatment regimen and in formulating national guidelines such as the 2000 and upcoming Surgeon's General's Report on Oral Health and the Office on Women's Health tobacco epidemic plans.

She has provided numerous presentations spanning many years, with the goal of reducing dental disparities and making quality dental care available to poor populations across the nation. These engagements include numerous presentations and workshops on dental management and the treatment of HIV, heart disease, sickle cell disease, kidney disease, and diabetes. She has also led panels on alternate opioid options, such as the prescribing of Tylenol and ibuprofen for complex dental surgical procedures.

Since joining the Howard University College of Dentistry (HUCD) faculty, has served as the director of dental public health and associate professor. She oversees clinic sessions, teaches several courses, and leads a large part of HUCD's student community outreach and cultural event activities. Students participate in more than thirty such events biannually, including health fairs, mission trips, externships, remote-area medical events, community chronic disease and screening events, and clinical rotations, in underserved areas across the United States.

In addition to the commitments listed above, Dr. Cherry-Peppers serves as a consultant to the US Public Health Service (USPHS) for disasters and critical emergencies and as a Howard University liaison. Dr. Cherry-Peppers is also on the infection control and COVID-19 teams at the College of Dentistry. She volunteers to support military functions in the COVID-19 crisis, and she currently serves as a COVID-19 tester and has participated in leading site organization. Additionally, Dr. Cherry-Peppers serves as the dental coordinator of the national HIV curriculum, an AIDS Education and Training Center (AETC) National Coordinating Resource Center project with the Howard University HIV team.

Dr. Cherry-Peppers has received numerous prestigious awards for outstanding achievement while in the US Public Health Service: the Phenomenal Woman Award from the National Dental Association and numerous other awards from Oral Health America, from national AIDS Education and Training Centers, and from many other societies and organizations.

Agnes H. Donahue, DDS, MSD, MPH

♦ ♦ ♦

Agnes H. Donahue directed intergovernmental affairs in the Office of the Assistant Secretary for Health. She directed the OASH intergovernmental and regional activities. Dr. Donahue reported to the assistant secretary for health (ASH), provided advice and counsel to the ASH on matters of intergovernmental affairs for public health and science, and served as the point of contact for the regional health administrators. She was the liaison to the regional health administrators for policies; program decisions; and initiatives of the administration, the secretary, and the assistant secretary for health and the surgeon general. Dr. Donahue also provides advice on public health and science for the Secretary's Office of Intergovernmental Affairs and was liaison to the Association of State and Territorial Health Officials, the National Association of County and City Health Officials, and the American Public Health Association for the Department of Health and Human Services.

Agnes Donahue earned a bachelor of science degree at Xavier University of New Orleans, Louisiana; a doctorate of Dental Surgery from Meharry Medical College, Nashville, Tennessee; a master of science in dentistry and a certificate of advanced graduate study (pediatric dentistry) at the Boston University School of Graduate Dentistry; and a master of public health at the University of California at Berkeley. Dr. Donahue entered HHS as a staff fellow (immunology) at the National Institutes of Health of Health (NIH), National Institute of Dental Research, in Bethesda, Maryland. At NIH, her research involves the study of interference with attachment of Cytophaga species to calcium-containing particles using monoclonal antibodies as reagents. Her clinical work focused on the management of oral complications of primary and secondary immune deficiency disorders. Her research conducted at the Brookhaven National Laboratory prior to joining the NIH focused on the structure of and function of ribosomes in protein synthesis.

Dr. Donahue made her transition from basic research and clinical care through the NIH Grants Associate Program for the development of health scientist administrators. She then joined the National Institute of General Medical Sciences (NIGMS) as a scientific-review administrator, a position in which she served for four years. She served concurrently as the executive secretary, then executive director of the PHS Coordination Committee on Women's Health Issues, a PHS-wide policy body appointed by the ASH and cochaired by the ASH and the then-director of NIGMS. These functions led to the establishment of the PHS Office on Women's Health. She served as the first director of the department's Office of Women's Health.

Agnes Donahue has served and provided leadership on numerous task forces, committees, panels, and working groups, including, among others, the Secretary's Prevention Initiative Steering Committee; the Secretary's Diabetes Detection Initiative Steering Committee; Healthy People 2010 Steering Committee; the President's Interagency Task Force on the Economic Development of the Southwest Border; the Departmental Committee on Pandemic Influenza Preparedness, the Vice President's Reinventing Government Initiative, PHS Field Structure Working Group; the Coordinating Committee on Women's Health Issues; and as US representative to the Subcommittee on Women Health and development of the executive council of the Pan American Health Organization.

Dr. Donahue has received numerous awards, including the Sustained Superior Service Award, Secretary's Award for Distinguished Service, and the PHS and Secretary's awards for leadership. She has been recognized as an outstanding alumna of both Meharry Medical College and the Boston University Goldman School of Graduate Dentistry.

Agnes H. Donahue, DDS, MSD, MPH

Agnes Donahue came into the government in 1980 from academia, where she was an assistant professor and attending staff faculty member at the University of Mississippi Medical Center and School of Dentistry.

Cherae Farmer-Dixon, DDS, MSPH, MBA, FACD, FICD

❖ ❖ ❖

Dr. Cherae Farmer-Dixon has overcome barriers in race, gender, and academia, becoming the third woman to head the School of Dentistry at Meharry Medical College. She remains one of a few select women to lead in the role as dean of a superior dental program that produces 40 percent of the nation's currently practicing African American dentists.

Dean Farmer-Dixon has selflessly served in the dental school for twenty-nine years. Prior to assuming the role of dean, Dr. Farmer-Dixon was the associate dean for academic and student affairs at Meharry in the School of Dentistry. She sets the bar high for her students and faculty in the program and always works overtime to help them in achieving their goals with excellence. Dr. Farmer-Dixon also proudly serves her country as a lieutenant colonel in the US Army Reserve.

The dean is also an academic scholar who immerses herself in published research activities dealing with oral health disparities, caries in low-income children, and community outreach and intervention, and she works tirelessly to address disparities within minority dental school enrollment.

She serves on numerous councils and has received a myriad of awards from students as well as local, state, and national professional memberships in several organizations. Most recently, she was selected to assist and lead a team of volunteers at the COVID-19 testing site at Meharry. Her stellar performance led to Meharry acquiring two other testing sites in the greater Nashville area. The dean is also recognized by the *Nashville Business Journal* as one of the 2019 Women of Influence. She is a distinguished 2019 alumna of the Nashville Healthcare Council of Fellows.

Dr. Farmer-Dixon is a native of Indianola, Mississippi. She is recognized as an outstanding graduate of the 1986 class of Mississippi Valley State University. She has also received the following degrees and certifications: Meharry Medical College doctor of dental surgery (DDS) degree, 1990, and the School of Graduate Studies and Research master of science in public health degree (MSPH), 1994; Tennessee State University executive master of business administration (EXMBA), 2019; the Institute of Educational Management Program Certificate from Harvard University, 2017; and Boston University's Public Health Residency Certificate, 2014. Dr. Farmer-Dixon is a 2018 fellow of the International College of Dentists, a 2014 fellow of the American College of Dentists, a 2000 alumna of the Executive Leadership in Academic Medicine Program (ELAM), and a member of the American Dental Education Association Leadership Institute 2003–2004 class.

A. Isabel Garcia, DDS, MPH, FACD

♦ ♦ ♦

Dr. A. Isabel Garcia joined the University of Florida College of Dentistry as its seventh permanent dean on Feb. 16, 2015. Dr. Garcia's career spans forty years in public health, clinical practice, research, teaching, and administration at the local, state, and national levels. She retired from the US Public Health Service in 2014 as a rear admiral, lower half. Prior to joining UFCD, she was the deputy director of the National Institute of Dental and Craniofacial Research, part of the National Institutes of Health; directed dental care and public health programs in Virginia and Ohio; and worked in private practice in Richmond and Hopewell, Virginia.

She received a doctorate in dental surgery in 1980 from Virginia Commonwealth University, a master's degree in public health from the University of Michigan in 1988, and completed a residency in dental public health at the University of Michigan and a fellowship in primary care policy from the US Public Health Service.

A fellow of the American College of Dentists, the Pierre Fauchard Academy, and Omicron Kappa Upsilon dental honorary society, Dean Garcia is a diplomate and past president of the American Board of Dental Public Health and an active member of the American Dental Education Association, the International Association for Dental Research, and the American Dental Association.

Leslie E. Grant, DDS, MSPA, FACD

◆ ◆ ◆

Dr. Leslie E. Grant is passionate about advocating for equitable access to oral health care. She believes that interprofessional collaboration and direct engagement with policy makers are integral components of the tool kit that will advance improved oral health in the world community. She has a zeal for innovation, is committed to serving the dental profession, and recently coedited the book *Infection Control in the Dental Office—A Global Perspective* (Springer, 2020).

Dr. Grant is a past president of the National Dental Association. She received her bachelor of science from Boston University and her master of speech pathology and audiology degree from the University of Washington. Dr. Grant obtained her doctor of dental surgery degree from the University of Maryland School of Dentistry in 1986 and completed a general practice residency at Saint Joseph's Hospital in Paterson, New Jersey, in 1987.

Judy Greenlea Taylor, DDS, MPH, FACD, FICD

♦ ♦ ♦

Dr. Judy Greenlea Taylor thrives on authentic fulfillment that comes from contributing to the lives of others. In her contribution to this book, she discusses her foundational path to leadership in health care, public health, and advocacy, and lessons learned.

Dr. Greenlea Taylor served as the ninety-second president of the National Dental Association. She has practiced dentistry for twenty-eight years and is CEO of Greenlea Dental Center, PC. She served many years in the public sector as a public health practitioner and as a consultant to the Department of Health and Human Services (HHS) and other organizations. She is CEO of Greenlea Health Solutions, LLC, a public health consulting company that partners with organizations to advance health equity and improve health outcomes. Additionally, she serves as dental director for CareSource, a nationally recognized managed care plan, serving Medicaid and government program beneficiaries in several state markets. She recently served two governor-appointed terms to the Georgia Department of Public Health Board and is an esteemed fellow of the both the American College of Dentists and International College of Dentists. She has received numerous awards, including an Outstanding Citizen Award from the Georgia secretary of state, and esteemed proclamations and commendations from the state of Georgia, the city of Atlanta, city of Union City, and the Department of Public Health.

Dr. Greenlea Taylor earned her BS degree from Prairie View A&M University (Texas), Benjamin Banneker Honors College. She earned her DDS degree from University of Iowa, completed a general practice residency/oral surgery fellowship at Emory University, and earned a MPH from Emory University's Rollins School of Public Health. She has received course certification in health-disparities research from Columbia University's Mailman School of Public Health, certification by HHS as a program facilitator for the Cultural Competency Program for Oral Health Professionals (CCPOHP), certification by the Mental Health First Aid National Council for Behavioral Health, and certification as a Lean Six Sigma Healthcare Green Belt.

Hazel J. Harper, DDS, MPH, FACD

◆ ◆ ◆

Dr. Harper is a graduate of the Howard University College of Dentistry and the Johns Hopkins University School of Hygiene and Public Health. She maintains a part-time private practice in general dentistry in Washington, DC, and is president and CEO of Hazel J. Harper & Associates, LLC, management consultants. In 2008, she cofounded and directed the Deamonte Driver Dental Project (DDDP), a school-based, mobile dental project, in Prince George's County, Maryland, which was named in memory of the twelve-year-old boy who died in 2007 from untreated tooth decay. She is currently the founding director of the award-winning NDA-HEALTH NOW project and the architect of the Inter-Professional Student Leaders Colloquium and Summit. Her reputation for innovation and success has merited awards from several foundations, which has enabled her to design and direct many national projects.

Dr. Harper lectures and writes extensively, and she has been the lead author of numerous publications and book chapters. She was also selected to be a contributing author for the 2020 US Surgeon General's Report on Oral Health. Since Deamonte's death, Dr. Harper has devoted her energies and creative talents to developing, implementing, and supporting interprofessional health education programs and community outreach events in cities across America and the world. She is a member of Alpha Kappa Alpha Sorority and The Links, Incorporated.

Sandra G. Harris, DDS, FACD

◆ ◆ ◆

Dr. Sandra G. Harris was born in Nashville, Tennessee, where she still resides. However, she also lived for short periods of time in Saint Louis, Missouri; San Jose, California; and the Washington, DC, suburb of Silver Spring, Maryland. Most of her education occurred in Nashville, where she attended both public and private schools. Upon graduating from high school, she entered Fisk University at the age of sixteen, where she majored in sociology.

Dr. Harris then worked as a social worker in Nashville for several years after graduating from Fisk and also married and started a family. Several years later, the family moved to Saint Louis and then to California. While living in those places, she was a housewife who did not work outside the home. However, during this time she began thinking more and more of a career path that she had considered as a child and teenager: becoming a health-care professional. It was in California that Dr. Harris decided to return to college to take the prerequisite courses for application to dental school.

In 1980, she was accepted into dental school at Meharry Medical College. During her matriculation at Meharry, Dr. Harris decided to pursue a career in orthodontics. In 1984, she entered Howard University's College of Dentistry's postgraduate orthodontic program. During the 1980s and earlier, there were very few female dental specialists and even fewer who were a minority.

Upon completing the postgraduate program at Howard University, Dr. Harris joined the faculty in the dental school at Meharry Medical

College and also opened a part-time orthodontic private practice. She worked in the practice evenings and weekends until retiring in 2017. However, she still remains on faculty at Meharry Medical College and serves as an orthodontic consultant for Delta Dental Insurance of Tennessee.

In addition to the many activities associated with her academic career, Dr. Harris has been involved in many professional organizations, which include the World Federation of Orthodontists, American Association of Orthodontists, Southern Association of Orthodontists, Tennessee Association of Orthodontists, National Dental Association, American Dental Association, Tennessee Dental Association, Nashville Dental Society, American Association of Women Dentists, American Dental Education Association, and Continental Orthodontic Study Club. She also enjoys music, international travel, and spending time with her daughter, Tracey Hughes Royal.

Marja M. Hurley, MD, FASBMR

◆ ◆ ◆

Pioneering physician-scientist Dr. Marja Hurley, a professor of medicine and orthopedic surgery at UConn Health, is renowned for her three decades of NIH-funded bone research and inspiring the next generation of doctors and scientists. She is an elected fellow of the Connecticut Academy of Science and Engineering, the American Society for Bone and Mineral Research, and the Association of Osteobiology.

Hurley's research has advanced knowledge of the role fibroblast growth factor 2 (FGF2) plays in human bone and bone-mass maintenance. Her research has shown how reduced expression of FGF2 in bone during the aging process may contribute to osteoporosis and osteoarthritis and how FGF2 therapy can enhance bone cell function. Her widely published research has appeared in 193 peer-reviewed publications, including manuscripts, invited reviews, book chapters, and scientific abstracts.

Hurley was the first Black woman to receive a medical degree from UConn School of Medicine, the first to become a tenured full professor, and founded its Health Career Opportunity Programs, which she continues to direct now, two decades later, attracting more young people from across Connecticut, of all ethnic and socioeconomic backgrounds, to medicine and science.

In fact, of the nearly nine hundred youth from middle schools, high schools, and colleges participating in her fourteen distinct John and Valerie Rowe Aetna Health Professions Partnership Initiative–sponsored programs since 1996, more than seven hundred have gone on to enter medical, dental, or other health profession schools. She has nurtured the biomedical science career development of students at every level of the pipeline, substantially increasing the number of underrepresented and first-generation students attending the UConn Schools of Medicine and Dental Medicine. She has mentored more than fifty college, medical, dental, and graduate students, postdoctoral fellows, and junior faculty in her research laboratory.

Dr. Hurley has been the recipient of numerous awards for research, teaching, science, and STEM student mentoring. Some of her past accolades include the Connecticut Technology Council Women of Innovation and Leadership Award, the UConn Health Board of Directors Faculty Recognition Award, the UConn School of Medicine Alumni Outstanding Faculty Award, UConn's Carole and Ray Neag Medal of Honor, UConn's Martin Luther King Award for Achievement in Science, and the Lawrence G. Raisz Award from the American Society for Bone and Mineral Research (ASBMR) for outstanding achievements in preclinical and translational research. Plus, UConn named Hurley one of its most outstanding women in one hundred years, and she serves as its liaison to the AAMC Group on Women in Medicine and Science.

In addition, Dr. Hurley is recognized nationally as a leader in education equity and has been appointed to several key committees in education, both in medicine and dentistry, locally and nationally, and is an invited speaker at national meetings and to testify before Congress. Recently, she was named chair of the Oversight Board of NIH, NIDDK Network of Minority Health Research Investigators.

Dr. Hurley graduated from UConn with an undergraduate degree and a doctorate in medicine, and, in 1986, she joined its faculty after completing both her residency training in internal medicine and fellowship in endocrinology at UConn. Hurley serves as an associate dean at UConn's medical and dental schools and as a member of its Institute of Systems Genomics, and she is on the UConn graduate school's faculty in cell biology and skeletal biology and regeneration.

Andrea D. Jackson, DDS, MS, FACP, FACD, FICD

◆ ◆ ◆

As a three-time graduate of Howard University (BS), Howard University College of Dentistry (DDS), and Howard University Hospital GPR (GPR certificate), I am happy to share my story in dental education. After joining the faculty of the College of Dentistry, I was encouraged to pursue postdoctoral training, which enhanced my career in academia. I reached the milestone of becoming a board-certified prosthodontist, having completed a master of science degree in prosthodontics from Georgetown University School of Dentistry. I have been involved in dental education at Howard University College of Dentistry (HUCD) for more than thirty years. During my time at HUCD, I have held positions at every level and witnessed the growth and continued success of our dental program and our alumni. During my tenure as an educator, I have held several leadership positions, including department chair, associate dean for clinical affairs, interim dean, and now dean of the College of Dentistry.

I started my career in academia as an instructor in the Department of Restorative Dentistry and, after my specialty training, was promoted to assistant professor. Through perseverance and hard work, I became a tenured associate professor, then a professor of prosthodontics. I have been an active member of the American Dental Education Association for my entire career in academia and have represented Howard University on the Counsel of Faculties from 1995 until 2010. I am also a past president of the prosthodontics section and served on the Council of Sections for two different terms.

I am currently a member of the Council of Deans of the American Dental Education Association, the American Dental Association, the District of Columbia Dental Society, the National Dental Association, the Robert T. Freeman Dental Society, Omicron Kappa Upsilon (National Dental Honor Society), and I hold fellowships in the American College of Prosthodontists, the American College of Dentists, and the International College of Dentists. I also serve on numerous committees within the college and university and in various capacities in national dental organizations, as a member of the Prosthodontics Test Construction Committee for the Joint Commission on National Dental Board Examinations (JCNDE), as a consultant examiner and member of the Quality Assurance Committee for the Commission on Dental Competency Assessments (CDCA), as a clinical board examiner for the Council of Interstate Testing Agencies (CITA), and as a site visitor for the Commission on Dental Accreditation (CODA). I have always treated others the way I would want to be treated—listening to people, being willing to learn, building a team of individuals to work together for a common goal, and making them feel a part of the process. I believe this has been the key to my success.

Ernestine S. Lacy, DDS

♦ ♦ ♦

Dr. Ernie Lacy earned her bachelor of science degree (1973), master of art degree (1976), and certificate of advanced secondary education (1978) from the University of Alabama in Birmingham. She taught high school mathematics and science for seventeen years before earning a doctor of dental surgery degree (1994) and certificate of advanced education in general dentistry (1996) from Baylor College of Dentistry (now Texas A&M University College of Dentistry). Dr. Lacy has been on faculty at the college since 1994. She began her academic career as an assistant professor in the Department of Restorative Sciences. Subsequent positions include director of academic programs, director of the Office of Student Services, director of student development, and executive director of student development and multicultural affairs. She is currently the associate dean for student affairs and a tenured professor in the Department of Comprehensive Dentistry.

Since 1999, Ernie Lacy has been the principal investigator and project director on over $13 million of grant funding to support Bridge to Dentistry, the college's dental pipeline program. Bridge to Dentistry is designed to help increase the diversity of the College of Dentistry's student body and faculty. In 2017, the college was awarded its second five-year Center of Excellence (COE) grant from the Health Resources and Services Administration to support Bridge to Dentistry. The program has been instrumental in Texas A&M University College of Dentistry's accomplishment of being one of the most diverse dental schools in the country (excluding dental schools associated with HBCUs and HSUs) in terms of underrepresented minority student enrollment. On a national level, Dr. Lacy has served as a facilitator of the American Dental Education Association's (ADEA) admissions workshops, made numerous presentations at ADEA annual sessions and symposia and other professional meetings, authored multiple manuscripts that have been published in peer-reviewed journals, and reviewed manuscripts for the Journal of Dental Education and grant applications for the Health Resources and Services Administration.

Dr. Lacy is currently a member of the National Dental Association, the American Dental Education Association, and the Omicron Kappa Upsilon Honor Dental Society.

Ana López-Fuentes, DMD, MPH, FACD, FICD

◆ ◆ ◆

Dr. Ana López-Fuentes is a tenured professor at the community dentistry section of the University of Puerto Rico School of Dental Medicine (UPRSDM). She served as dean of the UPRSDM from 2014 to 2018. She is currently president of the Infection Control and Quality Assurance standing committees and the president of the UPRSDM task force on COVID-19. Dr. López-Fuentes is the cochair of ADEA's Diversity and Inclusion Advisory Committee, member of the ADEA Collaborative on Dental Education Climate Assessment (CDECA), the UPRSDM's ADEA women liaison officer since 2006, member of ADEA's Annual Session Program Committee, chair of ADEA's Women in Leadership Special Interest Group, site visitor for the ADA Commission on Dental Accreditation, and elected member of the Board of Trustees of the Hispanic Dental Association (HDA). From 2018 to 2019, she was member of the American Dental Association Presidents' Summit for Diversity and Inclusion, representing the HDA. Dr. López-Fuentes is faculty advisor to the Hedwig van Ameringen Executive Leadership in Academic Medicine (ELAM) fellowship program since 2018. She is faculty advisor to the HDA and the American Association of Women Dentists student chapters. Dr. López-Fuentes has served as faculty representative to the Academic Senate at the UPR Medical Sciences Campus, as faculty representative to ADEA's Council of Faculties, as UPRSDM curriculum director, community dentistry section chief, and executive associate dean. At the university level, she was the representative of the

Medical Sciences Campus (MSC), Academic Senate at the President's Board, and was appointed executive secretary to the UPR President's Board (2013). She implemented and directed the first dental assistant program at the University of Granada, Spain, as a result of a collaboration between the University of Puerto Rico and the University of Granada, Spain. Dr. López-Fuentes is an alumnus of several leadership programs, including ADEA's Summer Program for Emerging Academic Leaders, the Hedwig van Ameringen Executive Leadership in Academic Medicine (ELAM) program, and the Bell Leadership Institute. As dean of the UPRSDM, she was instrumental in the amendment of the local dental law, implementation of the electronic health record, and the approval of the periodontics graduate program. Additionally, she was the first dean of the UPRSDM to be elected to ADEA's Council of Deans Administrative Board. She received the 2018 Chair of the ADEA Board of Directors Citation for significant contributions to dental education. This citation recognized her outstanding leadership as dean of the dental school after Hurricane María devastated Puerto Rico, maintaining the school's accreditation, keeping it open, and helping affected communities, thanks to donations from academia and dental associations in the United States.

Melanie E. Mayberry, DDS, MS-HCM, FACD

◆ ◆ ◆

Dr. Melanie E. Mayberry is currently a clinical associate professor and the division director of practice essentials and interprofessional education at the University of Detroit Mercy School of Dentistry. Previously, she was the chairperson of the Department of Oral Health and Integrated Care and the director of the Pre-Doctoral Patient Care Clinic at the University Health Center on the Detroit Medical Center Campus. Dr. Mayberry is a member of the Michigan Department of Health and Human Services Perinatal Oral Health Education Taskforce and the Interprofessional Education Taskforce. She is also a member of the State of Michigan Infant Mortality Advisory Council and is the codeveloper of a grant-funded education and patient care program that integrates oral health into OB (obstetrics) practice. Dr. Mayberry has developed interprofessional educational training partnerships with multiple medical schools and other health-professions programs.

Dr. Mayberry is a fellow of the Academy of General Dentistry and was inducted into the Pierre Fauchard International Honor Dental Academy. She maintains a part-time private practice and has a strong interest in interprofessional education and collaborative care. Dr. Mayberry is a graduate of Meharry Medical College School of Dentistry. She completed a general practice residency in hospital dentistry at the University of Michigan Medical Center and earned her master's degree in health-care management from the Harvard School of Public Health.

Renee McCoy-Collins, DDS, FACD, FICD

◆ ◆ ◆

Dr. McCoy-Collins is a graduate of the Howard University College of Dentistry, where she was the first female to graduate as an oral and maxillofacial surgeon. She was the first dentist to be in the National Association of Public Hospitals Physician Leadership Program as a fellow at the New York University School of Government. She is a fellow of the American College of Dentists and the International College of Dentists.

Dr. McCoy-Collins has held a number of distinguished leadership positions, including director of dental residency programs at Howard University Hospital, chairperson for the Department of Dentistry for the District of Columbia Public Benefits Corporation, interim chief operating officer at DC General Hospital, and associate chief medical officer for quality and management at DC General Hospital. She served as president of the medical and dental staff at Howard University and DC General hospitals, which each had over two hundred physicians.

Along with Dr. McCoy-Collins's achievements, she has always had a special concern for the medically underserved population in the District of Columbia. She has initiated a number of strategic programs to improve access to both medical and dental care for low-income populations. She has worked with the poverty agency for the district to develop new multi-specialty health centers in underserved areas of the District of Columbia. She has worked to ensure these programs have all included health-care residency education in medicine, dentistry, and

HIT technology. At present, Dr. McCoy-Collins is the chairperson of the District of Columbia Board of Dentistry, serving the district since 2010. As such, she is a member of the American Association of Dental Boards (AADB), serving as liaison for the DC Board of Dentistry, and a member of the Program and Strategic Planning Committee. She also serves as examiner ICFE, vice chairperson of the Quality Assurance Committee, and member of the Ad Hoc Committee and Ad Hoc Steering Committee of the Commission on Dental Competency Assessments (CDCA).

Vivian W. Pinn, MD, FCAP

◆ ◆ ◆

Dr. Vivian W. Pinn has enjoyed a dual career, having been in academic pathology and medical school administration for about twenty-five years and then in research policy and women's health for almost thirty years. She was the inaugural full-time director of the Office of Research on Women's Health at the National Institutes of Health (NIH) from 1991 and associate director of NIH for Women's Health Research from 1994 until her retirement in 2011. Under her leadership, this new office led the implementation of NIH research inclusion policies for women and minorities in clinical research, developed the first and several additional national strategic plans for women's health research, and established many new research funding initiatives and career development programs. During that time, she also established and cochaired the NIH Committee on Women in Biomedical Careers with the NIH director. She has since been named as a senior scientist emerita at the NIH Fogarty International Center. She has presented her perceptions of women's health and sex/gender research, health disparities, as well as challenges in biomedical careers to national and international audiences and has served as a mentor to hundreds of young women and men of all races.

She came to the NIH from Howard University College of Medicine, where she had been professor and chair of the Department of Pathology, the third woman in the US—and the first African American woman—to hold such an appointment. Dr. Pinn also previously held teaching appointments in pathology at Harvard Medical School and Tufts University, where she was also assistant dean for student affairs. She now also holds the position of professor for the Institute for Advanced Discovery & Innovation at the University of South Florida.

She is a fellow of the American Academy of Arts and Sciences and was elected to the National Academy of Medicine (IOM) in 1995. She served several terms on the National Academies Committee on Women in Science, Engineering, and Medicine and was a member of the National Academies committee that prepared the report on "Promising Practices for Addressing the Underrepresentation of Women in Science, Engineering, and Medicine: Opening Doors," which was released in the spring of 2020. She is also a member of the National Academies Roundtable on Black Men and Black Women in Science, Engineering, and Medicine. A graduate and former trustee of Wellesley College, she earned her MD in 1967 from the University of Virginia School of Medicine, the only woman and only minority in her class. She completed her postgraduate training in pathology at the Massachusetts General Hospital before joining the faculty of Tufts. Dr. Pinn has over two hundred scientific publications and book chapters, including forewords, and has given more than five hundred keynote speeches, lectures, and presentations since 1991.

A native of Lynchburg, Virginia, and educated in segregated public schools, Dr. Pinn has received seventeen honorary degrees of science, law and medicine. The University of Virginia School of Medicine has named one of its four advisory medical student colleges as "The Pinn College" in her honor. In 2011, Tufts University School of Medicine announced the unveiling of "The Vivian W. Pinn Office of Student Affairs," named for her at the time her former medical students dedicated a scholarship in her name. She has held leadership positions in many professional organizations, including that as the eighty-eighth president of the National Medical Association (NMA), and is currently chair of the NMA Past Presidents Council.

Additionally, lectures in women's health named for Dr. Pinn have been established at the National Institutes of Health, the National Women's Health Congress, and the National Medical Association. One of her greatest honors has been the announcement by the University of Virginia in the fall of 2016 that the medical research and education building was renamed for her as "Pinn Hall." And in December 2016, the UVA medical school also announced the inaugural Pinn Scholars program to support and recognize midlevel faculty in efforts to take their research in novel directions. Her oral history is included in the National Library of Medicine's exhibit on women physicians, "Changing the Face of Medicine"; in the University of Virginia's project "Explorations in Black Leadership," conducted by Julian Bond; and in The History Makers collection, which is now housed in the Library of Congress.

Shelia S. Price, DDS, EdD, FACD

◆ ◆ ◆

Dr. Shelia S. Price is associate dean for admissions, recruitment, and access and professor of diagnostic sciences at West Virginia University (WVU) School of Dentistry. She is a three-time graduate of WVU, where she earned DDS, MA, and EdD degrees. She also holds a BS in biology from the University of Charleston in Charleston, West Virginia.

With over thirty years of experience in oral health education and advocacy, four "firsts" are attributed to Dr. Price: (1) the first woman dentist and African American in the WVU dental school to ascend ranks from instructor to professor, (2) the first female African American WVU dental graduate, (3) the first WVU dental faculty member to complete the nationally competitive women's Executive Leadership in Academic Medicine (ELAM) program, and (4) under her leadership as principal investigator and project director, WVU was one of the first US dental schools awarded the Robert Wood Johnson (RWJ) Foundation Pipeline, Profession, and Practice: Community-Based Dental Education multi-year grant (2002–2007) to reduce oral-health-access disparities.

Beginning in 1995, Dr. Price held leadership positions that ranged from director of admissions and student affairs, interim associate dean for academic and postdoctoral affairs, and assistant dean for admissions and student affairs, to associate dean for admissions, recruitment and access, a role that she holds currently. She pioneered early-admissions dental programs in partnership with universities located both inside and outside West Virginia. Her work with the American Dental Education

Association (ADEA) includes Dental School Admissions Officers Section chair (2012–2013), Minority Affairs Advisory Committee chair (2003–2005), and Women's Health in Interprofessional Education and Collaborative Care dental workgroup leader (2018). Dr. Price has also served on the RWJ Foundation Dental Pipeline II National Advisory Committee (2007–2010) and the expert panel on "Systematic Screening and Assessment of Workforce Interventions to Promote Oral Health" (2012–2013).

Dr. Price has published articles, served as a peer reviewer for dental journals, and presented locally and nationally. In 2012–2013, she served as invited cofacilitator of regional workshops to help dental schools prepare for the Commission on Dental Accreditation's (CODA) revised standards on diversity and humanistic culture. In her community, Dr. Price is a founding member of the Women's Giving Circle of North Central West Virginia and teacher in the Christian Help Jobs for Life Program. Dr. Price received several prestigious awards and honors, including fellowship in the American College of Dentists, the WVU Women in Science and Health Excellence Award, the National Dental Association Foundation (NDAF)/Colgate-Palmolive Recognition Award for Service, the WVU School of Dentistry Distinguished Alumnus Award, the WVU Neil S. Bucklew Award for Social Justice, and the NDA Foundation/Colgate-Palmolive Award for Excellence in Teaching.

Joyce A. Reese, DDS, MPH, FACD

♦ ♦ ♦

Dr. Joyce Reese is an experienced dentist with an extensive career in the field of dental public health. She served for thirty-three years as a health scientist administrator at the National Institutes of Health (NIH), National Institute of Dental Research (NIDR), and at the National Institutes of Standards and Technology (NIST). Her public sector career spanned more than fifty years in dentistry. In her early career, she worked as a dentist in private practice and with the District of Columbia Department of Public Health as a dental officer.

Dr. Reese has experience working with industry, academia, and other agencies to advance dental research. Her expertise has covered areas of dental amalgam, dental cements, composite restorative materials, external maxillofacial prosthesis, endodontic, dental implants, and tooth replantation and transplantation.

Dr. Reese was elected to serve on one of the four commissions of the Federation Dentaire International (FDI). She served as an active member of the Commission on Dental Products and later became chair of the commission. In this role, her meetings and lectures have taken her to many countries throughout the world. She later edited Restorative Dental Materials, published in 1985 by the FDI.

A member of several national and international organizations, Dr. Reese served as NIDR's liaison to the American Dental Association's Council on Dental Materials, Instruments, and Equipment, president of the dental materials group of the International Association for Dental

Research, and, in 1984, headed the FDI's working group for clinical products on materials performance.

Dr. Reese received her BS degree from Virginia Union University, her DDS degree from Howard University College of Dentistry, and her MPH degree from the University of Minnesota. Since retiring from NIDR as the director of its Small Business Innovative Program, she has been working with the Maryland Democratic Committee.

Dionne J. Richardson, DDS, MPH

◆ ◆ ◆

Dr. Richardson has served as a leader in public health and state oral health programs throughout her career. She focuses on addressing the oral health needs of minority populations, those with chronic diseases, and those with special health-care needs. She has twenty-five years of training and experience in oral health promotion, prevention, and directing oral health programs for vulnerable populations. Her quest to eliminate oral health disparities has been a guiding force throughout her career in public health. Developing and implementing interventions and strategies to address oral disease in populations have helped to develop her understanding of the impacts of social determinants of health and her perspectives on lessening the impacts to improve the oral health of the most vulnerable populations.

Dr. Richardson received undergraduate and dental degrees from a HBCU. She has a bachelor of science degree in chemistry from Xavier University of Louisiana and a doctor of dental surgery degree from Meharry Medical College School of Dentistry in Tennessee. She has also completed extensive postdoctoral training in general dentistry, research, public health, neurodevelopmental disabilities in special needs populations, and health policy. She received a master of public health degree from the University of Rochester Medical Center in Rochester New York.

Currently, she serves as state dental director with the New York State Department of Health, guiding programs that provide valuable public health services and preventive interventions to improve oral health across the lifespan.

Dr. Richardson's opinions, perspectives, and comments are her own and are not an official position of the New York State Department of Health.

Jessica A. Rickert, DDS

♦ ♦ ♦

Dr. Jessica Ann Rickert made history as the first female American Indian dentist in the world. Dr. Rickert attended the University of Michigan from 1968 to 1975. In 1975, she established a private dental practice; she also provided dental care for the Children's Aid Society, the Department of Corrections of the State of Michigan, and the Family Health Care Organization (FQHC). Recently retired, Dr. Rickert is the Anishinaabe dental outreach specialist with Delta Dental of Michigan.

Dr. Rickert's book, *Exploring Careers in Dentistry*, is published by the Rosen Publishing Company. Her published works are many and are featured in the journals of the Michigan Dental Association, Society of American Indian Dentists, Association of American Indian Physicians, American Association of Women Dentists, the Dentistry Today periodical, the journal of the Arizona Dental Association, and the Prairie Band Pottawatomi News; she has served as the health advisor for Native News Online. She was most recently included in Northern Michigan University Press's Voice on the Water.

The American Dental Association awarded her its Access Award, and the Michigan Women's Hall of Fame inducted her in 2009. She had the honor of participating in the University of Nebraska Medical School's Science Partnership Education Award.

She served on the Michigan Urban Indian Health Council Board of Directors and on the Board of Directors of the Society of American Indian Dentists. Dr. Rickert is an active member of the American Dental Association.

It has been her honor to have spoken in many national venues: the State of Michigan "Legends" series, the Medicine Wheel Symposium at Northern Michigan University, the North American Indian Center's symposium on Native Women, Northern Michigan College, and the American Association of Indian Physicians predental workshop for American Indian students at the A.T. Still University. Recently, she was the keynote speaker at the Tribal Epidemiology Conference, the University at Buffalo SOD, Des Moines University, Kalamazoo Community College, Michigan Oral Health Coalition, Lewis University, University of Missouri SOD, Sinclair College, and the Seneca Nation.

Rochelle L. Rollins, PhD, MPH

◆ ◆ ◆

Dr. Rollins champions equitable access to oral health for underserved populations and promotes federal service as a career path for improving community wellness. She is currently a public health advisor in the Office of Minority Health, US Department of Health and Human Services, in Rockville, Maryland.

Dr. Rollins received her BS from Wellesley College, her MPH from Boston University, and her doctorate (1995) from Brandeis University's Heller School for Social Policy and Management, where she was a Pew Health Policy fellow. This narrative was written in Rochelle's personal capacity, and the views expressed therein do not necessarily represent those of the Department of Health and Human Services, the Office of the Assistant Secretary for Health, the Office of Minority Health, or the federal government.

Frances Emelia Sam, DDS

◆ ◆ ◆

Dr. Sam stays focused on her mission to humanize health care. She currently lectures on her book, Compassionate Competency, sharing the importance of emotional intelligence, mindfulness, and compassion in health-care spaces.

Dr. Sam graduated with a bachelor of science degree with specialization in genetics at the University of Alberta. She then obtained her DDS from the Howard University College of Dentistry in Washington, DC, graduating at the top of her class. She went on to complete an oral and maxillofacial surgery residency at Howard University Hospital. She then continued as faculty at her alma mater, most recently as an associate clinical professor in the Department of Surgery.

Jeanne C. Sinkford, DDS, MS, PhD, DSc, FACD, FICD

◆ ◆ ◆

Dr. Sinkford is a nationally and internationally renowned dental educator, administrator, researcher, and clinician. She finished first in the dental class of 1958 at Howard University before pursuing graduate study at Northwestern University, where she received her MS (1962) and PhD (1963). She completed a pedodontic residency at Children's Hospital National Medical Center in 1975. Dr. Sinkford became the first woman dean of a dental school in the United States in 1975. She served in that capacity from 1975 to 1991.

She has served on numerous committees and advisory councils of national significance, including the council of the Institute of Medicine; the National Academy of Sciences NRC Governing Board; the National Advisory Dental Research Council; the Directors' Advisory Council, National Institutes of Health; the governing board of the American Society for Geriatric Dentistry; advisory board, Robert Wood Johnson Health Policy Program; Committee A, Council on Dental Education; chair, Appeal Board Council of Dental Education, American Dental Association; chair, Council of Deans American Association of Dental Schools; Council on Dental Research, American Dental Association; Tuskegee Study Advisory Panel; Special Medical Advisory Group (SMAG), Veterans Administration; National Academy of Sciences; chair, Anatomical Review Board of the District of Columbia and National Board of Directors of the Girl Scouts USA; and The Sullivan Alliance Advisory Board.

Dr. Sinkford has more than one hundred articles published in refereed journals and has written an instructional manual for crown and bridge prosthodontics. From 1992 to 2011, Dr. Sinkford was responsible for diversity programming and initiatives at the American Dental Education Association (formerly American Association of Dental Schools). Under her leadership, ADEA created numerous opportunities for the advancement of women and underrepresented minorities including the ADEA/Enid A. Neidle Scholar-in-Residence Program for women and the ADEA International Women's Leadership Conferences (1998, 2003, 2005, and 2010).

Dr. Sinkford holds honorary degrees from Howard University, the University of Michigan, Meharry Medical College, Georgetown University, the University of Medicine and Dentistry of New Jersey, and Detroit-Mercy University. She has received alumni achievement awards from Northwestern University and Howard University and numerous other citations for exceptional professional achievement. Dr. Sinkford was selected as an Outstanding Leader in Dentistry by the International College of Dentists. She is the first African American woman to be so honored. She has received the Lucy Hobbs Taylor Award from the Association of American Women Dentists and the Distinguished Service Award from the American Dental Association and the Society of American Indian Dentists.

Dr. Sinkford received the 2007 Trailblazer Award from the National Dental Association (NDA). She was also recognized with the distinguished 2009 Herbert W. Nickens Award from the Association of American Medical Colleges for her outstanding contribution to promoting justice in medical education and health care. In 2010, Dr. Sinkford received the Pierre Fauchard Academy Gold Medal Award for her outstanding contributions to the progress and standing of the dental profession. In 2015, Dr. Sinkford was presented with American Dental Education Association's William J. Gies Award for Vision, Innovation and Achievement for Outstanding Vision by a Dental Educator and the American Dental Association's Distinguished Service Award. In 2017, Dr. Sinkford received the Lifetime Achievement Award from the American College of Dentists. She is a life member in the American Dental Association and was elected to Life Membership in the National Dental Association in 2012. Dr. Sinkford has been a member of the Institute of Medicine, National Academy of Sciences, since 1975.

Janet H. Southerland, DDS, MPH, PhD, FACD, FICD

❖ ❖ ❖

Dr. Southerland is vice president of interprofessional education, institutional effectiveness, and the Health Education Center, a professor in the Department of Nutrition Metabolism, and clinical assistant professor in oral and maxillofacial surgery at the University of Texas Medical Branch (UTMB). She completed her undergraduate studies at the University of North Carolina at Chapel Hill. After receiving her DDS at the UNC School of Dentistry in 1989, Dr. Southerland completed a two-year general practice residency program in which she spent a third year as a fellow and completed an MPH with a focus on health policy and administration and completed a PhD in oral biology, all at UNC. Previously, she served as dean of the Meharry Medical College School of Dentistry, chief academic officer for the school, and professor of oral and maxillofacial surgery. Prior to her time at Meharry, Dr. Southerland served as the chair of the Department of Hospital Dentistry, chief of the Oral Medicine Service, and director of the hospital dental clinics at UNC School of Dentistry and UNC hospitals.

Dr. Southerland is actively involved in research that focuses on the relationship between oral disease and systemic health and patient-centered outcomes. Specifically, her studies have focused on the relationship between diabetes and periodontal disease, early detection and interventions for oral cancer, and management of oral complications associated with HIV disease and the impact of improved oral health on HIV health outcomes. Additionally, she has studied health disparities related to xerostomia in individuals suffering with diabetes, intimate partner violence/elder abuse, cardiovascular disease and periodontal disease, and the use of salivary proteomics in evaluating overall health and well-being. Dr. Southerland is currently focused on creating an educational environment that focuses on interprofessional education and team-based learning leveraging technology to provide increased opportunities for knowledge and skill development.

Dr. Southerland holds memberships in a number of professional organizations, such as the National Dental Association, the American Dental Association, Texas Dental Association, the American/International Association Dental Research (AADR/IADR), and she has previously held membership in the American and international colleges of dentists. Dr. Southerland holds, or has held, a number of leadership positions that include chair of the National Dental Association's Committee on Minority Faculty Education, Research and Development; member of the National Advisory Committee for the Robert Wood Johnson Foundation Clinical Scholars Program; second vice chair of the UNC General Alumni Association's Board and chair of its Enrichment Committee; chair of the UNC Light on the Hill Scholarship Committee; chair of the Meharry Institutional Review Board; and coleader for the Meharry Translational Research Center's grant collaborations and partnership and pilot projects cores, funded by NIMHD.

Dr. Southerland has four adult children and is married to Dr. Charles P. Mouton.

Carol G. Summerhays, DDS, FACD

♦ ♦ ♦

Dr. Summerhays believes it is every leader's responsibility to mentor and grow future leaders. She attributes her professional success to mentors throughout her life. While president of the American Dental Association, one of her priorities was to visit, connect, and inspire dental students at dental schools and student dental organizations throughout the United States.

Currently, Dr. Summerhays serves on the FDI World Federation of Dentists as a councilor and the University of Southern California Ostrow School of Dentistry Board of Councilors as chair of the board, and she consults for several nonprofit and for-profit companies.

Dr. Summerhays graduated from the University of San Francisco with a BS in biology and from the USC Ostrow School of Dentistry with a doctorate in dental surgery. She received a full scholarship to dental school through the Health Professions Scholarship

Among her many professional positions are former president of the American Dental Association, the oldest and largest national dental association in the world, and former president of the California Dental Association, the largest state dental association. For over ten years, she served on the Board of the LD Pankey Institute for Advanced Dental Education.

Dr. Summerhays has received honorary fellowships from the American College of Dentists (FACD), the International College of Dentists (FICD), the Academy of Dentistry International (FADI), the Pierre

Fauchard Academy of Dentistry, and the Academy of General Dentistry (FAGD). She went on to earn a Mastership in the Academy of General Dentistry.

National recognition for her contributions to dentistry include the Ellis Island Medal of Honor, National Gold Medal from the Pierre Fauchard Academy, the Lucy Hobbs Award from the American Association of Women Dentists, and inclusion in the Congressional Record of the House of Representatives as president of the American Dental Association (first Filipina).

Other honors include an honorary doctor in humane letters from the Western University of Health Sciences and participation in the Senior Dental Leader, Global Child Fund.

From an early age, Dr. Summerhays felt a commitment to improving the community. Much of that commitment to the involved philanthropic efforts within the profession of dentistry with various foundations and other nonprofits such as the Salvation Army and the American Cancer Society. In 2010, she was honored as "A Woman of Dedication" by the Salvation Army and one of the Girl Scouts' "10 Cool Women in San Diego."

Machelle Fleming Thompson, RDH, HCAP, MPH

◆ ◆ ◆

As an effective leader, Machelle Thompson finds trusting her inner voice and staying true to who you are an important pillar. In this book, she shares how leading with love continues to inspire and strengthen her as a servant leader to empower others to do the same.

Machelle Thompson currently serves as dean for compliance at the Meharry Medical College School of Dentistry in Nashville, Tennessee. She graduated with an AS in dental hygiene and BS in health-care administration and planning from Tennessee State University and received her master of science degree in public health from Meharry Medical College.

Jennifer Webster-Cyriaque, DDS, PhD

◆ ◆ ◆

Dr. Jennifer Webster-Cyriaque is a professor in the divisions of oral and craniofacial sciences and of craniofacial and surgical care at the University of North Carolina Adams School of Dentistry, professor in the Department of Microbiology and Immunology at the University of North Carolina School of Medicine, and director of the oral viral pathogenesis group. Dr. Webster-Cyriaque is passionate about training and mentoring and views these areas as critical to creating and informing the next generation of translational scientists. She has provided science mentorship to over seventy trainees, several of whom are now working in academia.

Dr. Webster-Cyriaque received her DDS from the State University of New York at Buffalo and her PhD in microbiology and immunology from the University of North Carolina Chapel Hill with Nancy Raab-Traub. As a clinician providing care to underserved populations, she is acutely aware of the need for oral health research. As a prior dental scientist awardee, her clinical focus was oral medicine/hospital dentistry. Simultaneously, her PhD related to studies on viral pathogenesis and oral diseases.

Marilyn P. Woolfolk, MS, DDS, MPH, FACD

◆ ◆ ◆

Dr. Woolfolk received a BA degree from Cornell University in 1971. Completing all her graduate and professional education at the University of Michigan, Dr. Woolfolk earned an MS in microbiology from the Horace H. Rackham School of Graduate Studies in 1972, a DDS in 1978 from the School of Dentistry, and a MPH in dental public health from the School of Public Health in 1982. She held active faculty status at the University of Michigan School of Dentistry from 1978 to 2014 and maintained a joint appointment in the School of Public Health in dental public health and community health programs from 1983 to 1998.

As a public-health dentist, she has served as dental consultant to local and state health departments, to Region V (Chicago) DHHS Head Start programs, and as external reviewer for the Robert Wood Johnson Pipeline monograph. She was a member of the Dental Advisory Committee of Blue Cross/Blue Shield of Michigan. Professor Woolfolk's scholarship and teaching combined interests in oral health status of special population groups, diversification of the health professions workforce, utilization of dental services, and reduction of oral health disparities among the underserved. She spent much of her career involved in efforts to provide direct dental services to underserved populations locally and to increase the diversity of the health professions' workforce nationally. As the principal investigator for multiple Health Careers Opportunity (HCOP) grants, Dr. Woolfolk led the planning and implementation of summer academic enrichment programs at the University of Michigan that developed the cadre of students from minority and disadvantaged backgrounds who successfully competed for entry into dental or medical schools from 1994 to 2014.

Additionally, Dr. Woolfolk served the School of Dentistry in an administrative role for many years, providing oversight of admissions, student services, and financial aid. Past leadership roles in professional organizations include the past chair of the Oral Health Section of the American Public Health Association, executive councilor of the American Association of Public Health Dentistry, ADA curriculum consultant, member of the Commission on Dental Accreditation (CODA), member of the ADA National Dental Education Task Force, and chair of the 2012 Annual Session Program Committee for the American Dental Education Association.

Currently professor emerita of dentistry in the Department of Periodontics and Oral Medicine and assistant dean emerita for student services at the School of Dentistry, she continues in a national consulting role as a site visitor for the Commission on Dental Accreditation and as a member of the National Advisory Committee for the Robert Wood Johnson Foundation's Summer Health Professions Education Program. Dr. Woolfolk has received various awards and special recognition, including selection as a PEW National Dental Education fellow, as an Executive Leadership in Academic Medicine (ELAM) fellow, and as a fellow of the American College of Dentists.

Minority Women Oral Health Pioneers

Spanning 130 years, this snapshot of forty minority women "firsts" commemorates trailblazing achievement motivated by purpose, resilience, and determination to make a positive difference through oral health leadership, advocacy, education, service, and research.

YEAR	NAME	PIONEERING ACHIEVEMENT
1890	Dr. Ida Gray Nelson Rollins	First Black female dentist, University of Michigan School of Dentistry
1896	Dr. Mary Imogene Williams	First female graduate, Howard University School of Dentistry
1902	Dr. Ollie Bryan-Davis	First female graduate, Meharry Medical College School of Dentistry
1909	Dr. Gertrude Curtis	First Negro woman to practice dentistry in the State of New York; Columbia University graduate

Undaunted Trailblazers

1918	Dr. Vada Watson Somerville	First Black female graduate, University of Southern California School of Dentistry
1919	Dr. Jessie G. Garnett	First Black woman to practice dentistry in Boston; Tufts University graduate
1923	Dr. Bessie Delany	First Black female graduate, Columbia University School of Dentistry
1924	Dr. Mary Jane Watkins	First woman dentist in the military; Howard University graduate
1948	Dr. Eugenia Mobley	First female to receive the MPH degree, University of Michigan School of Public Health; Meharry Medical College School of Dentistry graduate
1949	Dr. Vivian Tompkins Dowell	First Black woman to practice dentistry in Oklahoma; Howard University graduate
1956	Dr. Doris Marshall Harris	First Black dentist to graduate from Dalhousie University
195_	Dr. Evangeline Upshur Freeman	President of the Arkansas Medical Dental/Pharmacy Association; Meharry Medical College School of Dentistry graduate

Minority Women OralHealth Pioneers

196_	Dr. Jacqueline D. Guinn	First Black clinical instructor at Case Western Reserve; Meharry Medical College School of Dentistry graduate
1969	Dr. Camille Lee Young	First woman chief of dental services in DC; Howard University graduate
1973	Konnetta Putman, RDH	First Black president of the American Dental Hygienists Association; Howard University graduate
1975	Dr. Jessica Rickert	First American Indian female dentist in the US; University of Michigan graduate
1975	Dr. Jeanne Sinkford	First US female dental dean, Howard University School of Dentistry; Howard University graduate
1975	Dr. Jeanne Sinkford	First woman dentist elected to the Institute of Medicine; Howard University graduate
1977	Dr. Erma Freeman	First Black female graduate, Medical College of Virginia School of Dentistry
1979	Dr. Joan Lanier	First Black woman endodontist in the US; University of Michigan graduate

1979	Dr. Joan Lanier	First woman endodontist in the state of Michigan; University of Michigan graduate
1982	Dr. Renee McCoy Collins	First female graduate, Oral Surgery Program, Howard University
1986	Dr. Marja Hurley	Associate dean University of Connecticut Schools of Medicine and Dental Medicine; University of Connecticut School of Medicine graduate
1987	Dr. Cheryl Stanback Fryer	First Black woman to complete oral pathology master's program in the US, University of Michigan; Howard University graduate
1991	Dr. Agnes H. Donahue	Executive director of US Public Health Service Office of Women's Health; Meharry Medical College School of Dentistry graduate
1991	Dr. Vivian Pinn	First director of the Office of Research on Women's Health (ORWH) at the National Institutes of Health (NIH); University of Virginia School of Medicine graduate

Minority Women OralHealth Pioneers

1992	Dr. Juliann Bluitt Foster	First Black woman president of the Chicago Dental Society; Howard University graduate
1992	Josephine Rosa, RDH	First woman president of the Hispanic Dental Association (HDA)*
1993	Dr. Juliann Bluitt Foster	First Black woman elected president of the American College of Dentists
1993	Dr. Andrea Jackson and Dr. Linda Thornton	First Black women certified by the American Board of Prosthodontics; Howard University graduate and New York University graduate, respectively
1997	Dr. Hazel Harper	First woman president of the National Dental Association (NDA); Howard University graduate
1997	Dr. Marilyn Woolfolk	First Black woman assistant dean, University of Michigan School of Dentistry; University of Michigan graduate
1998	Dr. Shelia S. Price	First Black woman professor of dentistry, West Virginia University; West Virginia University graduate

2002	Dr. Marsha Butler	First Black woman vice president of Colgate-Palmolive Company; Howard University graduate
2002	Dr. Marilyn Woolfolk	First Black woman professor of dentistry, University of Michigan; University of Michigan graduate
2003	Dr. Shelia S. Price	First Black woman associate dean, West Virginia University School of Dentistry; West Virginia University graduate
2003	Dr. Yilda Rivera	First woman dean, University of Puerto Rico School of Dentistry; University of Puerto Rico graduate
2006	Dr. Sandra Harris	First Black president of the American Association of Women Dentists; Meharry Medical College School of Dentistry graduate
2008	Dr. Joanne Dawley	First woman president of the Michigan Dental Association; University of Michigan graduate
2010	Dr. Gillian Barclay	First Black woman vice president of the Aetna Foundation; University of Detroit Mercy graduate

2011	Dr. Ruth Bol	First woman president of the Society of American Indian Dentists (SAID); University of the Pacific graduate
2015	Dr. Carol Summerhays	First Filipina president of the American Dental Association (ADA); University of Southern California graduate
2019	Dr. Winifred Booker	First Black president of the Society of American Indian Dentists (SAID); Meharry Medical College School of Dentistry graduate
2020	Dr. Rena D'Souza	First minority woman appointed director of the NIH National Institute of Dental and Craniofacial Research (NIDCR); University of Texas Health Science Center at Houston graduate

Sources: Jessie Carney Smith, *Powerful Black Women*; Women in Dentistry, Alpha Kappa Alpha Sorority Heritage Series 5, 1972; Smith, *Notable Black American Women*; Clifford F. Loader and Shigeo Ryan Kishi, *NDA II: The Story of America's Second National Dental Association*; *Legacy, The Dental Profession*; Lori S. Wilson, *Black Women Dentists*; The HistoryMakers Digital Archive; Joseph B. Harris, "Michigan's Black Dental Heritage," *Journal of the Michigan Dental Association*, vol. 74, no.1 (1992): 28-34; Society of American Indian Dentists, 2020; *Data via Google search/Hispanic Dental Association website, accessed November 14, 2020, https://www.hdassoc.org/about-hda. © Copyright 2020

Epilogue

◆ ◆ ◆

This book is an amazing venture because one hundred years after the signing of the Nineteenth Amendment to the US Constitution, we are able to document the advancement of oral health by minority women through their real-life stories. This rendering focuses on the noteworthy achievement of contemporary women of color who have defied barriers of gender and race and have demonstrated an unwavering commitment to professionalism and service in previously male-dominated professions. They have lived through major wars and conflicts on foreign soils (World War II, the Cold War, Korean War, Vietnam War, Desert Storm, Afghanistan) and hardships pertaining thereto. Domestically, they have faced threats of civil unrest, discrimination of all forms, harassment, and have been denied inalienable rights. Yet they continue to believe in noble ideals of democracy that exist through our constitutional rights and are reinforced through Amendments XII, XIII, XIV, and XIX. When some of these contemporary women entered the dental profession, only 2 percent of practicing dentists were women, and some dental schools were still not admitting women. Today, enrollment of women in US dental schools exceeds 50 percent, and that number continues to increase annually.

The year 1975 was important for global attention to women's issues and gender equality. The United Nations proclaimed 1975 as International Women's Year and convened the World Conference on Women in Mexico City, Mexico. It was the first international conference held by the United Nations to focus solely on women's issues and marked a significant turning point in policy directives related to gender equality on the global level. Subsequently, the United Nations organized three additional World Conferences on Women: Copenhagen in 1980, Nairobi in 1985, and Beijing in 1995. The Fourth World Conference on Women: Action for Equality, Development and Peace was the name given for the Beijing conference convened by the United Nations Commission on the Status of Women. Twelve areas of concern were included in the conference objectives for the empowerment of women and achievement of gender equality. The policy document and action strategies were unanimously adopted by 189 countries and became known as the Beijing Declaration and the Platform for Action.

Twelve critical areas of concern are:

1. Women and poverty
2. Education and training of women
3. Women and health
4. Violence against women
5. Women and armed conflict
6. Women and the economy
7. Women in power and decision-making
8. Institutional mechanisms for the advancement of women
9. Human rights of women
10. Women in the media
11. Women and the environment
12. The girl child

The twenty-five-year review and appraisal of this comprehensive action platform was scheduled for March 2020. The originally identified areas of concern continue to be critical to both the health and advancement of women and overall global health today.

As dentistry benefited from, but was not included in, the global targets, the American Dental Education Association (ADEA) founded its first global health session in 1998 through sponsorship of the first

International Women's Leadership Conference (IWLC) in Cannes/Mandelieu, France. The IWLC's agenda included leadership and broad oral health targets similar to critical areas identified in Beijing. The IWLCs continue to be sponsored by the ADEA with overarching themes of "Global Health through Women's Leadership" and include gender neutrality. Conference proceedings are available online at the ADEA website. The global conferences have elevated the status and role of women in health and health outcomes for both developed and developing countries throughout the world.

During the past two decades, our nation has been challenged to act by the release of the landmark document "Oral Health in America: A Report of the Surgeon General" in 2000. This report, the first ever report to exclusively address oral health, was issued from the office of Admiral David Satcher, the physician who served as the sixteenth US Surgeon General. The dental profession diligently responded to the report and its findings in multiple ways. As a body, the profession continues to contribute to the oral health of US citizens through education, therapeutics, access to care, research, and technology advancements and by promoting diversity in the dental workforce.

We will also be guided by data-driven national objectives to improve the health and well-being of all Americans as included in Healthy People 2030 (https://healthypeople.gov).

Diversity in the health professions improves patient outcomes and increases opportunity for advancement for women of all backgrounds. The enactment of Title IX in 1972 by the US Congress, eliminating discrimination in education for any institution receiving federal funding, expanded the horizon to give equal opportunity for women in many career domains, including competitive athletics. As a result of that legislation, women began to aggressively and ambitiously pursue nontraditional occupations, and the pursuit of dentistry was an appealing option for those interested in health care. Women of all demographics have been entering the dental profession as dentists in greater numbers at a time when there has been an expansion in the positions and roles of advocacy and authority available to them. According to the ADA, as of 2020 women are now 29.8 percent of the dental workforce in the United States and 50 percent of US dental students. Underrepresented (African American, Hispanic, Native American) minorities represent 12 percent of US dentists, while women represent 36 percent. Women are more than a "critical mass" in the health workforce. They have become pillars of hope for access to oral health care.

Through their reflective contemplations, we hear the voices of contemporary women with much to be told as their lives and contributions continue to unfold. Beyond their professional degrees and achievement, they have included in their authentic stories the opportunities, risks, and behaviors that connect the intersectionality of both positive and negative contributory factors in their lives. In their leadership roles, they are both mentors and teachers to their families, students, colleagues, and friends. These pioneers have exhibited a wide range of flexibility and versatility in their career paths. They multitask as they lead, teach, inform, serve, and motivate others in a continuous effort to "level the playing field" and "bridge the gap" to justice and equity. They have shared their personal stories as expressions of gratitude, pride, resilience, and hope for the future.

We have seen, through these individual stories, what prepares minority women for leadership and what has propelled their trajectory—a strong work ethic from ancestors, an ability to sidestep forces that impeded their pathway, a willingness to find mentors, and a resourcefulness to develop solid networks of professional support, among other factors. A few of the women have participated in formal leadership development programs, such as Executive Leadership in Academic Medicine (ELAM), the Enid A. Neidle Scholar-in-Residence Program for Women (ENS), and the ADEA/AAL Institute for Teaching and Learning. But overwhelmingly, without a road map or manual, these women have achieved in amazing ways! Collectively, they have provided an eclectic anthology/textbook of success for women leaders of the future to study, to adopt as best practices where applicable, and feel empowered by as they soar toward excellence and go beyond to pave new frontiers.

Their individual stories document the work of "unsung heroes" who continue to contribute to the oral health of minority children and families throughout this country. Through their leadership, these accomplished women have helped promote professional values of prevention, intervention, and the relationship of oral health to general health and disease. Through their disclosure of personal triumphs and challenges innate to their unique experiences, these leaders will have helped those who read their stories appreciate how far we have come as a profession in both gender equity and preventive health care and how far we still can go.

These minority women leaders have accepted their roles as change agents, thereby being catalysts to help introduce new management approaches in the workplace. Older methods of "top-down" leadership are fading as we see the collaborative leadership style emerge through their stories. These women will continue to be important members of teams with creative efforts that remove barriers and facilitate the achievement of all children, especially the underserved. As we emerge from the scourge of the global COVID-19 pandemic and attempt to remedy the shortcomings of existing systems that disproportionately affect minorities, women will be at the forefront of these efforts. They will adapt skills of the past to newer interactive technologies and instructional tools as methods of education shift and place more emphasis on the student's responsibility in lifelong learning and the intersectionality of new data and knowledge.

"Aha" moments are not "touchy-feely" expressions of emotion. Rather, they are introspections or real-life events or moments in time where destiny confronts reality, where the past and present connect to shape the future. Writing these stories forced us to stop and reflect on people, places, events, and times that collectively influenced our subconscious minds and our behaviors. The stories are a mosaic of both opportunities and inequities that have contributed to our sense of self-worth and created the sense of urgency and energy needed to "lift as we lead."

These stories are "snapshots" from the past and present that are the ripples of the future. We have come from a history of invisibility but we are no longer invisible. The leaders in this book have faced enormous challenges of sexism, racism, and bigotry. Their stamina to succeed required strength, grace, faith, and a sense of a purposeful life.

The reflective contemplations in these stories are of historic value to the progress of women in the dental profession and to oral/systemic health. The stories are such impressive testaments of individual achievement. Yet it is even more awe inspiring to imagine the unwritten stories behind these women that would undoubtedly reveal that they also excel in their "off-camera" roles as spouses, partners, mothers, sisters, daughters, caregivers for aging parents, and progenitors of artistic, political, and intellectual movements of the future. They rarely can be completely "off duty," which makes all their professional accomplishments even more remarkable! Not one of them would trade their identity; they cherish their roles as the stewards of a lasting legacy that benefits all humankind.

As we read the "aha" moments shared in personal stories from the contributors, we were able to discern a few commonalities:

- Scarcity of Black female professional role models
- Mentoring from male colleagues and family members
- Ability to develop support systems that met their individual needs
- Pursuit of nontraditional career trajectories (pathways) for professional development and advancement
- Ability to minimize male dominance in the dental profession
- Strong sense and reliability on Divine support
- Representation as "first" in racial, ethnic, or gender-diversity space

Undoubtedly, women leaders will continue to contribute to the understanding of the relationship of oral health to general health as good health continues to be a national priority for all Americans. It would be an oversight not to recognize the fact that beyond mentors, advocates, and allies, the success of minority women leaders has been undergirded by strong personal networks of support such as dedicated infant and childcare providers, or perhaps caregivers for aging loved ones. Those networks included spouses, other family members, friends, day-care personnel, and other kindhearted souls who were reliable resources and willing to step in, whatever the need. They made it possible for us to seek opportunity, reach ambitious goals, and fulfill our potential in the workplace as professionals with peace of mind. Without this unwavering support, navigating the complexities of the working world and becoming leaders would be inconceivable. "May we never forget the shoulders upon which we humbly and gratefully stand."

Afterword

◆ ◆ ◆

Commentary by:
Paul E. Gates, DDS, MBA
Retired Chair, Department of Dentistry
Dr. Martin Luther King Jr. Community
Health Center and Department of Dentistry
BronxCare Health System

This compendium of directed narratives by highly successful underrepresented minority women is a living testament of intelligence, ingenuity, perseverance, and triumph in dentistry. These paragons have decoded or deconstructed their particular area of expertise to achieve at the highest levels within the profession. Each of the selected participants was provided a set of structured questions that would allow them to share their personal and/or professional paths and perspectives. This variation on the theme of oral tradition results in intersectionality-based narratives of how these individuals managed to overcome the historical set of obstacles/hindrances encountered by this segment of the dental profession and serves as a brilliant illumination for mentoring and leadership.

The narratives demonstrate the importance of understanding the written and unwritten rules of engagement. When one is able to analyze the system in which she/he is participating, one can then understand the culture of that environment. This understanding permits a proactive interface with the system as opposed to a reactive one. In the existing culture of male dominance, women are faced with becoming relevant as opposed to becoming equal. Progress and promotion are based on the value they bring to the male need. This secondary gain acts to prevent a ready and certain pathway to success. Currently, there exist a gender earnings gap between females and males of $0.82/$1.00 and a gender wealth gap of a single-digit number of pennies for Black women/$0.32 for men, according to Sallie Krawcheck of Ellevest. Within dentistry, Black women earn approximate $50,000 less per year than any other group.

There is the need for the evolution of a sustainable methodology to address the decades-old situation of the paucity of underrepresented minorities within dentistry. As stated in a *Health Affairs* article I coauthored with Mertz, et al., "Workforce diversity by design is rooted in social justice and provides adequate support and incentives to increase the delivery system's capacity to care for all patients . . ."[*] The number of underrepresented minority students admitted into dental school in 2018–2019 represents less than 2 percent of the number of underrepresented dentists needed for population parity within the present workforce system.

An example of one exemplary collaborative effort was the multiyear Robert Wood Johnson Foundation, W. K. Kellogg Foundation, and California Endowment pipeline project. The efforts of organizations such as the American Dental Association, the National Dental Association, the Santa Fe Group, and the American Dental Education Association have been primarily recruitment and faculty development/mentoring programs that increased numbers of individuals who are appropriately prepared academically and have the desire or interest to pursue the dental profession. The efforts of all of these entities continue to be needed, with increased strategies and resources, if this gargantuan task is to be achieved.

The outcomes of efforts by the nation's dental schools to attempt to address this lack of a critical mass reflects the fact that these institutions have become involved when there are external monies available, such as the capitation monies from the 1963 Health Professions Educational

---

[*] Jean Calvo, Paul Gates, Aubri Kottek, Elizabeth Mertz, and Cynthia Wides, "Underrepresented Minority Dentists: Quantifying Their Numbers and Characterizing the Communities They Serve," *Health Affairs* 35, no. 12 (2016): 2190–99.

Assisting Program (HPEA) or the combined efforts of the W. K. Kellogg Foundation, the California Endowment, and the Robert Wood Johnson Foundation minority pipeline projects. Once those dollars are no longer available, the commitment of many of those institutions to address this problem seems to wither or die. A demonstrated need for a paradigm shift in the recruitment of this segment of the population is evident. The shift must be away from pivotal change. Rather, transformational change is essential. This book can serve as a foundation for those efforts.

The principal authors of this book are each sterling examples of how one succeeds within the dental profession and perseveres against the tide of complacency prevalent in the dental-organizational approach in the realm of increasing the numbers of underrepresented individuals entering into the profession. They understand that the best way to bring about a change in the culture of an organization is to be a part of the leadership of said organization. Their dedication to task in attempting to bring about necessary change in the complexion of the dental provider is exemplary. They have individually and collectively worked for decades to inculcate inclusion as a necessary part of diversity. They understand the need for sustained efforts in leadership by those who have attained success to expand the number of underrepresented women and men in this profession.

Change in the issue of underrepresentation of minorities within the dental profession involves developing dentists who become not just a thread in the fabric but the actual designers and weavers of the cloth.

I am excited by the publication of this extraordinary tome by these remarkable individuals. The stories of the amazing women will serve as beacons for generations. The need is paramount. The timing is long overdue. I anticipate its dissemination and utilization across public libraries, secondary schools, and universities.

Acknowledgments

◆ ◆ ◆

Science has not measured how far back in time we must go to identify factors in our DNA that contribute to the thinking and behaviors of contemporary minority women leaders. We know that somewhere in our histories, many ancestors have sacrificed and given their lives so that we could have a better future. What we continue to contribute to the world is somewhere in our genes, our brains, and our hearts.

In unison, we, the principal coauthors, extend our appreciation to the project manager, Dr. Joseph West, and his assistant, Mr. Kensley Youte, as well as our story editors, Drs. Marita Inglehart and Anne Marie O'Keefe, for their collaboration and candid insights throughout the book-writing process. We are extremely grateful to the contributing authors who entrusted their stories to us for the benefit of future aspiring leaders. We are also extremely indebted to Dr. Paul Gates for his prepared commentary and to Dr. Louis Sullivan, Dr. Joan Reede, and Provost Pamela Zarkowski for their support and endorsement of the book and its value as historical documentation of lifetime contributions to the advancement of oral health by minority women leaders. Additionally, we acknowledge, with sincere gratitude, the support received from the American College of Dentists, the American Dental Education Association, the Colgate-Palmolive Company, the Howard University College of Dentistry, the Meharry Medical College School of Dentistry, and the Office of Research on Women's Health at the National Institutes of Health. Special thanks go to Mr. Taylor Price for his technical advice and graphic arts savvy; to Ms. Janet Jones and Ms. Linda Mabrey, who both helped with research and typing; and to Ms. Liz Weaver for her cover design input. All of these individuals or organizations have been invaluable to our efforts to take the germination of an idea to its satisfying culmination as a finished volume. Sadly, one of our contributing authors, Dr. Agnes Donahue, suddenly passed away just prior to final publication, and we extend our condolences to her family, friends, and colleagues. Thank you to Dr. Johnetta Stokes for her assistance on behalf of Dr. Donahue.

Visual Resources

♦ ♦ ♦

The reference documents included in this work reflect the leadership role of women in both general and oral health. The paradigm is included in the first Dental Curriculum Study (2011) devoted to women's health in dental curriculums. From: Women's Health in the Dental School Curriculum Survey Report and Recommendations. American Dental Education Association. Washington, DC, 2012.

The Dental Student Population Includes More Women and Is More Diverse Over Time

In the past five years, dental school enrollment has seen an overall rise in diversity. The majority of enrollees are women (50.5%), and there are observable increases in Asian, Hispanic or Latino, Black or African American, and Two or More Races enrollees.

ADEA Snapshot of Dental Education 2019-20

FIRST-YEAR ENROLLEES 2013 - 5,769
- White: 52.6%
- Asian: 23.0%
- Black or African American: 8.1%
- Hispanic or Latino: 4.6%
- Two or More Races: 4.3%
- Unknown: 3.0%
- American Indian or Alaska Native: 0.2%
- Native Hawaiian or Other Pacific Islander: 0.1%
- Non-resident Alien: 4.2%

2013 Enrollees by Gender
- Other: 1.1%
- Men: 52.8%
- Women: 46.1%

FIRST-YEAR ENROLLEES 2018 - 6,163
- White: 49.4%
- Asian: 23.6%
- Black or African American: 10.1%
- Hispanic or Latino: 5.4%
- Two or More Races: 4.7%
- Unknown: 3.3%
- American Indian or Alaska Native: 0.2%
- Native Hawaiian or Other Pacific Islander: 0.1%
- Non-resident Alien: 3.1%

2018 Enrollees by Gender
- Other: 0.7%
- Men: 48.7%
- Women: 50.5%

Note: ADEA adheres to the revised federal guidelines for collecting and reporting race and ethnicity. Percentages may add up to more than 100% due to rounding.
*The "Other" gender category includes students who prefer not to report gender, do not identify as either male or female or whose gender is not available.
Source: American Dental Education Association, U.S. Dental School Applicants and Enrollees, 2013 and 2018 Entering Classes

Visual Resources

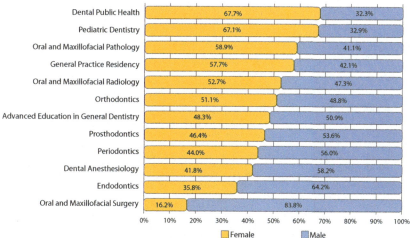

Percentage US Advanced Education Program Enrollment by Gender, 2018-2019 School Year

Source: ADA Health Policy Institute Infographic, "Dental School Grads and advanced Program Enrollment by Gender, 2018-2019." Available at: ADA.org/en/science-research/heatlth-policy-institute/publications/infographics, ADA News February 17, 2020

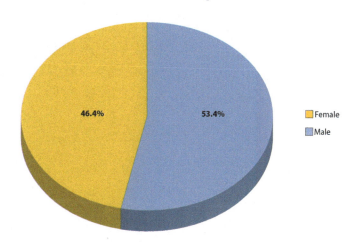

Percentage US Advanced Education Program Enrollment by Gender, 2018-2019 School Year (All Programs)

Source: ADA Health Policy Institute Infographic, "Dental School Grads and Advanced Program Enrollment by Gender, 2018-2019." Available at: ADA.org/en/science-research/heatlth-policy-institute/publications/infographics, ADA News February 17, 2020

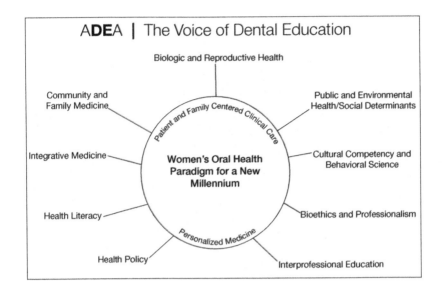

Source: American Dental Education Association. *Women's Health in the Dental Curriculum*. Bethesda, MD: National Institutes of Health, 2011.

Women's Health Resources 2018*

Organization	web address	free access	oral health	Attachment D women's oral health
Academy of General Dentistry-public section	www.knowyourteeth.com	yes	yes	yes
-profession section	www.agd.org	no	?	?
American Academy of Periodontology-public	www.perio.org	yes	yes	yes
-profession section	"	yes	yes	yes
American Association of Women Dentists	www.aawd.org	yes	no	no
American College of Obstetricians and Gynecologists	www.acog.org	yes	yes	yes
American Dental Association -public	www.mouthhealth.org	yes	yes	yes
-profession section	www.ada.org	yes	yes	yes
American Medical Women's Association	www.amwa-doc.org	yes	yes	yes
Centers for Disease Control and Prevention	www.cdc.gov	yes	yes	yes
Colgate Oral and Dental Health Resource Center	www.colgate.com	yes	yes	yes
Everyday Health	www.everydayhealth.com	yes	yes	yes
HealthCommunities	www.healthcommunities.com	yes	yes	yes
Health Resources and Services Administration	www.hrsa.gov/womenshealth/	yes	yes	yes
Journal of Women's Health	www.liebertpub.com	yes	yes	yes
MedEdPORTAL	www.mededportal.org	yes	yes	yes
MedicineNet	www.medicinenet.com	yes	yes	yes
MedlinePlus (US National Library of Medicine)	https://medlineplus.gov/womenshealth.html	yes	yes	yes
National Women's Health Network	www.womenshealthnetwork.com	yes	yes	yes
National Women's Health Resource Center	www.healthwomen.org	yes	yes	yes
OBGYN.net	www.obgyn.net	yes	yes	yes
Office of Women's Health, HHS, National Women's Health Information Center	www.4women.gov	yes	yes	yes
"	www.womenshealth.gov	yes	yes	yes
"	www.migrantclinician.org	yes	yes	yes
Society for Women's Health Research	www.swhr.org	yes	yes	yes
WebMD	www.webmd.com	yes	yes	yes
Wikipedia	www.en.wikipedia.org	yes	no	no
Women's Health Interactive	www.womens-health.com	yes	yes	yes
Women's Health Magazine	http://journals.sagepub.com/home/whe	yes	yes	yes
YouTube	www.youtube.com	yes	yes	yes

*Data from Google search: parameters were women's oral health, women' health, English language and data from 2005 and 2011 projects; about 223,000,000 hits! Links confirmed May 1, 2018

Wendy S. Hupp, DMD
Associate Professor of Oral Medicine (retired)
Department of General Dentistry and Oral Medicine
University of Louisville School of Dentistry

Source: ADEA | Women's Health in IPE and Collaborative Care, Attachment D, page 56, June 26, 2018.

Recommended Reading

♦ ♦ ♦

Books That Inform, Inspire, and Incite Thinking, Behavior, and Action of Leaders

Adams, Diane L. *Health Issues for Women of Color: A Cultural Diversity Perspective.* Thousand Oaks, CA: SAGE Publications, Inc., 1995.

American Dental Education Association. *Women's Health in the Dental Curriculum.* Bethesda, MD: National Institutes of Health, 2011. Includes: Women's Oral Health Paradigm for the New Millennium.

Bowen, W. G., and D. Bok. *The Shape of the River, Long-Term Consequences of Considering Race in College and University Admissions.* Princeton, NJ: Princeton University Press, 1999.

Briner, B. *The Management Methods of Jesus. Ancient Wisdom for Modern Business.* Nashville, Tennessee: Thomas Nelson, Inc., 1996.

Burton, V. *Successful Women Think Differently: 9 Habits to Make You Happier, Healthier and More Resilient.* Eugene, Oregon: Harvest House Publishers, 2012.

Collins, Jim. "Foreword." In *Seven Measures of Success*: What Remarkable Associations Do That Others Don't, pages vii-xi. Washington, DC: ASAE and the Center for Association Leadership, 2006.

Davis S., G. Jenkins, and R. Hunt. *The Pact.* New York, NY: Riverhead Books, 2002.

Dawson, P. L. *Forged by the Knife: The Experience of Surgical Residency from the Perspective of a Woman of Color.* Seattle, WA: Open Hand Publishing, Inc., 1999.

Delaney, S., and Delaney, A. E. *Having Our Say: The Delaney Sisters' First 100*

Years with A. H. Hearth. New York: Kodansha America, Inc., 1993.

Distinguished Black Women 1981–1985. Washington, DC: Black Women in Sisterhood for Action (BISA), Metropolitan Washington Area, Inc., 1986.

Dixon, B. *Good Health for African Americans.* New York: Crown Publishers, Inc., 1994.

Domar, A. D., and H. Dreher. *Healing Mind, Healthy Woman: Using the Mind-Body Connection to Manage Stress and Take Control of Your Life.* New York: Dell Publishing Group, Inc. 1996.

DuBois, W. E. B. *The Souls of Black Folk.* New York: Barnes & Noble Classics, 2003. (First published 1903.)

Duke University Center for Integrative Medicine. *The Duke Encyclopedia of New Medicine: Conventional and Alternative Medicine for All Ages.* Emmaus, PA: Rodale Books International, 2006.

Edelman, M. W. *The Measure of Our Success: A Letter to My Children and Yours.* Boston: Beacon Press, 1992.

Friedman, T. *The World Is Flat: A Brief History of the Twenty-First Century.* New York: Farrar, Straus and Giroux, 2005.

Fluker, W. E. *Ethical Leadership. The Quest for Character, Civility and Community.* Minneapolis, MN: Fortress Press, 2009.

Gaston, M. H., and G. Porter. *Prime Time.* New York: Random House Publishing Group, 2001.

Gawande, A. *Better: A Surgeon's Notes on Performance.* New York: Henry Holt and Company, 2007.

Gladwell, M. *The Tipping Point: How Little Things Can Make a Big Difference.* Boston: Little, Brown and Company, 2000.

Harari, Y. *Sapiens: A Brief History of Humankind.* New York: HarperCollins, 2015.

Jaworski, J. *Synchronicity: The Inner Path of Leadership.* San Francisco: Berrett-Koehler Publishers, Inc., 1996.

Kaplan, R. S., and D. P. Norton. *The Balanced Scorecard: Translating Strategy into Action.* Boston: Harvard Business School Press, 1996.

Kammen, M. *American Culture, American Tastes: Social Change the 20th Century.* New York: Basic Books, 1999.

Keohane, N. O. *Higher Ground: Ethics and Leadership in the Modern University*. Durham, NC: Duke University Press, 2006.

Klagsbrun, F. *The First Ms. Reader*. New York: Warner Paperback Library, 1973.

Lama, D., and D. Tutu. *The Book of Joy*. New York: Penguin Random House, 2016.

Morris, J. A. *Ignite: Inspiring Courageous Leaders*. Detroit, MI: Integral Coaching LLC, 2013.

Northrup, C. *Women's Bodies, Women's Wisdom: Creating Emotional Health and Healing*. New York: Bantam Books, 1998.

Page, S. E. *The Difference: How the Power of Diversity Creates Better Groups, Firms, Schools, and Societies*. Princeton, NJ: Princeton University Press, 2007.

Pinn, V. W. "Women's Health Research for the Twenty-First Century." ADEA First International Women's Leadership Conference Proceedings. *Journal of the American Association of Dental Schools* 63 no. 3 (1999): 223–230.

Roizen, M. F. *Real Age*. New York: HarperCollins, 1999.

Satcher, D., and R. Pamies. "Dentistry and Oral Health." In *Multicultural Medicine and Health Disparities*, 305–320. New York: McGraw-Hill, Medical Publishing Division, 2006.

Senge, P. M. *The Fifth Discipline: The Art and Practice of the Learning Organization*. New York: Currency Doubleday, 1990.

Sullivan, L. W. *Breaking Ground: My Life in Medicine*. Athens, GA: University of Georgia Press, 2014.

Tannen, D. *Talking from 9 to 5*. New York: William Morrow and Company, Inc., 1994.

Klagsbrun, F. The First Ms. Reader. *How Women are Changing Their Lives—in Work, Sex, Politics, Love, Power, and Life Styles*. An Anthology of Articles. Warner Paperback Library, 1973.

The Healthy Woman: A Complete Guide for All Ages. Washington, DC: US Department of Health and Human Services, Office on Women's Health, 2008.

Thomas, R. R. Jr. *Beyond Race and Gender, Unleashing the Power of Your Total Workforce by Managing Diversity*. Washington, DC: American Management Association, 1991.

Tocqueville, A. *Democracy in America*. New York: Alfred A. Knopf, Inc., 1945.

Toffler, A. *Future Shock*. New York: Random House, 1970.

Valian, V. *Why So Slow? The Advancement of Women*. Boston: Massachusetts Institute of Technology, 1998.

West, J. F. *Trod the Stony Road: A Young Man's Journey from the Mississippi to the Charles*. Charleston, SC: BookSurge Publishing, 2010.

Wilkerson, I. *Caste: The Origins of Our Discontents*. New York: Random House, 2020.

National Institutes of Health Office of Research on Women's Health website. https://orwh.od.nih.gov/. Accessed April 6, 2021.

Dental History Resources

♦ ♦ ♦

Books and Publications

150 Years of the American Dental Association: A Pictorial History, 1859–2009. Chicago: the Donning Company Publishers. American Dental Association, 2009.

Alpha Kappa Alpha Sorority. Heritage Series #5. Women In Dentistry. Chicago: Alpha Kappa Alpha Sorority, Inc. 1972.

American Dental Association. *Future of Dentistry.* Chicago: American Dental Association, Health Policy Resources Center, 2001.

Distinguished Black Women 1981–1985, Volume 1. Washington, DC: Black Women in Sisterhood for Action Metropolitan Washington Area, Inc., 1986.

Dummett, C. O., and L. D. Dummett. *Afro-Americans in Dentistry, Sequence and Consequences of Events.* Los Angeles: C. Dummett., 1978.

Dummett, C. O., and L. D Dummett. *National Dental Association II: The Story of America's Second National Dental Association.* Washington, DC: National Dental Association, 2000.

Exploring Biological Contributions to Human Health: Does Sex Matter? Washington, DC: Institute of Medicine National Academy Press, 2001.

Field, M. J., ed. *Dental Education at the Crossroads, Challenges and Change. Timeline of Selected Dates in Dentistry and Dental Education.* (Table 2.1, pages 36, 37). Washington, DC: Institute of Medicine National Academy Press, 1995.

Harper, H. J., C. E. Hodge, C. G. Manning, and M. W. Woolfolk. "African-American Women: Leadership in Transition." *J Dent Educ* 63, no. 3 (1999): 281–87.

Harris, J. B., contributing ed. "Michigan's Black Dental Heritage." *J Mich Dent Assn* 74, no. 1 (1992): 28–34.

In the Nation's Compelling Interest: Ensuring Diversity in the Health-Care Workforce. Washington, DC: Institute of Medicine, National Academy Press, 2004.

Manning, C. G., H. P. Haynes, H. J. Harper, S. S. Price, and M. W. Woolfolk. "Issues in Women's Oral Health: The Quest for Answers Continues." *J Nat Dent Assn* 48 (1997):17–22.

"Oral Conditions—Healthy People 2030." US Department of Health and Human Services, October 8, 2020. https://healthypeople.gov.

Oral Health in America: A Report of the Surgeon General. Rockville, MD: US Department of Health and Human Services, National Institutes of Health, National Institute of Dental and Craniofacial Research, 2000.

Oral Health in America: A Report of the Surgeon General. Rockville, MD: US Department of Health and Human Services, National Institutes of Health, National Institute of Dental and Craniofacial Research, pending release 2021.

Raja, Z., C. Wides, A. Kottek, P. Gates, and E. Mertz. *The Evolving Pipeline of Hispanic Dentists in the United States: Practice and Policy Implications.* Rensselaer, NY: Oral Health Workforce Research Center, Center for Health Workforce Studies, School of Public Health, SUNY Albany, August 2017.

Razzoog, M., and E Robinson. *Black Dentistry in the 21st Century.* Ann Arbor, MI: University of Michigan School of Dentistry, 1991.

Ring, M. E. *Dentistry: An Illustrated History.* New York: Abrams, Inc.; Mosby-Year Book, Inc., 1985.

Simonsen, R. J. *Dentistry in the 21st Century: A Global Perspective.* Chicago: Quintessence Publishing Co. Inc., 1991.

Sinkford, J. C., and R. W. Valachovic. *Growing Our Own: The ADEA Minority Dental Faculty Development Program: A Manual for Institutional Leadership in Diversity.* Washington, DC: the American Dental Education Association, 2011.

Smith, J. C. *Notable Black American Women.* Detroit: Gale Research Inc., 1992.

Smith, J. C. *Powerful Black Women.* Detroit: Gale Research, 1996.

Solomon, E. S., C. R. Williams, and J. C. Sinkford. "Practice Location Characteristics of Black Dentists in Texas." *J Dent Educ* 65 no. 6 (2001): 571–74.

Sullivan Commission on Diversity in the Health Workforce. "Missing Persons: Minorities in the Health Professions." Washington, DC: Hyde Park Communications, September 2004.

Wilson, L. S. *Black Women Dentists*. Richmond, VA: Northlight Publishing Company, 2014.

Woolfolk, M. W, and S. S. Price. "Dental Education: Evolving Student Trends." *J Dent Educ* 76, no. 1 (2012): 51–64.

Web Access

"Web Portal for Information on Disparities in Oral Health." Division of Oral Health, Centers for Disease Control and Prevention, US Department of Health and Human Services. Accessed September 22, 2020. www.cdc.gov/oralhealth/oral_health_disparities.htm.

"Web Portal for Information on Native American Professional Role Models." Nebraska Department of Education, Multicultural/Diversity Education. Accessed November 19, 2020. https://nativeamericanrole.wixsite.com/rolemodels.

Museums and Library Collections

"Women Dentists Exhibit." Sindecuse Museum of Dentistry University of Michigan. 1011 North University, Ann Arbor, MI. December 13, 2012 through July 8, 2016.

"The Future is Now: African Americans in Dentistry." National Museum of Dentistry. Baltimore, MD. September 27, 2002. NDA Foundation/Colgate-Palmolive Co. Exhibit Tour, July 30, 2004 during the NDA Convention, Los Angeles, CA. Louis Stokes Health Sciences Library Howard University.

Made in the USA
Coppell, TX
05 November 2022